ENSIGN KNIGHTLEY

AND OTHER STORIES

A. E. W. MASON

1st WORLD
LIBRARY
Literary Society

Ensign Knightley and Other Stories

A. E. W. Mason

© 1st World Library, 2007
PO Box 2211
Fairfield, IA 52556
www.1stworldlibrary.com
First Edition

LCCN: 2007934077

Softcover ISBN: 978-1-4218-9602-1
Hardcover ISBN: 978-1-4218-9702-8
eBook ISBN: 978-1-4218-9502-4

Purchase *"Ensign Knightley and Other Stories"*
as a traditional bound book at:
www.1stWorldLibrary.com/purchase.asp?ISBN=978-1-4218-9602-1

1st World Library is a literary, educational organization
dedicated to:

- Creating a free internet library of downloadable ebooks

- Hosting writing competitions and offering book publishing
  scholarships.

Interested in more 1st World Library books? contact:
literacy@1stworldlibrary.com
Check us out at: www.1stworldlibrary.com

1ˢᵗ World Library Literary Society

Giving Back to the World

"If you want to work on the core problem, it's early school literacy."

- James Barksdale, former CEO of Netscape

"No skill is more crucial to the future of a child, or to a democratic and prosperous society, than literacy."

- Los Angeles Times

"Literacy... means far more than learning how to read and write... The aim is to transmit... knowledge and promote social participation."

- UNESCO

"Literacy is not a luxury, it is a right and a responsibility. If our world is to meet the challenges of the twenty-first century we must harness the energy and creativity of all our citizens."

- President Bill Clinton

"Parents should be encouraged to read to their children, and teachers should be equipped with all available techniques for teaching literacy, so the varying needs and capacities of individual kids can be taken into account."

- Hugh Mackay

CONTENTS

ENSIGN KNIGHTLEY

It was eleven o'clock at night when Surgeon Wyley of His Majesty's ship *Bonetta* washed his hands, drew on his coat, and walked from the hospital up the narrow cobbled street of Tangier to the Main-Guard by the Catherine Port. In the upper room of the Main-Guard he found Major Shackleton of the Tangier Foot taking a hand at bassette with Lieutenant Scrope of Trelawney's Regiment and young Captain Tessin of the King's Battalion. There were three other officers in the room, and to them Surgeon Wyley began to talk in a prosy, medical strain. Two of his audience listened in an uninterested stolidity for just so long as the remnant of manners, which still survived in Tangier, commanded, and then strolling through the open window on to the balcony, lit their pipes.

Overhead the stars blazed in the rich sky of Morocco; the riding-lights of Admiral Herbert's fleet sprinkled the bay; and below them rose the hum of an unquiet town. It was the night of May 13th, 1680, and the life of every Christian in Tangier hung in the balance. The Moors had burst through the outposts to the west, and were now entrenched beneath the walls. The Henrietta Redoubt had fallen that day; to-morrow the little fort at Devil's Drop, built on the edge of the sand where the sea rippled up to the palisades, must fall; and Charles Fort, to the southwest, was hardly in a better case.

However, a sortie had been commanded at daybreak as a last effort to relieve Charles Fort, and the two officers on the balcony speculated over their pipes on the chances of success.

Meanwhile, inside the room Surgeon Wyley lectured to his remaining auditor, who, too tired to remonstrate, tilted his chair against the wall and dozed.

"A concussion of the brain," Wyley went on, "has this curious effect, that after recovery the patient will have lost from his consciousness a period of time which immediately preceded the injury. Thus a man may walk down a street here in Tangier; four, five, six hours afterwards, he mounts his horse, is thrown on to his head. When he wakes again to his senses, the last thing he remembers is—what? A sign, perhaps, over a shop in the street he walked down, or a leper pestering him for alms. The intervening hours are lost to him, and forever. It is no question of an abeyance of memory. There is a gap in the continuity of his experience, and that gap he will never fill up."

"Except by hearsay?"

The correction came from Lieutenant Scrope at the bassette table. It was quite carelessly uttered while the Lieutenant was picking up his cards. Surgeon Wyley shifted his chair towards the table, and accepted the correction.

"Except, of course, by hearsay."

Wyley was a new-comer to Tangier, having sailed into the bay less than a week back; but he had been long enough in the town to find in Scrope a subject at once of interest and perplexity. Scrope was in years nearer forty than thirty, dark of complexion, aquiline of feature, and though a trifle below the middle height he redeemed his stature by the litheness of his figure. What interested Wyley was that he seemed a man in whom strong passions were always desperately at war with a strong will. He wore habitually a mask of reserve; behind it, Wyley was aware of sleeping fires. He spoke habitually in a quiet, decided voice, like one that has the soundings of his nature; beneath it, Wyley detected, continually recurring, continually subdued, a note of turbulence. Here, in a word, was a man whose hand was against the world but who would not strike at random. What perplexed Wyley, on the other hand, was Scrope's subordinate rank of lieutenant in a garrison where, from the frequency of death, promotion was of the quickest. He sat there at the table, a lieutenant; a boy of twenty-four faced him, and the boy was a captain and his superior.

It was to the Lieutenant, however, that Wyley resumed his discourse.

"The length of time lost is proportionate to the severity of the concussion. It may be only an hour; I have known it to be a day." He leaned back in his chair and smiled. "A strange question that for a man to ask himself—What did he do during those hours?—a question to appal him."

Scrope chose a card from his hand and played it. Without looking up from the table, he asked: "To appal him? Why?"

"Because the question would be not so much what did he do, as what may he not have done. A man rides through life insecurely seated on his passions. Within a few hours the most honest man may commit a damnable crime, a damnable dishonour."

Scrope looked quietly at the Surgeon to read the intention of his words. Then: "I suppose so," he said carelessly. "But do you think that question would press?"

"Why not?" asked Wyley.

Scrope shrugged his shoulders. "I should need an example before I believed you."

The example was at the door. The corporal of the guard at the Catherine Port knocked and was admitted. He told his story to Major Shackleton, and as he told it the two officers lounged back into the room from the balcony, and the other who was dozing against the wall brought the legs of his chair with a bang to the floor and woke up.

It appeared that a sentry at the stockade outside the Catherine Port had suddenly noticed a flutter of white on the ground a few yards from the stockade. He watched this white object, and it moved. He challenged it, and was answered by a whispered prayer for admission in the English tongue and in an English voice. The sentry demanded the password, and received as a reply, "Inchiquin. It is the last password I have knowledge of. Let me in! Let me in!"

The sentry called the corporal, the corporal admitted the fugitive and brought him to the Main-Guard. He was now in the guard-room below.

"You did well," said the Major. "The man has come from the Moorish lines, and may have news which will profit us in the morning. Let him up!" and as the corporal retired, "'Inchiquin,'" he repeated thoughtfully: "I cannot call to mind that password."

Now Wyley had noticed that when the corporal first mentioned the word, Scrope, who was looking over his cards, had dropped one on the table as though his hand shook, had

A. E. W. Mason

raised his head sharply, and with his head his eyebrows, and had stared for a second fixedly at the wall in front of him. So he said to Scrope:

"You can remember."

"Yes, I remember the password," Scrope replied simply. "I have cause to. 'Inchiquin' and 'Teviot'—those were password and countersign on the night which ruined me—the night of January 6th two years ago."

There was an awkward pause, an interchange of glances. Then Major Shackleton broke the silence, though to no great effect.

"H'm—ah—yes," he said. "Well, well," he added, and laying an arm upon Scrope's sleeve. "A good fellow, Scrope."

Scrope made no response whatever, but of a sudden Captain Tessin banged his fist upon the table.

"January 6th two years ago. Why," and he leaned forward across the table towards Scrope, "Knightley fell in the sortie that morning, and his body was never recovered. The corporal said this fugitive was an Englishman. What if—"

Major Shackleton shook his head and interrupted.

"Knightley fell by my side. I saw the blow; it must have broken his skull."

There was a sound of footsteps in the passage, the door was opened and the fugitive appeared in the doorway. All eyes turned to him instantly, and turned from him again with looks of disappointment. Wyley remarked, however, that Scrope, who had barely glanced at the man, rose from his chair. He did not move from the table; only he stood where before he had sat.

The new-comer was tall; a beard plastered with mud, as if to disguise its colour, straggled over his burned and wasted cheeks, but here and there a wisp of yellow hair flecked with grey curled from his hood, a pair of blue eyes shone with excitement from hollow sockets, and he wore the violet-and-white robes of a Moorish soldier.

It was his dress at which Major Shackleton looked.

"One of our renegade deserters tired of his new friends," he said with some contempt.

"Renegades do not wear chains," replied the man in the doorway, lifting from beneath his long sleeves his manacled hands. He spoke in a weak, hoarse voice, and with a rusty accent; he rested a hand against the jamb of the door as though he needed support. Tessin sprang up from his chair, and half crossed the room.

The stranger took an uncertain step forward. His legs rattled as he moved, and Wyley saw that the links of broken fetters were twisted about his ankles.

"Have two years made so vast a difference?" he asked. "Well, they were years of the bastinado, and I do not wonder."

Tessin peered into his face. "By God, it is!" he exclaimed. "Knightley!"

"Thanks," said Knightley with a smile.

Tessin reached out to take Knightley's hands, then instantly

A. E. W. Mason

stopped, glanced from Knightley to Scrope and drew back.

"Knightley!" cried the Major in a voice of welcome, rising in his seat. Then he too glanced expectantly at Scrope and sat down again. Scrope made no movement, but stood with his eyes cast down on the table like a man lost in thought. It was evident to Wyley that both Shackleton and Tessin had obeyed the sporting instinct, and had left the floor clear for the two men. It was no less evident that Knightley remarked their action and did not understand it. For his eyes travelled from face to face, and searched each with a wistful anxiety for the reason of their reserve.

"Yes, I am Knightley," he said timidly. Then he drew himself to his full height. "Ensign Knightley of the Tangier Foot," he cried.

No one answered. The company waited upon Scrope in a suspense so keen that even the ringing challenge of the words passed unheeded. Knightley spoke again, but now in a stiff, formal voice, and slowly.

"Gentlemen, I fear very much that two years make a world of difference. It seems they change one who had your goodwill into a most unwelcome stranger."

His voice broke in a sob; he turned to the door, but staggered as he turned and caught at a chair. In a moment Major Shackleton was beside him.

"What, lad? Have we been backward? Blame our surprise, not us."

"Meanwhile," said Wyley, "Ensign Knightley's starving."

The Major pressed Knightley into a chair, called for an

orderly, and bade him bring food. Wyley filled a glass with wine from the bottle on the table, and handed it to the Ensign.

"It is vinegar," he said, "but—"

"But Tangier is still Tangier," said Knightley with a laugh. The Major's cordiality had strengthened him like a tonic. He raised the glass to his lips and drank; but as he tilted his head back his eyes over the brim of the glass rested on Scrope, who still stood without movement, without expression, a figure of stone, but that his chest rose and fell with his deep breathing. Knightley set down his glass half-full.

"There is something amiss," he said, "since even Captain Scrope retains no memory of his old comrade."

"Captain?" exclaimed Wyley. So Scrope had been more than a lieutenant. Here was an answer to the question which had perplexed him. But it only led to another question: "Had Scrope been degraded, and why?" He did not, however, speculate on the question, for his attention was seized the next moment. Scrope made no sort of answer to Knightley's appeal, but began to drum very softly with his fingers on the table. And the drumming, at first vague and of no significance, gradually took on, of itself as it seemed, a definite rhythm. There was a variation, too, in the strength of the taps—now they fell light, now they struck hard. Scrope was quite unconsciously beating out upon the table a particular tune, although, since there was but the one note sounded, Wyley could get no more than an elusive hint of its character.

Knightley watched Scrope for a little as earnestly as the rest. Then—"Harry!" he said, "Harry Scrope!" The name leaped from his lips in a pleading cry; he stretched out his hands towards Scrope, and the chain which bound them reached

A. E. W. Mason

down to the table and rattled on the wood.

There was a simultaneous movement, almost a simultaneous ejaculation of bewilderment amongst those who stood about Knightley. Where they had expected a deadly anger, they found in its place a beseeching humility. And Scrope ceased from drumming on the table and turned on Knightley.

"Don't shake your chains at me," he burst out harshly. "I am deaf to any reproach that they can make. Are you the only man that has worn chains? I can show as good, and better." He thrust the palm of his left hand under Knightley's nose. "Branded, d'ye see? Branded. There's more besides." He set his foot on the chair and stripped the silk stocking down his leg. Just above the ankle there was a broad indent where a fetter had bitten into the flesh. "I have dragged a chain, you see; not like you among the Moors, but here in Tangier, on that damned Mole, in sight of these my brother officers. By the Lord, Knightley, I tell you you have had the better part of it."

"You!" cried Knightley. "You dragged a chain on Tangier Mole? For what offence?" And he added, with a genuine tenderness, "There was no disgrace in't, I'll warrant."

Major Shackleton half checked an exclamation, and turned it into a cough. Scrope leaned right across the table and stared straight into Knightley's eyes.

"The offence was a duel," he answered steadily, "fought on the night of January 6th two years ago."

Knightley's face clouded for an instant. "The night when I was captured," he said timidly.

"Yes."

The officers drew closer about the table, and seemed to hold their breath, as the strange catechism proceeded.

"With whom did you fight?" asked Knightley.

"With a very good friend of mine," replied Scrope, in a hard, even voice.

"On what account?"

"A woman."

Knightley laughed with a man's amused leniency for such escapades when he himself is in no way hurt by them.

"I said there would be no disgrace in't, Harry," he said, with a smile of triumph.

The heads of the listeners, which had bunched together, were suddenly drawn back. A dark flush of anger overspread Scrope's face, and the veins ridged up upon his forehead. Some impatient speech was on the tip of his tongue, when the Major interposed.

"What's this talk of penalties? Where's the sense of it? Scrope paid the price of his fault. He was admitted to the ranks afterwards. He won a lieutenancy by sheer bravery in the field. For all we know he may be again a captain to-morrow. Anyhow he wears the King's uniform. It is a badge of service which levels us all from Ensign to Major in an equality of esteem."

Scrope bowed to the Major and drew back from the table. The other officers shuffled and moved in a welcome relief from the strain of their expectancy, and Knightley's thoughts were diverted by Shackleton's words to a quite different

A. E. W. Mason

subject. For he picked with his fingers at the Moorish robe he wore and "I too wore the King's uniform," he pleaded wistfully.

"And shall do so again, thank God," responded the Major heartily.

Knightley started up from his chair; his face lightened unaccountably.

"You mean that?" he asked eagerly. "Yes, yes, you mean it! Then let it be to-night—now—even before I sup. As long as I wear these chains, as long as I wear this dress, I can feel the driver's whip curl about my shoulders." He parted the robe as he spoke, and showed that underneath he wore only a coarse sack which reached to his knees, with a hole cut in it for his head.

"True, you have worn the chains too long," said the Major. "I should have had them knocked off before, but—" he paused for a second, "but your coming so surprised me that of a truth I forgot," he continued lamely. Then he turned to Tessin. "See to it, Tessin! Ensign Barbour of the Tangier Foot was killed to-day. He was quartered in the Main-Guard. Take Knightley to his quarters and see what you can do. By the way, Knightley, there's a question I should have put to you before. By what road did you come in?"

"Down Teviot Hill past the Henrietta Fort. The Moors brought me down from Mequinez to interpret between them and their prisoners. I escaped last night."

"Past the Henrietta Fort?" replied the Major. "Then you can help us, for that way we make our sortie."

"To relieve the Charles Fort?" said Knightley. "I guessed the

Charles Fort was surrounded, for I heard one man on the Tangier wall shouting through a speaking trumpet to the Charles Fort garrison. But it will not be easy to relieve them. The Moors are entrenched between. There are three trenches. I should never have crawled through them, but that I stripped a dead Moor of his robe."

"Three trenches," said Tessin, with a shrug of the shoulders.

"Yes, three. The two nearest to Tangier may be carried. But the third—it is deep, twelve feet at the least, and wide, at the least eight yards. The sides are steep and slippery with the rain."

"A grave, then," said Scrope carelessly; "a grave that will hold many before the evening falls. It is well they made it wide and deep enough."

The sombre words knocked upon every heart like a blow on a door behind which conspirators are plotting. The Major was the first to recover his speech.

"Curse your tongue, Scrope!" he said angrily. "Let who will lie in your grave when the evening falls. Before that time comes, we'll show these Moors so fine a powder-play as shall glut some of them to all eternity. *Bon chat, bon rat*; we are not made of jelly. Tessin, see to Knightley."

The two men withdrew. Major Shackleton scribbled a note and despatched it to Sir Palmes Fairborne, the Lieutenant-Governor. Scrope took a turn or two across the room while the Major was writing the news which Knightley had brought. Then—"What game is this he's playing?" he said, with a jerk of his head to the door by which Knightley had gone out. "I have no mind to be played with."

"But is he playing a game at all?" asked Wyley.

Scrope faced him quickly, looked him over for a second, and replied: "You are a new-comer to Tangier, or you would not have asked that question."

"I should," rejoined Wyley with complete confidence. "I know quite enough to be sure of one thing. I know there lies some deep matter of dispute between Ensign Knightley and Lieutenant Scrope, and I am sure that there is one other person more in the dark than myself, and that person is Ensign Knightley. For whereas I know there is a dispute, he is unaware of even that."

"Unaware?" cried Scrope. "Why, man, the very good friend I fought with was Ensign Knightley. The woman on whose account we fought was Knightley's wife." He flung the words at the Surgeon with almost a gesture of contempt. "Make the most of that!" And once again he began to pace the room.

"I am not in the least surprised," returned Wyley with an easy smile. "Though I admit that I am interested. A wife is sauce to any story." He looked placidly round the company. He alone held the key to the puzzle, and since he was now become the centre of attraction he was inclined to play with his less acute brethren. With a wave of the hand he stilled the requests for an explanation, and turned to Scrope.

"Will you answer me a question?"

"I think it most unlikely."

The curt reply in no way diminished the Surgeon's suavity.

"I chose my words ill. I should have asked, Will you confirm an assertion? The assertion is this: Ensign Knightley had no suspicion before he actually discovered the—well, the lamentable truth."

Scrope stopped his walk and came back to the table.

"Why, that is so," he agreed sullenly. "Knightley had no suspicions. It angered me that he had not."

Wyley leaned back in his chair.

"Really, really," he said, and laughed a little to himself. "On the night of January 6th Ensign Knightley discovers the lamentable truth. At what hour?" he asked suddenly.

Scrope looked to the Major. "About midnight," he suggested.

"A little later, I should think," corrected Major Shackleton.

"A little after midnight," repeated Wyley. "Ensign Knightley and Lieutenant Scrope, I understand, immediately fight a duel, which seems to have been interrupted before any hurt was done."

The Major and Scrope agreed with a nod of their heads.

"In the morning," continued Wyley, "Ensign Knightley takes part in a skirmish, and is clubbed on the head so fiercely that Major Shackleton thought his skull must be broken in. At what hour was he struck?" Again he put the question quickly.

"'Twixt seven and eight of the morning," replied the Major.

"Quite so," said Wyley. "The incidents fit to a nicety. Two years afterwards Ensign Knightley comes home. He knows nothing of the duel, or any cause for a duel. Lieutenant

A. E. W. Mason

Scrope is still 'Harry' to him, and his best of friends. It is all very clear."

He gazed about him. Perplexity sat on each face except one; that face was Scrope's.

"I spoke to you all some half an hour since concerning the effects of a concussion. I could not have hoped for so complete an example," said Wyley.

Captain Tessin whistled; Major Shackleton bounced on to his feet.

"Then Knightley knows nothing," cried Tessin in a gust of excitement.

"And never will know," cried the Major.

"Except by hearsay," sharply interposed Scrope. "Gentlemen, you go too fast, Except by hearsay. That, Mr. Wyley, was the phrase, I think. By what spells, Major," he asked with irony, "will you bind Tangier to silence when there's scandal to be talked? Let Knightley walk down to the water-gate to-morrow; I'll warrant he'll have heard the story a hundred times with a hundred new embellishments before he gets there."

Major Shackleton resumed his seat moodily.

"And since that's the truth, why, he had best hear the story nakedly from me."

"From you?" exclaimed Tessin. "Another duel, then. Have you counted the cost?"

"Why, yes," replied Scrope quietly.

"Two years of the bastinado," said the Major. "That was what he said. He comes back to Tangier to find—who knows?—a worse torture here. Knightley, Knightley, a good officer marked for promotion until that infernal night. Scrope, I could turn moralist and curse you!"

Scrope dropped his head as though the words touched him. But it was not long before he raised it again.

"You waste your pity, I think, Major," he said coldly. "I disagree with Mr. Wyley's conclusions. Knightley knows the truth of the matter very well. For observe, he has made no mention of his wife. He has been two years in slavery. He escapes, and he asks for no news of his wife. That is unlike any man, but most of all unlike Knightley. He has his own ends to serve, no doubt, but he knows."

The argument appeared cogent to Major Shackleton.

"To be sure, to be sure," he said. "I had not thought of that."

Tessin looked across to Wyley.

"What do you say?"

"I am not convinced," replied Wyley. "Indeed, I was surprised that Knightley's omission had not been remarked before. When you first showed reserve in welcoming Knightley, I noticed that he became all at once timid, hesitating. He seemed to be afraid."

Major Shackleton admitted the Surgeon's accuracy. "Well, what then?"

"Well, I go back to what I said before Knightley appeared. A man has lost so many hours. The question, what he did

A. E. W. Mason

during those hours, is one that may well appal any one. Lieutenant Scrope doubted whether that question would trouble a man, and needed an instance. I believe here is the instance. I believe Knightley is afraid to ask any questions, and I believe his reason to be fear of how he lived during those lost hours."

There was a pause. No one was prepared to deny, however much he might doubt, what Wyley said.

Wyley continued:

"At some point of time before this duel Knightley's recollections break off. At what precise point we are not aware, nor is it of any great importance. The sure thing is he does not know of the dispute between Lieutenant Scrope and himself, and it is of more importance for us to consider whether he cannot after all be kept from knowing. Could he not be sent home to England? Mrs. Knightley, I take it, is no longer in Tangier?"

Major Shackleton stood up, took Wyley by the arm and led him out on to the balcony. The town beneath them had gone to sleep; the streets were quiet; the white roofs of the houses in the star-shine descended to the water's edge like flights of marble steps; only here and there did a light burn. To one of the lights close by the city wall the Major directed Wyley's attention. The house in which it burned lay so nearly beneath them that they could command a corner of the square open *patio* in the middle of it; and the light shone in a window set in that corner and giving on to the *patio*.

"You see that house?" said the Major.

"Yes," said Wyley. "It is Scrope's. I have seen him enter and come out."

"No doubt," said the Major; "but it is Knightley's house."

"Knightley's! Then the light burning in the window is—"

The Major nodded. "She is still in Tangier. And never a care for him has troubled her for two years, not so much as would bring a pucker to her pretty forehead—all my arrears of pay to a guinea-piece."

Wyley leaned across the rail of the balcony, watching the light, and as he watched he was aware that his feelings and his thoughts changed. The interest which he had felt in Scrope died clean away, or rather was transferred to Knightley; and with this new interest there sprang up a new sympathy, a new pity. The change was entirely due to that one yellow light burning in the window and the homely suggestions which it provoked. It brought before him very clearly the bitter contrast: so that light had burned any night these last two years, and Scrope had gone in and out at his will, while up in the barbarous inlands of Morocco the husband had had his daily portion of the bastinado and the whip. It was her fault, too, and she made her profit of it. Wyley became sensible of an overwhelming irony in the disposition of the world.

"You spoke a true word to-night, Major," he said bitterly. "That light down there might turn any man to a moralist, and send him preaching in the market-places."

"Well," returned the Major, as though he must make what defence he could for Scrope, "the story is not the politest in the world. But, then, you know Tangier—it is only a tiny outpost on the edges of the world where we starve behind broken walls forgotten of our friends. We have the Moors ever swarming at our gates and the wolf ever snarling at our heels, and so the niceties of conduct are lost. We have so

A. E. W. Mason

little time wherein to live, and that little time is filled with the noise of battle. Passion has its way with us in the end, and honour comes to mean no more than bravery and a gallant death."

He remained a few moments silent, and then disconnectedly he told Wyley the rest of the story.

"It was only three years ago that Knightley came to Tangier. He should never have brought his wife with him. Scrope and Knightley became friends. All Tangier knew the truth pretty soon, and laughed at Knightley's ignorance.... I remember the night of January 6th very well. I was Captain of the Guard that night too. A spy brought in news that we might expect a night attack. I sent Knightley with the news to Lord Inchiquin. On the way back he stepped into his own house. It was late at night. Mrs. Knightley was singing some foolish song to Scrope. The two men came down into the street and fought then and there. The quarter was aroused, the combatants arrested and brought to me.... There are two faults which our necessities here compel us to punish beyond their proper gravity: duelling, for we cannot afford to lose officers that way; and brawling in the streets at night, because the Moors lie *perdus* under our walls; ready to take occasion as it comes. Of Scrope's punishment you have heard. Knightley I released for that night. He was on guard—I could not spare him. We were attacked in the morning, and repulsed the attack. We followed up our success by a sortie in which Knightley fell."

Wyley began again to wonder at what particular point in this story Knightley's recollection broke off; and, further, what particular fear it was that kept him from all questions even concerning his wife.

Knightley's voice was heard behind them, and they turned

back into the room. The Ensign had shaved his matted beard and combed out his hair, which now curled and shone graciously about his head and shoulders; his face, too, for all that it was wasted, had taken almost a boyish zest, and his figure, revealed in the graceful dress of his regiment, showed youth in every movement. He was plainly by some years a younger man than Scrope.

He saluted the Major, and Wyley noticed that with his uniform he seemed to have drawn on something of a soldierly confidence.

"There's your supper, lad," said Shackleton, pointing to a few poor herrings and a crust of bread which an orderly had spread upon the table. "It is scanty."

"I like it the better," said Knightley with a laugh; "for so I am assured I am at home, in Tangier. There is no beef, I suppose?"

"Not so much as a hoof."

"No butter?"

"Not enough to cover a sixpence."

"There is cheese, however." He lifted up a scrap upon a fork.

"There will be none to-morrow."

"And as for pay?" he asked slyly.

"Two years and a half in arrears."

Knightley laughed again.

A. E. W. Mason

"Moreover," added Shackleton, "out of our nothing we may presently have to feed the fleet. It is indeed the pleasantest joke imaginable."

"In a week, no doubt," rejoined Knightley, "I shall be less sensible of its humour. But to-night—well, I am home in Tangier, and that contents me. Nothing has changed." At that he stopped suddenly. "Nothing has changed?" This time the phrase was put as a question, and with the halting timidity which he had shown before. No one answered the question. "No, nothing has changed," he said a third time, and again his eyes began to travel wistfully from face to face.

Tessin abruptly turned his back; Shackleton blinked his eyes at the ceiling with altogether too profound an unconcern; Scrope reached out for the wine, and spilt it as he filled his glass; Wyley busily drew diagrams with a wet finger on the table.

All these details Knightley remarked. He laid down his fork, he rested his elbow on the table, his forehead upon his hand. Then absently he began to hum over to himself a tune. The rhythm of it was somehow familiar to the Surgeon's ears. Where had he heard it before? Then with a start he remembered. It was this very rhythm, that very tune, which Scrope's fingers had beaten out on the table when he first saw Knightley. And as he had absently drummed it then, so Knightley absently hummed it now.

Surely, then, the tune had some part in the relations of the two men—perhaps a part in this story. "A foolish song." The words flashed into Wyley's mind.

"She was singing a foolish song." What if the tune was the tune of that song? But then—Wyley's argument came to a sudden conclusion. For if the tune *was* the tune of that song, why, then Knightley must know the truth, since he remembered that song. Was Scrope right after all? Was Knightley playing with him? Wyley glanced at Knightley in the keenest excitement. He wanted words fitted to that tune, and in a little the words came—first one or two fitted here and there to a note, and murmured unconsciously, then an entire phrase which filled out a bar, finally this verse in its proper sequence:

"No, no, fair heretick, it needs must be
But an ill love in me,
And worse for thee;
For were it in my power
To love thee now this hour
More than I did the last,
'Twould then so fall
I might not love at all.
Love that can flow...."

And then the song broke off, and silence followed. Wyley looked again at Knightley, but the latter had not changed his position. He still sat with his face shaded by his hand.

The Surgeon was startled by a light touch on the arm. He turned with almost a jump, and he saw Scrope bending across the table towards him, his eyes ablaze with an excitement no less keen than his own.

"He knows, he knows!" whispered Scrope. "It was that song she was singing; at that word 'flow' he pushed open the door of the room."

Knightley raised his head and drew his hand across his forehead, as though Scrope's whisper had aroused him. Scrope seated himself hurriedly.

"Nothing has changed, eh?" Knightley asked, like a man fresh from his sleep. Then he stood, and quietly, slowly, walked round the table until he stood directly behind Scrope's chair. Scrope's face hardened; he laid the palms of his hands upon the edge of the table ready to spring up; he looked across to Wyley with the expectation of death in his eyes.

One of the officers shuffled his feet. Tessin said "Hush!" Knightley took a step forward and dropped a hand on Scrope's shoulder, very lightly; but none the less Scrope started and turned white as though he had been stabbed.

"Harry," said the Ensign, "my—my wife is still in Tangier?"

Scrope drew in a breath. "Yes."

"Ah, waiting for me! You have shown her what kindness you could during my slavery?"

He spoke in a wavering voice, as if he were not sure of his ground, and as he spoke he felt Scrope shiver beneath his hand, and saw upon the faces of his companions an unmistakable shrinking. He turned away and staggered, rather than walked, to the window, where he stood leaning against the sill.

"The day is breaking," he said quietly. Wyley looked up; outside the window the colour was fading down the sky. It was purple still towards the zenith, but across the Straits its edges rested white upon the hills of Spain.

"Love that can flow ..." murmured Knightley, and of a sudden he flung back into the room. "Let me have the truth of it," he burst out, confronting his brother-officers gathered about the table—"the truth, though it knell out my damnation. If you only knew how up there, at Fez, at Mequinez, I have pictured your welcome when I should get back! I made of my anticipation a very anodyne. The cudgelling, the chains, the hunger, the sun, hot as though a burning glass was held above my head—it would all make a good story for the guard-room when I got back—when I got back. And yet I do get back, and one and all of you draw away from me as though I were one of the Tangier lepers we jostle in the streets. 'Love that can flow ...'" he broke off. "I ask myself"—he hesitated, and with a great cry, "I ask you, did I play the coward on that night I was captured two years ago?"

"The coward?" exclaimed Shackleton in bewilderment.

Wyley, for all his sympathy, could not refrain from a triumphant glance at Scrope. "Here is the instance you needed," he said.

"Yes, did I play the coward?" Knightley seated himself sideways on the edge of the table, and clasping his hands between his knees, went on in a quick, lowered voice. "'Love that can flow'—those are the last words I remember. You sent me, Major, to the Governor with a message. I delivered it; I started back. On my way back I passed my house. I went in. I stood in the *patio*. My wife was singing that song. The window of the room in which she sang opened on to the *patio*. I stood there listening for a second. Then I went upstairs. I turned the handle of the door. I remember quite clearly the light upon the room wall as I opened the door. Those words 'love that can flow' came swelling through the opening; and—and—the next thing I am aware of, I was riding chained upon a camel into slavery."

Tessin and Major Shackleton looked suddenly towards Wyley in recognition of the accuracy of his guess. Scrope simply wiped the perspiration from his forehead and waited.

A. E. W. Mason

"But how does that—forgetfulness, shall we say?—persuade you to the fear that you played the coward?" asked Wyley.

"Well," replied Knightley, and his voice sank to a whisper, "I played the coward afterwards at Mequinez. At the first it used to amuse me to wonder what happened after I opened the door and before I was captured outside Tangier; later it only puzzled me, and in the end it began to frighten me. You see, I could not tell; it was all a blank to me, as it is now; and a man overdriven—well, he nurses sickly fancies. No need to say what mine were until the day I played the coward in Mequinez. They set me to build the walls of the Emperor's new Palace. We used the stones of the old Roman town and built them up in Mequinez, and in the walls we were bidden to build Christian slaves alive to the glory of Allah. I refused. They stripped the flesh off my feet with their bastinadoes, starved me of food and drink, and brought me back again to the walls. Again I refused." Knightley looked up at his audience, and whether or no he mistook their breathless silence for disbelief,—"I did," he implored. "Twice I refused, and twice they tortured me. The third time—I was so broken, the whistle of a cane in the air made me cry out with pain—I was sunk to that pitch of cowardice—" He stopped, unable to complete the sentence. He clasped and unclasped his hands convulsively, he moistened his dry lips with his tongue, and looked about him with a weak, almost despairing laugh. Then he began in another way. "The Christian was a Portuguee from Marmora. He was set in the wall with his arms outstretched on either side—the attitude of a man crucified. I built in his arms—his right arm first—and mortised the stones, then his left arm in the same way. I was careful not to look in his face. No, no! I didn't look in his face." Knightley repeated the words with a horrible leer of cunning, and hugged himself with his arms. To Wyley's thinking he was strung almost to madness. "After his arms I built in his feet, and upwards from his feet I built in his legs and his body until I came to his neck. All this while he had been crying out for pity, babbling prayers, and the rest of it. When I reached his neck he ceased his clamour. I suppose he was dumb with horror. I did not know. All I knew was that now I should have to meet his eyes as I built in his face. I thought for a moment of blinding him. I could have done it quite easily with a stone. I picked up a stone to do it, and then, well—I could not help looking at him. He drew my eyes to his like a steel filing to a magnet. And once I had looked, once I had heard his eyes speaking, I—I tore down the stones. I freed his body, his legs, his feet and one arm. When the guards noticed what I was doing I cannot tell. I could not tell you when their sticks began to beat me. But they dragged me away when I had freed only one arm. I remember seeing him tugging at the other. What happened to me,"—he shivered,—"I could not describe to you. But you see I had played the coward finely at Mequinez, and when that question recurred to me as to what had happened after I had opened the door, I began to wonder whether by any chance I had played the coward at Tangier. I dismissed the thought as a sickly fancy, but it came again and again; and I came back here, and you draw aloof from me with averted faces and forced welcomes on your lips. Did I play the coward on that night I was captured? Tell me! Tell me!" And so the torrent of his speech came to an end.

The Major rose gravely from his seat, walked round the table and held out his hand.

"Put your hand there, lad," he said gravely.

Knightley looked at the outstretched hand, then at the Major's face. He took the hand diffidently, and the Major's grasp was of the heartiest.

"Neither at Mequinez nor at Tangier did you play the

A. E. W. Mason

coward," said the Major. "You fell by my side in the van of the attack."

And then Knightley began to cry. He blubbered like a child, and with his blubbering he mixed apologies. He was weak, he was tired, his relief was too great; he was thoroughly ashamed.

"You see," he said, "there was need that I should know. My wife is waiting for me. I could not go back to her bearing that stigma. Indeed, I hardly dared ask news of her. Now I can go back; and, gentlemen, I wish you good-night."

He stood up, made his bow, wiped his eyes, and began to walk to the door. Scrope rose instantly.

"Sit down, Lieutenant," said the Major sharply, and Scrope obeyed with reluctance.

The Major watched Knightley cross the room. Should he let the Ensign go? Should he keep him? He could not decide. That Knightley would seek his wife at once might of course have been foreseen; and yet it had not been foreseen either by the Major or the others. The present facts, as they had succeeded one after another had engrossed their minds.

Knightley's hand was on the door, and the Major had not decided. He pushed the door open, he set a foot in the passage, and then the roar of a gun shook the room.

"Ah!" remarked Wyley, "the signal for your sortie."

Knightley stopped and listened. Major Shackleton stood in a fixed attitude with his eyes upon the floor. He had hit upon an issue, it seemed to him by inspiration. The noise of the gun was followed by ten clear strokes of a bell.

"That's for the King's Battalion," said Knightley with a smile.

"Yes," said Tessin, and picking up his sword from a corner he slung the bandolier across his shoulder.

The bell rang out again; this time the number of the strokes was twenty.

"That's for my Lord Dunbarton's Regiment," said Knightley.

"Yes," said two of the remaining officers. They took their hats and followed Captain Tessin down the stairs.

A third time the bell spoke, and the strokes were thirty.

"Ah!" said Knightley, "that's for the Tangier Foot. Well, good luck to you, Major!" and he passed through the door.

"A moment, Knightley. The regiment first. You wear Ensign Barbour's uniform. You must do more than wear his uniform. The regiment first."

Major Shackleton spoke in a husky voice and kept his eyes on the floor. Scrope looked at him keenly from the table. Knightley hardly looked at him at all. He stepped back into the room.

"With all my heart, Major: the regiment first."

"Your station is at Peterborough Tower. You will go there— at once."

"At once," replied Knightley cheerfully. "So she would wish," and he went down the stairs into the street. Major Shackleton picked up his hat.

"I command this sortie," he said to Wyley; but as he turned he found himself confronted by Scrope.

"What do you intend?" asked Scrope.

Major Shackleton looked towards Wyley. Wyley understood the look and also what Shackleton intended. He went from the room and left the two men together.

The grey light poured through the window; the candles still burnt yellow on the table.

"What do you intend?"

The Major looked Scrope straight in the face.

"I have heard a man speak to-night in a man's voice. I mean to do that man the best service that I can. These two years at Mequinez cannot mate with these two years at Tangier. Knightley knows nothing now; he never shall know. He believes his wife a second Penelope; he shall keep that belief. There is a trench—you called it very properly a grave. In that trench Knightley will not hear though all Tangier scream its gossip in his ears. I mean to give him his chance of death."

"No, Major," cried Scrope. "Or listen! Give me an equal chance."

"Trelawney's Regiment is not called out. Again, Lieutenant, I fear me you will have the harder part of it."

Shackleton repeated Scrope's own words in all sincerity, and hurried off to his post.

Scrope was left alone in the guard-room. A vision of the

trench, twelve feet deep, eight yards wide, yawned before his eyes. He closed them, but that made no difference; he still saw the trench. In imagination he began to measure its width and depth. Then he shook his head to rid himself of the picture, and went out on to the balcony. His eyes turned instinctively to a house by the city wall, to a corner of the *patio* the house and the latticed shutter of a window just seen from the balcony.

He stepped back into the room with a feeling of nausea, and blowing out the candles sat down alone, in the twilight, amongst the empty chairs. There were dark corners in the room; the broadening light searched into them, and suddenly the air was tinged with warm gold. Somewhere the sun had risen. In a little, Scrope heard a dropping sound of firing, and a few moments afterwards the rattle of a volley. The battle was joined. Scrope saw the trench again yawn up before his eyes. The Major was right. This morning, again, Lieutenant Scrope had the harder part of it.

A. E. W. Mason

THE MAN OF WHEELS

When Sir Charles Fosbrook was told by Mr. Pepys that Tangier had been surrendered to the Moors, he asked at once after the fate of his gigantic mole; and when he was informed that his mole had been, before the evacuation, so utterly blown to pieces that its scattered blocks made the harbour impossible for anchorage, he forbade so much as the mention in his presence of the name of Africa. But if he had done with Tangier, Tangier had not done with him, and five years afterwards he became concerned in the most unexpected way with certain tragic consequences of that desperate siege.

He received a letter from an acquaintance of whom he had long lost sight, a Mr. Mardale of the Quarry House near Leamington, imploring him to give his opinion upon some new inventions. The value of the inventions could be easily gauged; Mr. Mardale claimed to have invented a wheel of perpetual rotation. Sir Charles, however, had his impulses of kindness. He knew Mr. Mardale to be an old and gentle person, a little touched in the head perhaps, who with money enough to surfeit every instinct of pleasure, had preferred to live a shy secluded life, busily engaged either in the collection of curiosities or the invention of toy-like futile machines. There was a girl too whom Sir Charles remembered, a weird elfin creature with extraordinary black eyes and hair and a clear white face. Her one regret in those days had been that she was not born a horse, and she had lived in the stables, in as horse like a fashion as was possible. Her ankle indeed still must bear an unnecessary scar through the application of a fierce horse-liniment to a sprain. No doubt, however, she had long since changed her ambitions. Sir Charles calculated her age. Resilda Mardale must be twenty-five years old and a deuced fine woman into the bargain. Sir Charles took a glance at his figure in his cheval-glass. He had reached middle-age to be sure, but he had a leg that many a spindle-shanked youngster might envy, nor was there any unbecoming protuberance at his waist. He wrote a letter accepting the invitation and a week later in the dusk of a June evening, drove up the long avenue of trees to the terrace of the Quarry House.

The house was a solid square mansion built upon the side of a hill, and the ground in front of it fell away very quickly from the terrace to what Sir Charles imagined must be a pond, for a light mist hung at the bottom. On the other side of the pond the ground rose again in a steep hill. But Sir Charles had no opportunity at this moment to get any accurate knowledge of the house and its surroundings. For apart from the darkness, it was close upon supper-time and Miss Resilda Mardale must assuredly not be kept waiting. His valet subsequently declared that Sir Charles had seldom been so particular in the choice of his coat and small-clothes; and the supper-bell certainly rang out before he was satisfied with the set of his cravat.

He could not, however, consider his pains wasted when once he was set down opposite to Resilda. She was taller than he had expected her to be, but he did not count height a fault so long as there was grace to carry it off, and grace she had in plenty. Her face had gained in delicacy and lost nothing of its brilliancy, or of its remarkable clearness of complexion. Her hair too if it was less rebellious, and more neatly coiled,

A. E. W. Mason

had retained its glory of profusion, and her big black eyes, though to be sure they were grown a trifle sedate, no doubt could sparkle as of old. Sir Charles set himself to make them sparkle. Old Mr. Mardale prattled of his inventions to his heart's delight—he described the wheel, and also a flying machine and besides the flying machine, an engine by which steam might be used to raise water to great altitudes. Sir Charles was ready from time to time with a polite, if not always an appropriate comment, and for the rest he paid compliments to Resilda. Still the eyes did not sparkle, indeed a pucker appeared and deepened on her forehead. Sir Charles accordingly redoubled his gallantries, he was slyly humorous about the horse-liniment, and thereupon came the remark which so surprised him and was the beginning of his strange discoveries. For Resilda suddenly leaned towards him and said frankly:

"I would much rather, Sir Charles, you told me something of your great mole at Tangier."

Sir Charles had reason for surprise. The world had long since forgotten his mole, if ever it had been concerned in it. Yet here was a girl whose thoughts might be expected to run on youths and ribands talking of it in a little village four miles from Leamington as though there were no topic more universal. Sir Charles Fosbrook answered her gravely.

"I thought never to speak of Tangier and the mole again. I spent many years upon the devising and construction of that great breakwater. It could have sheltered every ship of his Majesty's navy. It was wife and children to me. My heart lay very close to it. I fancied indeed my heart was disrupted with the disruption of the mole, and it has at all events, lain ever since as heavy as King Charles' Chest."

"Yes, I can understand that," said Resilda.

Sir Charles had vowed never to speak of the matter again. But he had kept his vow for five long years, and besides here was a girl of a remarkable beauty expressing sympathy and asking for information. Sir Charles broke his vow and talked, and the girl helped him. A suspicion that she might have primed herself with knowledge in view of his coming, vanished before the flame of her enthusiasm. She knew the history of its building almost as well as he did himself, and could even set him right in his dates. It was she who knew the exact day on which King Charles' Chest, that great block of mortised stones, which formed as it were the keystone of the breakwater, had been lowered into its place. Sir Charles abandoned all reserve, and talked freely of his hopes and fears as the pier ran farther out and out into the currents of the Straits, of his bitter disappointment when his labours were destroyed. He forgot his gallantries, he showed himself the man he was. Neither he nor Resilda noticed a low rumble of thunder or the beating of sudden rain upon the windows, so occupied were they with the theme of their talk; and at last Sir Charles, leaning back in his chair, cried out with astonishment and delight.

"But how is it that my mole is so familiar a thing to you? Explain it if you please! Never have I spent so agreeable an evening."

A momentary embarrassment seemed to follow upon his words. Resilda looked at her father who chuckled and explained.

"Sir, an old soldier years ago came over the hill in front of the house and begged for alms. He found my daughter on the terrace in a lucky moment for himself. He had all sorts of wonderful stories of Tangier and the great mole which was then a building. Resilda was set on fire that day, and though the King and the Parliament might shut their eyes to the sore

A. E. W. Mason

straits of that town and the gallantry of its defenders, no one was allowed to forget them in the Quarry House. To tell the truth I sometimes envied the obliviousness of Parliament," and he laughed gently. "So from the first my daughter was primed with the history of that siege, and lately we have had further means of knowledge—" He began to speak warily and with embarrassment—"For two years ago Resilda married an officer of The King's Battalion, Major Lashley."

"Here are two surprises," cried Sir Charles. "For in the first place, Madam, I had no thought you were wed. Blame a bachelor's stupidity!" and he glanced at her left hand which lay upon the table-cloth with the band of gold gleaming upon a finger. "In the second place I knew Major Lashley very well, though it is news to me that he ever troubled his head with my mole. A very gallant officer, who defended Charles Fort through many nights of great suspense, and cleft his way back to Tangier when his ammunition was expended. I shall be very glad to shake the Major once more by the hand."

At once Sir Charles was aware that he had uttered the most awkward and unsuitable remark. Resilda Lashley, as he must now term her, actually flinched away from him and then sat with a vague staring look of pain as though she had been shocked clean out of her wits. She recovered herself in a moment, but she did not speak, neither had Sir Charles any words. He looked at her dress which was white and had not so much as a black riband dangling anywhere about it.

But there were other events than death which could make the utterance of his wish a *gaucherie*. Sir Charles prided himself upon his tact, particularly with a good-looking woman, and he was therefore much abashed and confused. The only one who remained undisturbed was Mr. Mardale. His mind was never for very long off his wheels, or his works of art. It was the turn of his pictures now. He had picked up a genuine

Rubens in Ghent, he declared. It was standing somewhere in the great drawing-room on the carpet against the back of a chair, and Sir Charles must look at it in the morning, if only it could be found. He had clean forgotten all about his daughter it appeared. She, however, had a mind to clear the mystery up, and interrupting her father.

"It is right that you should know," she said simply, "Major Lashley disappeared six months ago."

"Disappeared!" exclaimed Sir Charles in spite of himself, and the astonishment in his voice woke the old gentleman from his prattle.

"To be sure," said he apologetically, "I should have told you before of the sad business. Yes, Sir, Major Lashley disappeared, utterly from this very house on the eleventh night of last December, and though the country-side was scoured and every ragamuffin for miles round brought to question, no trace of him has anywhere been discovered from that day to this."

An intuition slipped into Sir Charles Fosbrook's mind, and though he would have dismissed it as entirely unwarrantable, persisted there. The thought of the steep slope of ground before the house and the mist in the hollow between the two hills. The mist was undoubtedly the exhalation from a pond. The pond might have reeds which might catch and gather a body. But the pond would have been dragged. Still the thought of the pond remained while he expressed a vague hope that the Major might by God's will yet be restored to them.

He had barely ended before a louder gust of rain than ordinary smote upon the windows and immediately there followed a knocking upon the hall-door. The sound was violent, and it

A. E. W. Mason

came with so opposite a rapidity upon the heels of Fosbrook's words that it thrilled and startled him. There was something very timely in the circumstances of night and storm and that premonitory clapping at the door. Sir Charles looked towards the door in a glow of anticipation. He had time to notice, however, how deeply Resilda herself was stirred; her left hand which had lain loose upon the table-cloth was now tightly clenched, and she had a difficulty in breathing. The one strange point in her conduct was that although she looked towards the door like Sir Charles Fosbrook, there was more of suspense in the look than of the eagerness of welcome. The butler, however, had no news of Major Lashley to announce. He merely presented the compliments of Mr. Gibson Jerkley who had been caught in the storm near the Quarry House and ten miles from his home. Mr. Jerkley prayed for supper and a dry suit of clothes.

"And a bed too," said Resilda, with a flush of colour in her cheeks, and begging Sir Charles' permission she rose from the table. Sir Charles was disappointed by the mention of a strange name. Mr. Mardale, however, to whom that loud knocking upon the door had been void of suggestion, now became alert. He looked with a strange anxiety after his daughter, an anxiety which surprised Fosbrook, to whom this man of wheels and little toys had seemed lacking in the natural affections.

"And a bed too," repeated Mr. Mardale doubtfully, "to be sure! To be sure!" And though he went into the hall to welcome his visitor, it was not altogether without reluctance.

Mr. Gibson Jerkley was a man of about thirty years. He had a brown open personable countenance, a pair of frank blue eyes, and the steady restful air of a man who has made his account with himself, and who neither speaks to win praise nor is at pains to escape dislike. Sir Charles Fosbrook was from the first taken with the man, though he spoke little with him for the moment. For being tired with his long journey from London, he retired shortly to his room.

But however tired he was, Sir Charles found that it was quite impossible for him to sleep. The cracking of the rain upon his windows, the groaning trees in the park, and the wail of the wind among the chimneys and about the corners of the house were no doubt for something in a Londoner's sleeplessness. But the mysterious disappearance of Major Lashley was at the bottom of it. He thought again of the pond. He imagined a violent kidnapping and his fancies went to work at devising motives. Some quarrel long ago in the crowded city of Tangier and now brought to a tragical finish amongst the oaks and fields of England. Perhaps a Moor had travelled over seas for his vengeance and found his way from village to village like that Baracen lady of old times. And when he had come to this point of his reflections, he heard a light rapping upon his door. He got out of bed and opened it. He saw Mr. Gibson Jerkley standing on the threshold with a candle in one hand and a finger of the other at his lip.

"I saw alight beneath your door," said Jerkley, and Sir Charles made room for him to enter. He closed the door cautiously, and setting his candle down upon a chest of drawers, said without any hesitation:

"I have come, Sir, to ask for your advice. I do not wonder at your surprise, it is indeed a strange sort of intrusion for a man to make upon whom you have never clapped your eyes before this evening. But for one thing I fancy Mrs. Lashley wishes me to ask you for the favour. She has said nothing definitely, in faith she could not as you will understand when you have heard the story. But that I come with her approval I am very sure. For another, had she disapproved, I should none the less have come of my own accord. Sir, though I

A. E. W. Mason

know you very well by reputation, I have had the honour of few words with you, but my life has taught me to trust boldly where my eyes bid me trust. And the whole affair is so strange that one more strange act like this intrusion of mine is quite of apiece. I ask you therefore to listen to me. The listening pledges you to nothing, and at the worst, I can promise you, my story will while away a sleepless hour. If when you have heard, you can give us your advice, I shall be very glad. For we are sunk in such a quandary that a new point of view cannot but help us."

Sir Charles pointed to a chair and politely turned away to hide a yawn. For the young man's lengthy exordium had made him very drowsy. He could very comfortably had fallen asleep at this moment. But Gibson Jerkley began to speak, and in a short space of time Sir Charles was as wide-awake as any house-breaker.

"Eight years ago," said he, "I came very often to the Quarry House, but I always rode homewards discontented in the evening. Resilda at that time had a great ambition to be a boy. The sight of any brown bare-legged lad gipsying down the hill with a song upon his lips, would set her viciously kicking the toes of her satin slippers against the parapet of the terrace, and clamouring at her sex. Now I was not of the same mind with Resilda."

"That I can well understand," said Sir Charles drily. "But, my young friend, I can remember a time when Resilda desired of all things to be a horse. There was something hopeful because more human in her wish to be a boy, had you only known."

Mr. Jerkley nodded gravely and continued:

"I was young enough to argue the point with her, which did

me no good, and then to make matters worse, the soldier from Tangier came over the hill, with his stories of Major Lashley—Captain he was then."

"Major Lashley," exclaimed Sir Charles. "I did not hear the soldier was one of Major Lashley's men!"

"But he was and thenceforward the world went very ill with me. Reports of battles, and sorties came home at rare intervals. She was the first to read of them. Major Lashley's name was more than once mentioned. We country gentlemen who stayed at home and looked after our farms and our tenants, having no experience of war, suffered greatly in the comparison. So at the last I ordered my affairs for a long voyage, and without taking leave of any but my nearest neighbours and friends, I slipped off one evening to the wars."

"You did not wish your friends at the Quarry House good-bye?" said Fosbrook.

"No. It might have seemed that I was making claims, and, after all, one has one's pride. I would never, I think, ask a woman to wait for me. But she heard of course after I had gone and—I am speaking frankly—I believe the news woke the woman in her. At all events there was little talk after of Tangier at the Quarry House."

Mr. Jerkley related his subsequent history. He had sailed at his own charges to Africa; he had enlisted as a gentleman volunteer in The King's Battalion; he had served under Major Lashley in the Charles Fort where he was in charge of the great speaking-trumpet by which the force received its orders from the Lieutenant-Governor in Tangier Castle; he took part in the desperate attempt to cut a way back through the Moorish army into the town. In that fight he was wounded

A. E. W. Mason

and left behind for dead.

"A year later peace was made. Tangier was evacuated, Major Lashley returned to England. Now the Major and I despite the difference in rank had been friends. I had spoken to him of Miss Mardale's admiration, and as chance would have it, he came to Leamington to take the waters."

"Chance?" said Sir Charles drily.

"Well it may have been intention," said Jerkley. "There was no reason in the world why he should not seek her out. She was not promised to me, and very likely I had spoken of her with enthusiasm. For a long time she would not consent to listen to him. He was, however, no less persistent—he pleaded his suit for three years. I was dead you understand, and what man worth a pinch of salt would wish a woman to waste her gift of life in so sterile a fidelity.... You follow me? At the end of three years Resilda yielded to his pleadings, and the persuasions of her friends. For Major Lashley quickly made himself a position in the country. They were married, Major Lashley was not a rich man, it was decided that they should both live at the Quarry House."

"And what had Mr. Mardale to say to it?" asked Fosbrook.

"Oh, Sir," said Gibson Jerkley with a laugh. "Mr. Mardale is a man of wheels, and little steel springs. Let him sit at his work-table in that crowded drawing-room on the first floor, without interruption, and he will be very well content, I can assure you.... Hush!" and he suddenly raised his hand. In the silence which followed, they both distinctly heard the sound of some one stirring in the house. Mr. Jerkley went to the door and opened it. The door gave on to the passage which was shut off at its far end by another door from the square tulip-wood landing, at the head of the stairs. He came back into the bedroom.

"There is a light on the other side of the passage-door," said he. "But I have no doubt it is Mr. Mardale going to his bed. He sits late at his work-table."

Sir Charles brought him back to his story.

"Meanwhile you were counted for dead, but actually you were taken prisoner. There is one thing which I do not understand. When peace was concluded the prisoners were freed and an officer was sent up into Morocco to secure their release."

"There were many oversights like mine, I have no doubt. The Moors were reluctant enough to produce their captives. We who were supposed to be dead were not particularly looked for. I have no doubt there is many a poor English soldier sweating out his soul in the uplands of that country to this day. I escaped two years ago, just about the time, in fact, when Miss Resilda Mardale became Mrs. Lashley. I crept down over the hillside behind Tangier one dark evening, and lay all night beneath a bush of tamarisks dreaming the Moors were still about me. But an inexplicable silence reigned and nowhere was the darkness spotted by the flame of any camp-fire. In the morning I looked down to Tangier. The first thing which I noticed was your broken stump of mole, the second that nowhere upon the ring of broken wall could be seen the flash of a red coat or the glitter of a musket-barrel. I came down into Tangier, I had no money and no friends. I got away in a felucca to Spain. From Spain I worked my passage to England. I came home nine months ago. And here is the trouble. Three months after I returned Major Lashley disappeared. You understand?"

"Oh," cried Sir Charles, and he jumped in his chair. "I

A. E. W. Mason

understand indeed. Suspicion settled upon you," and as it ever will upon the least provocation suspicion passed for a moment into Fosbrook's brain. He was heartily ashamed of it when he looked into Jerkley's face. It would need, assuredly, a criminal of an uncommon astuteness to come at this hour with this story. Mr. Jerkley was not that criminal.

"Yes," he answered simply, "I am looked at askance, devil a doubt of it. I would not care a snap of the fingers were I alone in the matter; but there is Mrs. Lashley ... she is neither wife nor widow ... and," he took a step across the room and said quickly—and were she known for a widow, there is still the suspicion upon me like a great iron door between us."

"Can you help us, Sir Charles! Can you see light?"

"You must tell me the details of the Major's disappearance," said Sir Charles, and the following details were given.

On the eleventh of December and at ten o'clock of the evening Major Lashley left the house to visit the stables which were situated in the Park and at the distance of a quarter of a mile from the house. A favourite mare, which he had hunted the day before, had gone lame, and all day Major Lashley had shown some anxiety; so that there was a natural reason why he should have gone out at the last moment before retiring to bed. Mrs. Lashley went up to her room at the same time, indeed with so exact a correspondence of movement that as she reached the polished tulip-wood landing at the top of the stairs, she heard the front door latch as her husband drew it to behind him. That was the last she heard of him.

"She woke up suddenly," said Jerkley, "in the middle of the night, and found that her husband was not at her side. She waited for a little and then rose from her bed. She drew the window-curtains aside and by the glimmering light which came into the room, was able to read the dial of her watch. It was seven minutes past three of the morning. She immediately lighted her candle and went to rouse her father. Her door opened upon the landing, it is the first door upon the left hand side as you mount the stairs; the big drawing-room opens on to the landing too, but faces the stairs. Mrs. Lashley at once went to that room, knowing how late Mr. Mardale is used to sit over his inventions, and as she expected, found him there. A search was at once arranged; every servant in the house was at once impressed, and in the morning every servant on the estate. Major Lashley had left the stable at a quarter past ten. He has been seen by no one since."

Sir Charles reflected upon this story.

"There is a pond in front of the house," said he.

"It was dragged in the morning," replied Jerkley.

Sir Charles made various inquiries and received the most unsatisfactory answers for his purpose. Major Lashley had been a favourite alike at Tangier, and in the country. He had a winning trick of a smile, which made friends for him even among his country's enemies. Mr. Jerkley could not think of a man who had wished him ill.

"Well, I will think the matter over," said Sir Charles, who had not an idea in his head, and he held the door open for Mr. Jerkley. Both men stood upon the threshold, looked down the passage and then looked at one another.

"It is strange," said Jerkley.

"The light has been a long while burning on the landing," said Sir Charles. They walked on tiptoe down the passage to

A. E. W. Mason

the door beneath which one bright bar of light stretched across the floor. Jerkley opened the door and looked through; Sir Charles who was the taller man looked over Jerkley's head and never were two men more surprised. In the embrasure of that door to the left of the staircase, the door behind which Resilda Lashley slept, old Mr. Mardale reclined, with his back propped against the door-post. He had fallen asleep at his post, and a lighted candle half-burnt flamed at his side. The reason of his presence then was clear to them both.

"A morbid fancy!" he said in a whisper, but with a considerable anger in his voice. "Such a fancy as comes only to a man who has lost his judgment through much loneliness. See, he sits like any negro outside an Eastern harem! Sir, I am shamed by him."

"You have reason I take the liberty to say," said Sir Charles absently, and he went back to his room puzzling over what he had seen, and over what he could neither see nor understand. The desire for sleep was altogether gone from him. He opened his window and leaned out. The rain had ceased, but the branches still dripped and the air was of an incomparable sweetness. Blackbirds and thrushes on the lawns, and in the thicket-depths were singing as though their lives hung upon the full fresh utterance of each note. A clear pure light was diffused across the world. Fosbrook went back to his old idea of some vengeful pursuit sprung from a wrong done long ago in Tangier. The picture of Major Lashley struck with terror as he got news of his pursuers, and slinking off into the darkness. Even now, somewhere or another, on the uplands or the plains of England, he might be rising from beneath a hedge to shake the rain from his besmeared clothes, and start off afresh on another day's aimless flight. The notion caught his imagination and comforted him to sleep. But in the morning he woke to recognise its unreality. The unreality became yet more vivid to him at the breakfast-table, when he sat with two pairs of young eyes turning again and again trustfully towards him. The very reliance which the man and woman so clearly placed in him spurred him. Since they looked to him to clear up the mystery, why he must do it, and there was an end of the matter.

He was none the less glad, however, when Mr. Jerkley announced his intention of returning home. There would at all events be one pair of eyes the less. He strolled with Mr. Jerkley on the terrace after breakfast with a deep air of cogitation, the better to avoid questions. Gibson Jerkley, however, was himself in a ruminative mood. He stopped, and gazing across the valley to the riband of road descending the hill:

"Down that road the soldier came," said he, "whose stories brought about all this misfortune."

"And very likely down that road will come the bearer of news to make an end of it," rejoined Fosbrook sententiously. Mr. Jerkley looked at him with a sudden upspringing of hope, and Sir Charles nodded with ineffable mystery, never guessing how these lightly spoken words were to return to his mind with the strength of a fulfilled prophecy.

As he nodded, however, he turned about towards the house, and a certain disfigurement struck upon his eyes. Two windows on the first floor were entirely bricked up, and as the house was square with level tiers of windows, they gave to it an unsightly look. Sir Charles inquired of his companion if he could account for them.

"To be sure," said Jerkley, with the inattention of a man diverted from serious thought to an unimportant topic. "They

A. E. W. Mason

are the windows of the room in which Mrs. Mardale died a quarter of a century ago. Mr. Mardale locked the door as soon as his wife was taken from it to the church, and the next day he had the windows blocked. No one but he has entered the room during all these years, the key has never left his person. It must be the ruin of a room by now. You can imagine it, the dust gathering, the curtains rotting, in the darkness and at times the old man sitting there with his head running on days long since dead. But you know Mr. Mardale, he is not as other men."

Sir Charles swung round alertly to his companion. To him at all events the topic was not an indifferent one.

"Yet you say, you believe that he is void of the natural affections. Last night we saw a proof, a crazy proof if you will, but none the less a proof of his devotion to his daughter. To-day you give me as sure a one of his devotion to his dead wife," and almost before he had finished, Mr. Mardale was calling to him from the steps of the house.

He spent all that morning in the great drawing-room on the first floor. It was a room of rich furniture, grown dingy with dust and inattention, and crowded from end to end with tables and chairs and sofas, on which were heaped in a confused medley, pictures, statues of marble, fans and buckles from Spain, queer barbaric ornaments, ivory carvings from the Chinese. Sir Charles could hardly make his way to the little cleared space by the window, where Mr. Mardale worked, without brushing some irreplaceable treasure to the floor. Once there he was fettered for the morning. Mr. Mardale with all the undisciplined enthusiasm of an amateur, jumping from this invention to that, beaming over his spectacles. Sir Charles listened with here and there a word of advice, or of sympathy with the labour of creation. But his thoughts were busy elsewhere, he was pondering over his discovery of the morning, over the sight which he and Jerkley had seen last night, he was accustoming himself to regard the old man in a strange new light, as an over-careful father and a sorely-stricken husband. Meanwhile he sat over against the window which was in the side of the house, and since the house was built upon a slope of hill, although the window was on the first floor, a broad terrace of grass stretched away from it to a circle of gravel ornamented with statues. On this terrace he saw Mrs. Lashley, and reflected uncomfortably that he must meet her at dinner and again sustain the inquiry of her eyes.

He avoided actual questions, however, and as soon as dinner was over, with a meaning look at the girl to assure her that he was busy with her business, he retired to the library. Then he sat himself down to think the matter over restfully. But the room, walled with books upon its three sides, fronted the Southwest on its fourth, and as the afternoon advanced, the hot June sun streamed farther and farther into the room. Sir Charles moved his chair back, and again back, and again, until at last it was pushed into the one cool dark corner of the room. Then Sir Charles closed his wearied eyes the better to think. But he had slept little during the last night, and when he opened them again, it was with a guilty start. He rubbed his eyes, then he reached a hand down quickly at his side, and lifted a book out of the lowest shelf in the corner. The book was a volume of sermons. Sir Charles replaced it, and again dipped his hand into the lucky-bag. He drew out a tome of Mr. Hobbes' philosophy; Sir Charles was not in the mood for Hobbes; he tried again. On this third occasion he found something very much more to his taste, namely the second Volume of Anthony Hamilton's Memoirs of Count Grammont. This he laid upon his knee, and began glancing through the pages while he speculated upon the mystery of the Major's disappearance. His thoughts, however, lagged in a now well-worn circle, they begot nothing new in the way

A. E. W. Mason

of a suggestion. On the other hand the book was quite new to him. He became less and less interested in his thoughts, more and more absorbed in the Memoirs. There were passages marked with a pencil-line in the margin, and marked, thought Sir Charles, by a discriminating judge. He began to look only for the marked passages, being sure that thus he would most easily come upon the raciest anecdotes. He read the story of the Count's pursuit by the brother of the lady he was affianced to. The brother caught up the Count when he was nearing Dover to return to France. "You have forgotten something," said the brother. "So I have," replied Grammont. "I have forgotten to marry your sister." Sir Charles chuckled and turned over the pages. There was an account of how the reprobate hero rode seventy miles into the country to keep a tryst with an *inamorata* and waited all night for no purpose in pouring rain by the Park gate. Sir Charles laughed aloud. He turned over more pages, and to his surprise came across, amongst the marked passages, a quite unentertaining anecdote of how Grammont lost a fine new suit of clothes, ordered for a masquerade at White Hall. Sir Charles read the story again, wondering why on earth this passage had been marked; and suddenly he was standing by the window, holding the book to the light in a quiver of excitement. Underneath certain letters in the words of this marked passage he had noticed dents in the paper, as though by the pressure of a pencil point. Now that he stood by the light, he made sure of the dents, and he saw also by the roughness of the paper about them, that the pencil-marks had been carefully erased. He read these underlined letters together— they made a word, two words—a sentence, and the sentence was an assignation.

Sir Charles could not remember that the critical moment in any of his great engineering undertakings, had ever caused him such a flutter of excitement, such a pulsing in his temples, such a catching of his breath—no, not even the lowering of Charles' Chest into the Waters of Tangier harbour. Everything at once became exaggerated out of its proportions, the silence of the house seemed potential and expectant, the shadows in the room now that the sun was low had their message, he felt a queer chill run down his spine like ice, he shivered. Then he hurried to the door, locked it and sat down to a more careful study. And as he read, there came out before his eyes a story—a story told as it were in telegrams, a story of passion, of secret meetings, of gratitude for favours.

Who was the discriminating judge who had marked these passages and underlined these letters? The book was newly published, it was in the Quarry House, and there were three occupants of the Quarry House. Was it Mr. Mardale? The mere question raised a laugh. Resilda? Never. Major Lashley then? If not Major Lashley, who else?

It flashed into his mind that here in this book he might hold the history of the Major's long courtship of Resilda. But he dismissed the notion contemptuously. Gibson Jerkley had told him of that courtship, and of the girl's reluctance to respond to it. Besides Resilda was never the woman in this story. Perhaps the first volume might augment it and give the clue to the woman's identity. Sir Charles hunted desperately through the shelves. Nowhere was the first volume to be found. He wasted half-an-hour before he understood why. Of course the other volume would be in the woman's keeping, and how in the world to discover her?

Things moved very quickly with Sir Charles that afternoon. He had shut up the volume and laid it on the table, the while he climbed up and down the library steps. From the top of the steps he glanced about the room in a despairing way, and his eyes lit upon the table. For the first time he remarked the binding which was of a brown leather. But all the books on

　　　　　A. E. W. Mason

the shelves were bound uniformly in marble boards with a red backing. He sprang down from the steps with the vigour of a boy, and seizing the book looked in the fly leaf for a name. There was a name, the name of a bookseller in Leamington, and as he closed the book again, some one rapped upon the door. Sir Charles opened it and saw Mr. Mardale. He gave the old gentleman no time to speak.

"Mr. Mardale," said he, "I am a man of plethoric habits, and must needs take exercise. Can you lend me a horse?"

Mr. Mardale was disappointed as his manner showed. He had perhaps at that very moment hit upon a new and most revolutionary invention. But his manners hindered him from showing more than a trace of the disappointment, and Sir Charles rode out to the bookseller at Leamington, with the volume beneath his coat.

"Can you show me the companion to this?" said he, dumping it down upon the counter. The bookseller seized upon the volume and fondled it.

"It is not fair," he cried. "In any other affair but books, it would be called at once sheer dishonesty. Here have been my subscribers clamouring for the Memoirs for six months and more."

"You hire out your books!" cried Sir Charles.

"Give would be the properer word," grumbled the man.

Sir Charles humbly apologised.

"It was the purest oversight," said he, "and I will gladly pay double. But I need the first volume."

"The first volume, Sir," replied the bookseller in a mollified voice, "is in the like case with the second. There has been an oversight."

"But who has it?"

The bookseller was with difficulty persuaded to search his list. He kept his papers in the greatest disorder, so that it was no wonder people kept his volumes until they forgot them. But in the end he found his list.

"Mrs. Ripley," he read out, "Mrs. Ripley of Burley Wood."

"And where is Burley Wood?" asked Sir Charles.

"It is a village, Sir, six miles from Leamington," replied the bookseller, and he gave some rough directions as to the road.

Sir Charles mounted his horse and cantered down the Parade. The sun was setting; he would for a something miss his supper; but he meant to see Burley Wood that day, and he would have just daylight enough for his purpose. As he entered the village, he caught up a labourer returning from the fields. Sir Charles drew rein beside him.

"Will you tell me, if you please, where Mrs. Ripley lives?"

The man looked up and grinned.

"In the churchyard," said he.

"Do you mean she is dead?"

"No less."

"When did she die?"

"Well, it may have been a month or two ago, or it may have been more."

"Show me her grave and there's a silver shilling in your pocket."

The labourer led Fosbrook to a corner of the churchyard. Then upon a head-stone he read that Mary Ripley aged twenty-nine had died on December 7th. December the 7th thought Sir Charles, five days before Major Lashley died. Then he turned quickly to the labourer.

"Can you tell me when Mrs. Ripley was buried?"

"I can find out for another shilling."

"You shall have it, man."

The labourer hurried off, discovered the sexton, and came back. But instead of the civil gentleman he had left, he found now a man with a face of horror, and eyes that had seen appalling things. Sir Charles had remained in the churchyard by the grave, he had looked about him from one to the other of the mounds of turf, his imagination already stimulated had been quickened by what he had seen; he stood with the face of a Medusa.

"She was buried when?" he asked.

"On December the 11th," replied the labourer.

Sir Charles showed no surprise. He stood very still for a moment, then he gave the man his two shillings, and walked to the gate where his horse was tied. Then he inquired the nearest way to the Quarry House, and he was pointed out a bridle-path running across fields to a hill. As he mounted he asked another question.

"Mr. Ripley is alive?"

"Yes."

"It must be Mr. Ripley," Sir Charles assured himself, as he rode through the dusk of the evening. "It must be ... It must be ..." until the words in his mind became a meaningless echo of his horse's hoofs. He rode up the hill, left the bridle-path for the road, and suddenly, and long before he had expected, he saw beneath him the red square of the Quarry House and the smoke from its chimneys. He was on that very road up which he and Gibson Jerkley had looked that morning. Down that road, he had said, would come the man who knew how Major Lashley had disappeared, and within twelve hours down that road the man was coming. "But it must be Mr. Ripley," he said to himself.

None the less he took occasion at supper to speak of his ride.

"I rode by Leamington to Burley Wood. I went into the churchyard." Then he stopped, but as though the truth was meant to come to light, Resilda helped him out.

"I had a dear friend buried there not so long ago," she said. "Father, you remember Mrs. Ripley."

"I saw her grave this afternoon," said Fosbrook, with his eyes upon Mr. Mardale. It might have been a mere accident, it was in any case a trifling thing, the mere shaking of a hand, the spilling of a spoonful of salt upon the table, but trifling things have their suggestions. He remembered that Resilda, when she had waked up on the night of December the 11th to find herself alone, had sought out her father, who was still up, and at work in the big drawing-room. He remembered

A. E. W. Mason

too that the window of that room gave on to a terrace of grass. A man might go out by that window—aye and return without a soul but himself being the wiser.

Of course it was all guess work and inference, and besides, it must be Mr. Ripley. Mr. Ripley might as easily have discovered the secret of the Memoirs as himself—or anyone else. Mr. Ripley would have justification for anger and indeed for more—yes for what men who are not affected are used to call a crime ... Sir Charles abruptly stopped his reasoning, seeing that it was prompted by a defence of Mr. Mardale. He made his escape from his hosts as soon as he decently could and retired to his room. He sat down in his room and thought, and he thought to some purpose. He blew out his candle, and stole down the stairs into the hall. He had met no one. From the hall he went to the library-door and opened it—ever so gently. The room was quite dark. Sir Charles felt his way across it to his chair in the corner. He sat down in the darkness and waited. After a time inconceivably long, after every board in the house had cracked a million times, he heard distinctly a light shuffling step in the passage, and after that the latch of the door release itself from the socket. He heard nothing more, for a little, he could only guess that the door was being silently opened by some one who carried no candle. Then the shuffling footsteps began to move gently across the room, towards him, towards the corner where he was sitting. Sir Charles had had no doubt but that they would, not a single doubt, but none the less as he sat there in the dark, he felt the hair rising on his scalp, and all his body thrill. Then a hand groped and touched him. A cry rang out, but it was Sir Charles who uttered it. A voice answered quietly:

"You had fallen asleep. I regret to have waked you."

"I was not asleep, Mr. Mardale."

There was a pause and Mr. Mardale continued.

"I cannot sleep to-night, I came for a book."

"I know. For the book I took back to Leamington to-day, before I went to visit Mrs. Ripley's grave."

There was a yet longer pause before Mr. Mardale spoke again.

"Stay then!" he said in the same gentle voice. "I will fetch a light." He shuffled out of the room, and to Sir Charles it seemed again an inconceivably long time before he returned. He came back with a single candle, which he placed upon the table, a little star of light, showing the faces of the two men shadowy and dim. He closed the door carefully, and coming back, said simply:

"You know."

"Yes."

"How did you find out?"

"I saw the grave. I noticed the remarkable height of the mound. I guessed."

"Yes," said Mr. Mardale, and in a low voice he explained. "I found the book here one day, that he left by accident. On December 11th Mrs. Ripley was buried, and that night he left the house—for the stables, yes, but he did not return from the stables. It seemed quite clear to me where he would be that night. People hereabouts take me for a man crazed and daft, I know that very well, but I know something of passion, Sir Charles. I have had my griefs to bear. Oh, I knew where he would be. I followed over the hill down to the churchyard of

Burley Wood. I had no thought of what I should do. I carried a stick in my hand, I had no thought of using it. But I found him lying full-length upon the grave with his lips pressed to the earth of it, whispering to her who lay beneath him.... I called to him to stand up and he did. I bade him, if he dared, repeat the words he had used to my face, to me, the father of the girl he had married, and he did—triumphantly, recklessly. I struck at him with the knob of my stick, the knob was heavy, I struck with all my might, the blow fell upon his forehead. The spade was lying on the ground beside the grave. I buried him with her. Now what will you do?"

"Nothing," said Sir Charles.

"But Mr. Jerkley asked you to help him."

"I shall tell a lie."

"My friend, there is no need," said the old man with his gentle smile. "When I went out for this candle I ..." Sir Charles broke in upon him in a whirl of horror.

"No. Don't say it! You did not!"

"I did," replied Mr. Mardale. "The poison is a kindly one. I shall be dead before morning. I shall sleep my way to death. I do not mind, for I fear that, after all, my inventions are of little worth. I have left a confession on my writing-desk. There is no reason—is there?—why he and she should be kept apart?"

It was not a question which Sir Charles could discuss. He said nothing, and was again left alone in the darkness, listening to the shuffling footsteps of Mr. Mardale as, for the last time, he mounted the stairs.

MR. MITCHELBOURNE'S LAST ESCAPADE

It was in the kitchen of the inn at Framlingham that Mr. Mitchelbourne came across the man who was afraid, and during the Christmas week of the year 1681. Lewis Mitchelbourne was young in those days, and esteemed as a gentleman of refinement and sensibility, with a queer taste for escapades, pardonable by reason of his youth. It was his pride to bear his part in the graceful tactics of a minuet, while a saddled horse waited for him at the door. He delighted to vanish of a sudden from the lighted circle of his friends into the byways where none knew him, or held him of account, not that it was all vanity with Mitchelbourne though no doubt the knowledge that his associates in London Town were speculating upon his whereabouts tickled him pleasurably through many a solitary day. But he was possessed both of courage and resource, qualities for which he found too infrequent an exercise in his ordinary life; and so he felt it good to be free for awhile, not from the restraints but from the safeguards, with which his social circumstances surrounded him. He had his spice of philosophy too, and discovered that these sharp contrasts,—luxury and hardship, treading hard upon each other and the new strange people with whom he fell in, kept fresh his zest of life.

Thus it happened that at a time when families were gathering cheerily each about a single fireside, Mr. Mitchelbourne was

A. E. W. Mason

riding alone through the muddy and desolate lanes of Suffolk. The winter was not seasonable; men were not tempted out of doors. There was neither briskness nor sunlight in the air, and there was no snow upon the ground. It was a December of dripping branches, and mists and steady pouring rains, with a raw sluggish cold, which crept into one's marrow.

The man who was afraid, a large, corpulent man, of a loose and heavy build, with a flaccid face and bright little inexpressive eyes like a bird's, sat on a bench within the glow of the fire.

"You travel far to-night?" he asked nervously, shuffling his feet.

"To-night!" exclaimed Mitchelbourne as he stood with his legs apart taking the comfortable warmth into his bones. "No further than from this fire to my bed," and he listened with enjoyment to the rain which cracked upon the window like a shower of gravel flung by some mischievous urchin. He was not suffered to listen long, for the corpulent man began again.

"I am an observer, sir. I pride myself upon it, but I have so much humility as to wish to put my observations to the test of fact. Now, from your carriage, I should judge you to serve His Majesty."

"A civilian may be straight. There is no law against it," returned Mitchelbourne, and he perceived that the ambiguity of his reply threw his questioner into a great alarm. He was at once interested. Here, it seemed, was one of those encounters which were the spice of his journeyings.

"You will pardon me," continued the stranger with a great

assumption of heartiness, "but I am curious, sir, curious as Socrates, though I thank God I am no heathen. Here is Christmas, when a sensible gentleman, as upon my word I take you to be, sits to his table and drinks more than is good for him in honour of the season. Yet here are you upon the roads to Suffolk which have nothing to recommend them. I wonder at it, sir."

"You may do that," replied Mitchelbourne, "though to be sure, there are two of us in the like case."

"Oh, as for me," said his companion shrugging his shoulders, "I am on my way to be married. My name is Lance," and he blurted it out with a suddenness as though to catch Mitchelbourne off his guard. Mitchelbourne bowed politely.

"And my name is Mitchelbourne, and I travel for my pleasure, though my pleasure is mere gipsying, and has nothing to do with marriage. I take comfort from thinking that I have no friend from one rim of this country to the other, and that my closest intimates have not an inkling of my whereabouts."

Mr. Lance received the explanation with undisguised suspicion, and at supper, which the two men took together, he would be forever laying traps. Now he slipped some outlandish name or oath unexpectedly into his talk, and watched with a forward bend of his body to mark whether the word struck home; or again he mentioned some person with whom Mitchelbourne was quite unfamiliar. At length, however, he seemed satisfied, and drawing up his chair to the fire, he showed himself at once in his true character, a loud and gusty boaster.

"An exchange of sentiments, Mr. Mitchelbourne, with a chance acquaintance over a pipe and a glass—upon my word

I think you are in the right of it, and there's no pleasanter way of passing an evening. I could tell you stories, sir; I served the King in his wars, but I scorn a braggart, and all these glories are over. I am now a man of peace, and, as I told you, on my way to be married. Am I wise? I do not know, but I sometimes think it preposterous that a man who has been here and there about the world, and could, if he were so meanly-minded, tell a tale or so of success in gallantry, should hamper himself with connubial fetters. But a man must settle, to be sure, and since the lady is young, and not wanting in looks or breeding or station, as I am told—"

"As you are told?" interrupted Mitchelbourne.

"Yes, for I have never seen her. No, not so much as her miniature. Nor have I seen her mother either, or any of the family, except the father, from whom I carry letters to introduce me. She lives in a house called 'The Porch' some miles from here. There is another house hard by to it, I understand, which has long stood empty and I have a mind to buy it. I bring a fortune, the lady a standing in the county."

"And what has the lady to say to it?" asked Mitchelbourne.

"The lady!" replied Lance with a stare. "Nothing but what is dutiful, I'll be bound. The father is under obligations to me." He stopped suddenly, and Mitchelbourne, looking up, saw that his mouth had fallen. He sat with his eyes starting from his head and a face grey as lead, an image of panic pitiful to behold. Mitchelbourne spoke but got no answer. It seemed Lance could not answer—he was so arrested by a paralysis of terror. He sat staring straight in front of him, and it seemed at the mantelpiece which was just on a level with his eyes. The mantelpiece, however, had nothing to distinguish it from a score of others. Its counterpart might be found to this day in the parlour of any inn. A couple of china figures disfigured it, to be sure, but Mitchelbourne could not bring himself to believe that even their barbaric crudity had power to produce so visible a discomposure. He inclined to the notion that his companion was struck by a physical disease, perhaps some recrudescence of a malady contracted in those foreign lands of which he vaguely spoke.

"Sir, you are ill," said Mitchelbourne. "I will have a doctor, if there is one hereabouts to be found, brought to your relief." He sprang up as he spoke, and that action of his roused Lance out of his paralysis. "Have a care," he cried almost in a shriek, "Do not move! For pity, sir, do not move," and he in his turn rose from his chair. He rose trembling, and swept the dust off a corner of the mantelpiece into the palm of his hand. Then he held his palm to the lamp.

"Have you seen the like of this before?" he asked in a low shaking voice.

Mitchelbourne looked over Lance's shoulder. The dust was in reality a very fine grain of a greenish tinge.

"Never!" said Mitchelbourne.

"No, nor I," said Lance, with a sudden cunning look at his companion, and opening his fingers, as he let the grain run between them. But he could not remove as easily from Mitchelbourne's memories that picture he had shown him of a shaking and a shaken man. Mitchelbourne went to bed divided in his feelings between pity for the lady Lance was to marry, and curiosity as to Lance's apprehensions. He lay awake for a long time speculating upon that mysterious green seed which could produce so extraordinary a panic, and in the morning his curiosity predominated. Since, therefore, he had no particular destination he was easily persuaded to ride to Saxmundham with Mr. Lance, who, for his part, was most earnest for a companion. On the journey Lance gave further evidence of his fears. He had a trick of looking backwards whenever they came to a corner of the road—an habitual trick, it seemed, acquired by a continued condition of fear. When they stopped at midday to eat at an ordinary, he inspected the guests through the chink at the hinges of the door before he would enter the room; and this, too, he did as though it had long been natural to him. He kept a bridle in his mouth, however; that little pile of grain upon the mantelshelf had somehow warned him into reticence, so that Mitchelbourne, had he not been addicted to his tobacco, would have learnt no more of the business and would have escaped the extraordinary peril which he was subsequently called upon to face.

But he *was* addicted to his tobacco, and no sooner had he finished his supper that night at Saxmundham than he called for a pipe. The maidservant fetched a handful from a cupboard and spread them upon the table, and amongst them was one plainly of Barbary manufacture. It had a straight wooden stem painted with hieroglyphics in red and green and a small reddish bowl of baked earth. Nine men out of ten would no doubt have overlooked it, but Mitchelbourne was the tenth man. His fancies were quick to kindle, and taking up the pipe he said in a musing voice:

"Now, how in the world comes a Barbary pipe to travel so far over seas and herd in the end with common clays in a little Suffolk village?"

He heard behind him the grating of a chair violently pushed back. The pipe seemingly made its appeal to Mr. Lance also.

"Has it been smoked?" he asked in a grave low voice.

"The inside of the bowl is stained," said Mitchelbourne.

Mitchelbourne had been inclined to believe that he had seen last evening the extremity of fear expressed in a man's face: he had now to admit that he had been wrong. Mr. Lance's terror was a Circe to him and sunk him into something grotesque and inhuman; he ran once or twice in a little tripping, silly run backwards and forwards like an animal trapped and out of its wits; and his face had the look of a man suffering from a nausea; so that Mitchelbourne, seeing him, was ashamed and hurt for their common nature.

"I must go," said Lance babbling his words. "I cannot stay. I must go."

"To-night?" exclaimed Mitchelbourne. "Six yards from the door you will be soaked!"

"Then there will be the fewer men abroad. I cannot sleep here! No, though it rained pistols and bullets I must go." He went into the passage, and calling his host secretly asked for his score. Mitchelbourne made a further effort to detain him.

"Make an inquiry of the landlord first. It may be a mere shadow that frightens you."

"Not a word, not a question," Lance implored. The mere suggestion increased a panic which seemed incapable of increase. "And for the shadow, why, that's true. The pipe's the shadow, and the shadow frightens me. A shadow! Yes! A shadow is a horrible, threatning thing! Show me a shadow cast by nothing and I am with you. But you might as easily hold that this Barbary pipe floated hither across the seas of its own will. No! 'Ware shadows, I say." And so he continued harping on the word, till the landlord fetched in the bill.

A. E. W. Mason

The landlord had his dissuasions too, but they availed not a jot more than Mr. Mitchelbourne's.

"The road is as black as a pauper's coffin," said he, "and damnable with ruts."

"So much the better," said Lance.

"There is no house where you can sleep nearer than Glemham, and no man would sleep there could he kennel elsewhere."

"So much the better," said Lance. "Besides, I am expected to-morrow evening at 'The Porch' and Glemham is on the way." He paid his bill, slipped over to the stables and lent a hand to the saddling of his horse. Mitchelbourne, though for once in his life he regretted the precipitancy with which he welcomed strangers, was still sufficiently provoked to see the business to its end. His imagination was seized by the thought of this fat and vulgar person fleeing in terror through English lanes from a Barbary Moor. He had now a conjecture in his mind as to the nature of that greenish seed. He accordingly rode out with Lance toward Glemham.

It was a night of extraordinary blackness; you could not distinguish a hedge until the twigs stung across your face; the road was narrow, great tree-trunks with bulging roots lined it, at times it was very steep—and, besides and beyond every other discomfort, there was the rain. It fell pitilessly straight over the face of the country with a continuous roar as though the earth was a hollow drum. Both travellers were drenched to the skin before they were free of Saxmundham, and one of them, when after midnight they stumbled into the poor tumble-down parody of a tavern at Glemham, was in an extreme exhaustion. It was no more than an ague, said Lance, from which he periodically suffered, but the two men slept in the same bare room, and towards morning Mitchelbourne was awakened from a deep slumber by an unfamiliar voice talking at an incredible speed through the darkness in an uncouth tongue. He started up upon his elbow; the voice came from Lance's bed. He struck a light. Lance was in a high fever, which increased as the morning grew.

Now, whether he had the sickness latent within him when he came from Barbary, or whether his anxieties and corpulent habit made him an easy victim to disease, neither the doctor nor any one else could determine. But at twelve o'clock that day Lance was seized with an attack of cholera and by three in the afternoon he was dead. The suddenness of the catastrophe shocked Mr. Mitchelbourne inexpressibly. He stood gazing at the still features of the man whom fear had, during these last days, so grievously tormented, and was solemnly aware of the vanity of those fears. He could not pretend to any great esteem for his companion, but he made many suitable reflections upon the shears of the Fates and the tenacity of life, in which melancholy occupation he was interrupted by the doctor, who pointed out the necessity of immediate burial. Seven o'clock the next morning was the hour agreed upon, and Mitchelbourne at once searched in Lance's coat pockets for the letters which he carried. There were only two, superscribed respectively to Mrs. Ufford at "The Porch" near Glemham, and to her daughter Brasilia. At "The Porch" Mitchelbourne remembered Lance was expected this very evening, and he thought it right at once to ride thither with his gloomy news.

Having, therefore, sprinkled the letters plentifully with vinegar and taken such rough precautions as were possible to remove the taint of infection from the letters, he started about four o'clock. The evening was most melancholy. For, though no rain any longer fell, there was a continual pattering of drops from the trees and a ghostly creaking of branches in a light and almost imperceptible wind. The day, too, was falling, the grey overhang of cloud was changing to black, except for one wide space in the west, where a pale spectral light shone without radiance; and the last of that was fading when he pulled up at a parting of the roads and inquired of a man who chanced to be standing there his way to "The Porch." He was directed to ride down the road upon his left hand until he came to the second house, which he could not mistake, for there was a dyke or moat about the garden wall. He passed the first house a mile further on, and perhaps half a mile beyond that he came to the dyke and the high garden wall, and saw the gables of the second house loom up behind it black against the sky. A wooden bridge spanned the dyke and led to a wide gate. Mitchelbourne stopped his horse at the bridge. The gate stood open and he looked down an avenue of trees into a square of which three sides were made by the high garden wall, and the fourth and innermost by the house. Thus the whole length of the house fronted him, and it struck him as very singular that neither in the lower nor the upper windows was there anywhere a spark of light, nor was there any sound but the tossing of the branches and the wail of the wind among the chimneys. Not even a dog barked or rattled a chain, and from no chimney breathed a wisp of smoke. The house in the gloom of that melancholy evening had a singular eerie and tenantless look; and oppressive silence reigned there; and Mitchelbourne was unaccountably conscious of a growing aversion to it, as to something inimical and sinister.

He had crossed the mouth of a lane, he remembered, just at the first corner of the wall. The lane ran backwards from the road, parallel with the side wall of the garden. Mitchelbourne had a strong desire to ride down that lane and inspect the back of the house before he crossed the bridge into the garden. He was restrained for a moment by the thought that such a proceeding must savour of cowardice. But only for a moment. There had been no doubting the genuine nature of Lance's fears and those fears were very close to Mr. Mitchelbourne now. They were feeling like cold fingers about his heart. He was almost in the icy grip of them.

He turned and rode down the lane until he came to the end of the wall. A meadow stretched behind the house. Mitchelbourne unfastened the catch of a gate with his riding whip and entered it. He found himself upon the edge of a pool, which on the opposite side wetted the house wall. About the pool some elder trees and elms grew and overhung, and their boughs tapped like fingers upon the window-panes. Mitchelbourne was assured that the house was inhabited, since from one of the windows a strong yellow light blazed, and whenever a sharper gust blew the branches aside, swept across the face of the pool like a flaw of wind.

The lighted window was in the lowest storey, and Mitchelbourne, from the back of his horse, could see into the room. He was mystified beyond expression by what he saw. A deal table, three wooden chairs, some ragged curtains drawn back from the window, and a single lamp made up the furniture. The boards of the floor were bare and unswept; the paint peeled in strips from the panels of the walls; the discoloured ceiling was hung with cobwebs; the room in a word matched the outward aspect of the house in its look of long disuse. Yet it had occupants. Three men were seated at the table in the scarlet coats and boots of the King's officers. Their faces, though it was winter-time, were brown with the sun, and thin and drawn as with long privation and anxiety. They had little to say to one another, it seemed. Each man sat stiffly in a sort of suspense and expectation, with now and then a restless movement or a curt word as curtly answered.

A. E. W. Mason

Mitchelbourne rode back again, crossed the bridge, fastened his horse to a tree in the garden, and walked down the avenue to the door. As he mounted the steps, he perceived with something of a shock, that the door was wide open and that the void of the hall yawned black before him. It was a fresh surprise, but in this night of surprises, one more or less, he assured himself, was of little account. He stepped into the hall and walked forwards feeling with his hands in front of him. As he advanced, he saw a thin line of yellow upon the floor ahead of him. The line of yellow was a line of light, and it came, no doubt, from underneath a door, and the door, no doubt, was that behind which the three men waited. Mitchelbourne stopped. After all, he reflected, the three men were English officers wearing His Majesty's uniform, and, moreover, wearing it stained with their country's service. He walked forward and tapped upon the door. At once the light within the room was extinguished.

It needed just that swift and silent obliteration of the slip of light upon the floor to make Mitchelbourne afraid. He had been upon the brink of fear ever since he had seen that lonely and disquieting house; he was now caught in the full stream. He turned back. Through the open doorway, he saw the avenue of leafless trees tossing against a leaden sky. He took a step or two and then came suddenly to a halt. For all around him in the darkness he seemed to hear voices breathing and soft footsteps. He realised that his fear had overstepped his reason; he forced himself to remember the contempt he had felt for Lance's manifestations of terror; and swinging round again he flung open the door and entered the room.

"Good evening, gentlemen," said he airily, and he got no answer whatsoever. In front of him was the grey panel of dim twilight where the window stood. The rest was black night and an absolute silence. A map of the room was quite clear in his recollections. The three men were seated he knew at the table on his right hand. The faint light from the window did not reach them, and they made no noise. Yet they were there. Why had they not answered him, he asked himself. He could not even hear them breathing, though he strained his ears. He could only hear his heart drumming at his breast, the blood pulsing in his temples. Why did they hold their breath? He crossed the room, not knowing what he did, bereft of his wits. He had a confused, ridiculous picture of himself wearing the flaccid, panic stricken face of Mr. Lance, like an ass' head, not holding the wand of Titania. He reached the window and stood in its embrasure, and there one definite, practical thought crept into his mind. He was visible to these men who were invisible to him. The thought suggested a precaution, and with the trembling haste of a man afraid, he tore at the curtains and dragged them till they met across the window so that even the faint grey glimmer of the night no longer had entrance. The next moment he heard the door behind him latch and a key turn in the lock. He crouched beneath the window and did not stand up again until a light was struck, and the lamp relit.

The lighting of the lamp restored Mr. Mitchelbourne, if not to the full measure of his confidence, at all events to an appreciation that the chief warrant for his trepidation was removed. What he had with some appearance of reason feared was a sudden attack in the dark. With the lamp lit, he could surely stand in no danger of any violence at the hands of three King's officers whom he had never come across in all his life. He took, therefore, an easy look at them. One, the youngest, now leaned against the door, a youth of a frank, honest face, unremarkable but for a firm set of the jaws. A youth of no great intellect, thought Mitchelbourne, but tenacious, a youth marked out for a subordinate command, and never likely for all his sterling qualities to kindle a woman to a world-forgetting passion, or to tread with her the fiery heights where life throbs at its fullest. Mr. Mitchelbourne began to feel quite sorry for this young officer of the limited capacities, and he was still in the sympathetic mood when one of the two men at the table spoke to him. Mitchelbourne turned at once. The officers were sitting with a certain air of the theatre in their attitudes, one a little dark man and the other a stiff, light complexioned fellow with a bony, barren face, unmistakably a stupid man and the oldest of the three. It was he who was speaking, and he spoke with a sort of aggravated courtesy like a man of no breeding counterfeiting a gentleman upon the stage.

"You will pardon us for receiving you with so little ceremony. But while we expected you, you on the other hand were not expecting us, and we feared that you might hesitate to come in if the lamp was burning when you opened the door."

Mitchelbourne was now entirely at his ease. He perceived that there was some mistake and made haste to put it right.

"On the contrary," said he, "for I knew very well you were here. Indeed, I knocked at the door to make a necessary inquiry. You did not extinguish the lamp so quickly but that I saw the light beneath the door, and besides I watched you some five minutes through the window from the opposite bank of the pool at the back of the house."

The officers were plainly disconcerted by the affability of Mr. Mitchelbourne's reply. They had evidently expected to carry off a triumph, not to be taken up in an argument. They had planned a stroke of the theatre, final and convincing, and behold the dialogue went on! There was a riposte to their thrust.

The spokesman made some gruff noises in his throat. Then

his face cleared.

"These are dialectics," he said superbly with a wave of the hand.

"Good," said the little dark fellow at his elbow, "very good!"

The youth at the door nodded superciliously towards Mitchelbourne.

"True, these are dialectics," said he with a smack of the lips upon the word. It was a good cunning scholarly word, and the man who could produce it so aptly worthy of admiration.

"You make a further error, gentlemen," continued Mitchelbourne, "you no doubt are expecting some one, but you were most certainly not expecting me. For I am here by the purest mistake, having been misdirected on the way." Here the three men smiled to each other, and their spokesman retorted with a chuckle.

"Misdirected, indeed you were. We took precautions that you should be. A servant of mine stationed at the parting of the roads. But we are forgetting our manners," he added rising from his chair. "You should know our names. The gentleman at the door is Cornet Lashley, this is Captain Bassett and I am Major Chantrell. We are all three of Trevelyan's regiment."

"And my name," said Mitchelbourne, not to be outdone in politeness, "is Lewis Mitchelbourne, a gentleman of the County of Middlesex."

At this each of the officers was seized with a fit of laughter; but before Mitchelbourne had time to resent their behavior, Major Chantrell said indulgently:

A. E. W. Mason

"Well, well, we shall not quarrel about names. At all events we all four are lately come from Tangier."

"Oh, from Tangier," cried Mitchelbourne. The riddle was becoming clear. That extraordinary siege when a handful of English red-coats unpaid and ill-fed fought a breached and broken town against countless hordes for the honour of their King during twenty years, had not yet become the property of the historian. It was still an actual war in 1681. Mitchelbourne understood whence came the sunburn on his antagonists' faces, whence the stains and the worn seams of their clothes. He advanced to the table and spoke with a greater respect than he had used.

"Did one of you," he asked, "leave a Moorish pipe behind you at an inn of Saxmundham?"

"Ah," said the Major with a reproachful glance at Captain Bassett. The Captain answered with some discomfort:

"Yes. I made that mistake. But what does it matter? You are here none the less."

"You have with you some of the Moorish tobacco?" continued Mitchelbourne.

Captain Bassett fetched out of his pocket a little canvas bag, and handed it to Mitchelbourne, who untied the string about the neck, and poured some of the contents into the palm of his hand. The tobacco was a fine, greenish seed.

"I thought as much," said Mitchelbourne, "you expected Mr. Lance to-night. It is Mr. Lance whom you thought to misdirect to this solitary house. Indeed Mr. Lance spoke of such a place in this neighbourhood, and had a mind to buy it."

Captain Bassett suddenly raised his hand to his mouth, not so quickly, however, but Mitchelbourne saw the grim, amused smile upon his lips. "It is Mr. Lance for whom you now mistake me," he said abruptly.

The young man at the door uttered a short, contemptuous laugh, Major Chantrell only smiled.

"I am aware," said he, "that we meet for the first time to-night, but you presume upon that fact too far. What have you to say to this?" And dragging a big and battered pistol from his pocket, he tossed it upon the table, and folded his arms in the best transpontine manner.

"And to this?" said Captain Bassett. He laid a worn leather powder flask beside the pistol, and tapped upon the table triumphantly.

Mr. Mitchelbourne recognised clearly that villainy was somehow checkmated by these proceedings and virtue restored, but how he could not for the life of him determine. He took up the pistol.

"It appears to have seen some honourable service," said he. This casual remark had a most startling effect upon his auditors. It was the spark to the gun-powder of their passions. Their affectations vanished in a trice.

"Service, yes, but honourable! Use that lie again, Mr. Lance, and I will ram the butt of it down your throat!" cried Major Chantrell. He leaned forward over the table in a blaze of fury. Yet his face did no more than match the faces of his comrades.

Mitchelbourne began to understand. These simple soldier-men had endeavoured to conduct their proceedings with

A. E. W. Mason

great dignity and a judicial calmness; they had mapped out for themselves certain parts which they were to play as upon a stage; they were to be three stern imposing figures of justice; and so they had become simply absurd and ridiculous. Now, however, that passion had the upper hand of them, Mitchelbourne saw at once that he stood in deadly peril. These were men.

"Understand me, Mr. Lance," and the Major's voice rang out firm, the voice of a man accustomed to obedience. "Three years ago I was in command of Devil's Drop, a little makeshift fort upon the sands outside Tangier. In front the Moors lay about us in a semicircle. Sir, the diameter was the line of the sea at our backs. We could not retire six yards without wetting our feet, not twenty without drowning. One night the Moors pushed their trenches up to our palisades; in the dusk of the morning I ordered a sortie. Nine officers went out with me and three came back, we three. Of the six we left behind, five fell, by my orders, to be sure, for I led them out; but, by the living God, you killed them. There's the pistol that shot my best friend down, an English pistol. There's the powder flask which charged the pistol, an English flask filled with English powder. And who sold the pistol and the powder to the Moors, England's enemies? You, an Englishman. But you have come to the end of your lane to-night. Turn and turn as you will you have come to the end of it."

The truth was out now, and Mitchelbourne was chilled with apprehension. Here were three men very desperately set upon what they considered a mere act of justice. How was he to dissuade them? By argument? They would not listen to it. By proofs? He had none to offer them. By excuses? Of all unsupported excuses which can match for futility the excuse of mistaken identity? It springs immediate to the criminal's lips. Its mere utterance is almost a conviction.

"You persist in error, Major Chantrell," he nevertheless began.

"Show him the proof, Bassett," Chantrell interrupted with a shrug of the shoulders, and Captain Bassett drew from his pocket a folded sheet of paper.

"Nine officers went out," continued Chantrell, "five were killed, three are here. The ninth was taken a prisoner into Barbary. The Moors brought him down to their port of Marmora to interpret. At Marmora your ship unloaded its stores of powder and guns. God knows how often it had unloaded the like cargo during these twenty years—often enough it seems, to give you a fancy for figuring as a gentleman in the county. But the one occasion of its unloading is enough. Our brother officer was your interpreter with the Moors, Mr. Lance. You may very likely know that, but this you do not know, Mr. Lance. He escaped, he crept into Tangier with this, your bill of lading in his hand," and Bassett tossed the sheet of paper towards Mitchelbourne. It fell upon the floor before him but he did not trouble to pick it up.

"Is it Lance's death that you require?" he asked.

"Yes! yes! yes!" came from each mouth.

"Then already you have your wish. I do not question one word of your charges against Lance. I have reason to believe them true. But I am not Lance. Lance lies at this moment dead at Great Glemham. He died this afternoon of cholera. Here are his letters," and he laid the letters on the table. "I rode in with them at once. You do not believe me, but you can put my words to the test. Let one of you ride to Great Glemham and satisfy himself. He will be back before morning."

A. E. W. Mason

The three officers listened so far with impassive faces, or barely listened, for they were as indifferent to the words as to the passion with which they were spoken.

"We have had enough of the gentleman's ingenuities, I think," said Chantrell, and he made a movement towards his companions.

"One moment," exclaimed Mitchelbourne. "Answer me a question! These letters are to the address of Mrs. Ufford at a house called 'The Porch.' It is near to here?"

"It is the first house you passed," answered the Major and, as he noticed a momentary satisfaction flicker upon his victim's face, he added, "But you will not do well to expect help from 'The Porch'—at all events in time to be of much service to you. You hardly appreciate that we have been at some pains to come up with you. We are not likely again to find so many circumstances agreeing to favour us, a dismantled house, yourself travelling alone and off your guard in a country with which you are unfamiliar and where none know you, and just outside the window a convenient pool. Besides—besides," he broke out passionately, "There are the little mounds about Tangier, under which my friends lie," and he covered his face with his hands. "My friends," he cried in a hoarse and broken voice, "my soldier-men! Come, let's make an end. Bassett, the rope is in the corner. There's a noose to it. The beam across the window will serve;" and Bassett rose to obey.

But Mitchelbourne gave them no time. His fears had altogether vanished before his indignation at the stupidity of these officers. He was boiling with anger at the thought that he must lose his life in this futile ignominious way for the crime of another man, who was not even his friend, and who besides was already dead. There was just one chance to escape, it seemed to him. And even as Bassett stooped to lift the coil of rope in the corner he took it.

"So that's the way of it," he cried stepping forward. "I am to be hung up to a beam till I kick to death, am I? I am to be buried decently in that stagnant pool, am I? And you are to be miles away before sunrise, and no one the wiser! No, Major Chantrell, I am not come to the end of my lane," and before either of the three could guess what he was at, he had snatched up the pistol from the table and dashed the lamp into a thousand fragments.

The flame shot up blue and high, and then came darkness.

Mitchelbourne jumped lightly back from his position to the centre of the room. The men he had to deal with were men who would follow their instincts. They would feel along the walls; of so much he could be certain. He heard the coil of rope drop down in a corner to his left; so that he knew where Captain Bassett was. He heard a chair upset in front of him, and a man staggered against his chest. Mitchelbourne had the pistol still in his hand and struck hard, and the man dropped with a crash. The fall followed so closely upon the upsetting of the chair that it seemed part of the same movement and accident. It seemed so clearly part, that a voice spoke on Mitchelbourne's left, just where the empty hearth would be.

"Get up! Be quick!"

The voice was Major Chantrell's and Mitchelbourne had a throb of hope. For since it was not the Major who had fallen nor Captain Bassett, it must be Lashley. And Lashley had been guarding the door, of which the key still remained in the lock. If only he could reach the door and turn the key! He heard Chantrell moving stealthily along the wall upon his left hand and he suffered a moment's agony; for in the darkness he could not surely tell which way the Major moved. For if he moved to the window, if he had the sense to move to the window and tear aside those drawn curtains, the grey twilight would show the shadowy moving figures. Mitchelbourne's chance would be gone. And then something totally unexpected and unhoped for occurred. The god of the machine was in a freakish mood that evening. He had a mind for pranks and absurdities. Mitchelbourne was strung to so high a pitch that the ridiculous aspect of the occurrence came home to him before all else, and he could barely keep himself from laughing aloud. For he heard two men grappling and struggling silently together. Captain Bassett and Major Chantrell had each other by the throat, and neither of them had the wit to speak. They reserved their strength for the struggle. Mitchelbourne stepped on tiptoe to the door, felt for the key, grasped it without so much as a click, and then suddenly turned it, flung open the door and sprang out. He sprang against a fourth man—the servant, no doubt, who had misdirected him—and both tumbled on to the floor. Mitchelbourne, however, tumbled on top. He was again upon his feet while Major Chantrell was explaining matters to Captain Bassett; he was flying down the avenue of trees before the explanation was finished. He did not stop to untie his horse; he ran, conscious that there was only one place of safety for him—the interior of Mrs. Ufford's house. He ran along the road till he felt that his heart was cracking within him, expecting every moment that a hand would be laid upon his shoulder, or that, a pistol shot would ring out upon the night. He reached the house, and knocked loudly at the door. He was admitted, breathless, by a man, who said to him at once, with the smile and familiarity of an old servant:

"You are expected, Mr. Lance."

Mitchelbourne plumped down upon a chair and burst into uncontrollable laughter. He gave up all attempt for that night to establish his identity. The fates were too heavily against him. Besides he was now quite hysterical.

The manservant threw open a door.

"I will tell my mistress you have come, sir," said he.

"No, it would never do," cried Mitchelbourne. "You see I died at three o'clock this afternoon. I have merely come to leave my letters of presentation. So much I think a proper etiquette may allow. But it would never do for me to be paying visits upon ladies so soon after an affair of so deplorable a gravity. Besides I have to be buried at seven in the morning, and if I chanced not to be back in time, I should certainly acquire a reputation for levity, which since I am unknown in the county, I am unwilling to incur," and, leaving the butler stupefied in the hall, he ran out into the road. He heard no sound of pursuit.

A. E. W. Mason

THE COWARD

I

"Geoffrey," said General Faversham, "look at the clock!"

The hands of the clock made the acutest of angles. It was close upon midnight, and ever since nine the boy had sat at the dinner-table listening. He had not spoken a word, indeed had barely once stirred in the three hours, but had sat turning a white and fascinated face upon speaker after speaker. At his father's warning he waked with a shock from his absorption, and reluctantly stood up.

"Must I go, father?" he asked.

The General's three guests intervened in a chorus. The conversation was clear gain for the lad, they declared,—a first taste of powder which might stand him in good stead at a future time. So Geoffrey was allowed furlough from his bed for another half-hour, and with his face supported between his hands he continued to listen at the table. The flames of the candles were more and more blurred with a haze of tobacco smoke, the room became intolerably hot, the level of the wine grew steadily lower in the decanters, and the boy's face took a strained, quivering look, his pallour increased, his dark, wide-opened eyes seemed preternaturally large.

The stories were all of that terrible winter in the Crimea, now ten years past, and a fresh story was always in the telling before its predecessor was ended. For each of the four men had borne his share of that winter's wounds and privations. It was still a reality rather than a memory to them; they could feel, even in this hot summer evening and round this dinner-table, the chill of its snows, and the pinch of famine. Yet their recollections were not all of hardships. The Major told how the subalterns, of whom he had then been one, had cheerily played cards in the trenches three hundred yards from the Malakoff. One of the party was always told off to watch for shells from the fort's guns. If a black speck was seen in the midst of the cannon smoke, then the sentinel shouted, and a rush was made for safety, for the shell was coming their way. At night the burning fuse could be seen like a rocket in the air; so long as it span and flew, the card-players were safe, but the moment it became stationary above their heads it was time to run, for the shell was falling upon them. The guns of the Malakoff were not the rifled guns of a later decade. When the Major had finished, the General again looked at the clock, and Geoffrey said good-night.

He stood outside the door listening to the muffled talk on the other side of the panels, and, with a shiver, lighted his candle, and held it aloft in the dark and silent hall. There was not one man's portrait upon the walls which did not glow with the colours of a uniform,—and there were the portraits of many men. Father and son the Faversham's had been soldiers from the very birth of the family. Father and son,— no steinkirks and plumed hats, no shakos and swallow tails, no frogged coats and no high stocks. They looked down upon the boy as though summoning him to the like service.

A. E. W. Mason

No distinction in uniform could obscure their resemblance to each other: that stood out with a remarkable clearness. The Favershams were men of one stamp,—lean-faced, hard as iron—they lacked the elasticity of steel—, rugged in feature; confident in expression, men with firm, level mouths but rather narrow at the forehead, men of resolution and courage, no doubt; but hardly conspicuous for intellect, men without nerves or subtlety, fighting-men of the first-class, but hardly first-class soldiers. Some of their faces, indeed, revealed an actual stupidity. The boy, however, saw none of their defects. To him they were one and all portentous and terrible; and he had an air of one standing before his judges and pleading mutely for forgiveness. The candle shook in his hand.

These Crimean knights, as his father termed them, were the worst of torturers to Geoffrey Faversham. He sat horribly thralled, so long as he was allowed; he crept afterwards to bed and lay there shuddering. For his mother, a lady who some twenty years before had shone at the Court of Saxe-Coburg, as much by the refinement of her intellect as by the beauty of her person, had bequeathed to him a very burdensome gift of imagination. It was visible in his face, marking him off unmistakably from his father, and from the study portraits in the hall. He had the capacity to foresee possibilities, and he could not but exercise that capacity. A hint was enough for the boy. Straightway he had a vivid picture before his mind, and as he listened to the men at the dinner-table, their rough clipped words set him down in the midst of their battlefields, he heard the drone of bullets, he quivered expecting the shock of a charge. But of all the Crimean nights this had been fraught with the most torments.

His father had told a story with a lowered voice, and in his usual jerky way. But the gap was easy to fill up.

"A Captain! Yes, and he bore one of the best names in all England. It seemed incredible, and mere camp rumour. But the rumour grew with every fight he was engaged in. At the battle of Alma the thing was proved. He was acting as galloper to his General. I believe, upon my soul, that the General chose him for this duty so that the man might set himself right. He was bidden to ride with a message a quarter of a mile, and that quarter of a mile was bullet-swept. There were enough men looking on to have given him a reputation, had he dared and come through. But he did not dare, he refused, and was sent under arrest to his tent. He was court-martialled and broken. He dropped out of his circle like a plummet of lead; the very women in Piccadilly spat if he spoke to them. He blew his brains out three years later in a back bedroom off the Haymarket. Explain that if you can. Turns tail, and says 'I daren't!' But you, can you explain it? You can only say it's the truth, and shrug your shoulders. Queer, incomprehensible things happen. There's one of them."

Geoffrey, however, understood only too well. He was familiar with many phases of warfare of which General Faversham took little account, such as, for instance, the strain and suspense of the hours between the parading of the troops and the first crack of a rifle. He took that story with him up the great staircase, past the portraits to his bed. He fell asleep only in the grey of the morning, and then only to dream of a crisis in some hard-fought battle, when, through his cowardice, a necessary movement was delayed, his country worsted, and those dead men in the hall brought to irretrievable shame. Geoffrey's power to foresee in one flash all the perils to be encountered, the hazards to be run, had taught him the hideous possibility of cowardice. He was now confronted with the hideous fact. He could not afterwards clear his mind of the memory of that evening.

A. E. W. Mason

He grew up with it; he looked upon himself as a born coward, and all the time he knew that he was destined for the army. He could not have avoided his destiny without an explanation, and he could not explain. But what he could do, he did. He hunted deliberately, hoping that familiarity with danger would overcome the vividness of his anticipations. But those imagined hours before the beginnings of battles had their exact counterpart in the moments of waiting while the covers were drawn. At such times he had a map of the country-side before his eyes, with every ditch and fence and pit underlined and marked dangerous; and though he rode straight when the hounds were off, he rode straight with a fluttering heart. Thus he spent his youth. He passed into Woolwich and out of it with high honours; he went to India with battery, and returned home on a two years' furlough. He had not been home more than a week when his father broke one morning into his bedroom in a great excitement—

"Geoff," he cried, "guess the news to-day!"

Geoffrey sat up in his bed:—"Your manner, Sir, tells me the news. War is declared."

"Between France and Germany."

Geoffrey said slowly:—

"My mother, Sir, was of Germany."

"So we can wish that country all success."

"Can we do no more?" said Geoffrey. And at breakfast-time he returned to the subject. The Favershams held property in Germany; influence might be exerted; it was only right that those who held a substantial stake in a country should venture something for its cause. The words came quite easily from Geoffrey's lips; he had been schooling himself to speak them ever since it had become apparent that Germany and France were driving to the collision of war. General Faversham laughed with content when he heard them.

"That's a Faversham talking," said he. "But there are obstacles, my boy. There is the Foreign Enlistment Act, for instance. You are half German, to be sure, but you are an English subject, and, by the Lord! you are all Faversham. No, I cannot give you permission to seek service in Germany. You understand. I cannot give you permission," he repeated the words, so that the limit as well as the extent of their meaning might be fully understood; and as he repeated them, he solemnly winked. "Of course, you can go to Germany; you can follow the army as closely as you are allowed. In fact, I will give you some introductions with that end in view. You will gain experience, of course; but seek service,—no! To do that, as I have said, I cannot give you permission."

The General went off chuckling to write his letters; and with them safely tucked away in his pocket, Geoffrey drove later in the day to the station.

General Faversham did not encourage demonstrations. He shook his son cordially by the hand—

"There's no way I would rather you spent your furlough. But come back, Geoff," said he. He was not an observant man except in the matter of military detail; and of Geoffrey's object he had never the slightest suspicion. Had it been told him, however, he would only have considered it one of those queer, inexplicable vagaries, like the history of his coward in the Crimea.

Geoffrey's action, however, was of a piece with the rest of

A. E. W. Mason

his life: it was due to no sudden, desperate resolve. He went out to the war as deliberately as he had ridden out to the hunting-field. The realities of battle might prove his anticipations mere unnecessary torments of the mind.

"If only I can serve,—as a volunteer, as a private, in any capacity," he thought, "I shall at all events know. And if I fail, I fail not in the company of my fellows. I disgrace only myself, not my name. But if I do not fail—" He drew a great breath, he saw himself waking up one morning without oppression, without the haunting dread that he was destined one day to slink in forgotten corners of the world a forgotten pariah, destitute even of the courage to end his misery. He went out to the war because he was afraid of fear.

II

On the evening of the capitulation of Paris, two subalterns of German Artillery were seated before a camp fire on a slope of hill overlooking the town. To both of them the cessation of alarm was as yet strange and almost incomprehensible, and the sudden silence after so many months lived amongst the booming of cannon had even a disquieting effect. Both were particularly alert on this night when vigilance was never less needed. If a gust of wind caught the fire and drove the red flare of the flame like a ripple across the grass, one would be sure to look quickly over his shoulder, the other perhaps would lift a warning finger and listen to the shivering of the trees behind them. Then with a relaxation of his attitude he would say "All right" and light his pipe again at the fire. But after one such gust, he retained his position.

"What is it, Faversham?" asked his companion.

"Listen, Max," said Geoffrey; and they heard a faint jingle. The jingle became more distinct, another sound was added to it, the sound of a horse galloping over hard ground. Both officers turned their faces away from the yellow entrenchment with its brown streak of gun, below them and looked towards a roofless white-walled farmhouse on the left, of which the rafters rose black against the sky like a gigantic gallows. From behind that farmhouse an aide-de-camp galloped up to the fire.

"I want the officer in command of this battery," he cried out and Geoffrey stood up.

"I am in command."

A. E. W. Mason

The aide-de-camp looked at the subaltern in an extreme surprise.

"You!" he exclaimed. "Since when?"

"Since yesterday," answered Faversham.

"I doubt if the General knows you have been hit so hard," the aide-de-camp continued. "But my orders are explicit. The officer in command is to take sixty men and march to-morrow morning into St. Denis. He is to take possession of that quarter, he is to make a search for mines and bombs, and wait there until the German troops march in." There was to be no repetition, he explained, of a certain unfortunate affair when the Germans after occupying a surrendered fort had been blown to the four winds. He concluded with the comforting information that there were 10,000 French soldiers under arms in St. Denis and that discretion was therefore a quality to be much exercised by Faversham during his day of search. Thereupon he galloped back.

Faversham remained standing a few paces from the fire looking down towards Paris. His companion petulantly tossed a branch upon the fire.

"Luck comes your way, my friend," said he enviously.

Geoffrey looked up to the stars and down again to Paris which with its lights had the look of a reflected starlit firmament. Individual lights were the separate stars and here and there a gash of fire, where a wide thoroughfare cleaved, made a sort of milky way.

"I wonder," he answered slowly.

Max started up on his elbow and looked at his friend

in perplexity.

"Why, you have sixty men and St. Denis to command. To-morrow may bring you your opportunity;" and again with the same slowness, Geoffrey answered, "I wonder."

"You joined us after Gravelotte," continued Max, "Why?"

"My mother was German," said Faversham, and turning suddenly back to the fire he dropped on the ground beside his companion.

"Tell me," he said in a rare burst of confidence, "Do you think a battle is the real test of courage? Here and there men run away to be sure. But how many fight and fight no worse than the rest by reason of a sort of cowardice? Fear of their companions in arms might dominate fear of the enemy."

"No doubt," said Max. "And you infer?"

"That the only touchstone is a solitary peril. When danger comes upon a man and there is no one to see whether he shirks—when he has no friends to share his risks—that I should think would be the time when fear would twist a man's bowels."

"I do not know," said Max. "All I am sure of is that luck comes your way and not mine. To-morrow you march into St. Denis."

Geoffrey Faversham marched down at daybreak and form-ally occupied the quarter. The aide-de-camp's calculations were confirmed. There were at the least 10,000 French soldiers crowded in the district. Geoffrey's discretion warned against any foolish effort to disarm them; he simply ignored their chassepots and bulging pouches, and searched the

A. E. W. Mason

barracks, which the Germans were to occupy, from floor to ceiling. Late in the afternoon he was able to assure himself that his duty was ended. He billeted his men, and inquired whether there was a hotel where he could sleep the night. A French sergeant led him through the streets to an Inn which matched in every detail of its appearance that dingy quarter of the town. The plaster was peeling from its walls, the window panes were broken, and in the upper storey and the roof there were yawning jagged holes where the Prussian shells had struck. In the dusk the building had a strangely mean and sordid look. It recalled to Faversham's mind the inns in the novels of the elder Dumas and acquired thus something of their sinister suggestions. In the eager and arduous search of the day he had forgotten these apprehensions to which he had given voice by the camp fire. They now returned to him with the relaxation of his vigilance. He looked up at the forbidding house. "I wonder," he said to himself.

He was met in the hall by a little obsequious man who was full of apologies for the disorder of his hostelry. He opened a door into a large and dusty room.

"I will do my best, Monsieur," said he, "but food is not yet plentiful in Paris."

In the centre of the room was a large mahogany table surrounded by chairs. The landlord began to polish the table with his napkin.

"We had an ordinary, Sir, every day before the war broke out. But most cheerful, every chair had its regular occupant. There were certain jokes, too, which every day were repeated. Ah, but it was like home. However, all is changed as you see. It has not been safe to sit in this room for many a long month."

Faversham unstrapped his sword and revolver from his belt and laid them on the table.

"I saw that your house had unfortunately suffered."

"Suffered!" said the garrulous little man. "It is ruined, sir, and its master with it. Ah, war! It is a fine thing no doubt for you young gentlemen, but for me? I have lived in a cellar, Sir, under the ground ever since your guns first woke us from our sleep. Look, I will show you."

He went out from the dining-room into the hall and from the hall into the street; Faversham followed him. There was a wooden trap in the pavement close by the wall with an iron ring. The landlord pulled at the ring and raised the trap disclosing a narrow flight of stone steps. Faversham bent forward and peered down into a dark cellar.

"Yes it is there that I have lived. Come down, Sir, and see for yourself;" and the landlord moved down a couple of steps. Faversham drew back. At once the landlord turned to him.

"But there is nothing to fear, Sir," he said with a deprecatory smile. Faversham coloured to the roots of his hair.

"Of course there is nothing," said he and he followed the landlord. The cellar was only lighted by the trap-door and at first Faversham coming out of the daylight could distinguish nothing at all. He stood, however, with his back to the light and in a little he began to see. A little truckle-bed with a patchwork counterpane stood at the end, the floor was merely hard earth, the furniture consisted of a stove, a stool and a small deal table. And as Faversham took in the poverty of this underground habitation, he suddenly found himself in darkness again. The explanation came to him at once, the entrance to the cellar had been blocked from the light. Yet he

A. E. W. Mason

had heard no sound except the footsteps of people in the street above his head. He turned and faced the stair steps. As he did so, the light streamed down again; the obstruction had been removed, and that obstruction had not been the trap-door as Faversham had suspected, but merely the body of some inquisitive passer-by. He recognised this with relief and immediately heard voices speaking together, and as it seemed to him in lowered tones.

A sword rattled on the pavement, the entrance was again darkened, but Faversham had just time to see that the man who stooped down wore the buttons of a uniform and a soldier's kepi. He kept quite still, holding his breath while the man peered down into the cellar. He remembered with a throb of hope that he had himself been unable to distinguish a thing in the gloom. And then the landlord knocked against the table and spoke aloud. At once the man at the head of the steps stood up. Faversham heard him cry out in French, "They are here," and he detected a note of exultation in the cry. At the same moment a picture flashed before his eyes, the picture of that dusty desolate dining-room up the steps, and of a long table surrounded by chairs, upon which lay a sword and a revolver,—his sword, his revolver. He had dismissed his sixty soldiers, he was alone.

"This is a trap," he blurted out.

"But, Sir, I do not understand," began the landlord, but Faversham cut him short with a whispered command for silence.

The cellar darkened again, and the sound of boots rang upon the stone steps. A rifle besides clanged as it struck against the wall. The French soldiers were descending. Faversham counted them by the light which escaped past their legs; there were three. The landlord kept the silence which had been enjoined upon him but he fancied in the darkness that he heard some one's teeth chattering.

The Frenchmen descended into the cellar and stood barring the steps. Their leader spoke.

"I have the honour to address the Prussian officer in command of St. Denis."

The Frenchman got no reply whatever to his words but he seemed to hear some one sharply draw in a breath. He spoke again into the darkness; for it was now impossible for any one of the five men in the cellar to see a hand's breadth beyond his face.

"I am the Captain Plessy of Mon Vandon's Division. I have the honour to address the Prussian officer."

This time he received an answer, quietly spoken yet with an inexplicable note of resignation.

"I am Lieutenant Faversham in command of St. Denis."

Captain Plessy stepped immediately forward, and bowed. Now as he dipped his shoulders in the bow a gleam of light struck over his head into the cellar, and—he could not be sure—but it seemed to him that he saw a man suddenly raise his arm as if to ward off a blow. Captain Plessy continued.

"I ask Lieutenant Faversham for permission for myself and my two officers to sleep to-night at this hotel;" and now he very distinctly heard a long, irrepressible sigh of relief. Lieutenant Faversham gave him the permission he desired in a cordial, polite way. Moreover he added an invitation. "Your name, Captain Plessy, is well known to me as to all on both sides who have served in this campaign and to many

A. E. W. Mason

more who have not. I beg that you and your officers will favour me with your company at dinner."

Captain Plessy accepted the invitation and was pleased to deprecate the Lieutenant's high opinion of his merits. But his achievement none the less had been of a redoubtable character. He had broken through the lines about Metz and had ridden across France into Paris without a single companion. In the sorties from that beleaguered town he had successively distinguished himself by his fearless audacity. His name and reputation had travelled far as Lieutenant Faversham was that evening to learn. But Captain Plessy, for the moment, was all for making little of his renown.

"Such small exploits should be expected from a soldier. One brave man may say that to another,—is it not so?—and still not be thought to be angling for praise," and Captain Plessy went up the steps, wondering who it was that had drawn the long sharp breath of suspense, and uttered the long sigh of immense relief. The landlord or Lieutenant Faversham? Captain Plessy had not been in the cellar at the time when the landlord had seemed to hear the chatter of a man's teeth.

The dinner was not a pronounced success, in spite of Faversham's avoidance of any awkward topic. They sat at the long table in the big, desolate and shabby room, lighted only by a couple of tallow candles set up in their candlesticks upon the cloth. And the two junior officers maintained an air of chilly reserve and seldom spoke except when politeness compelled them. Faversham himself was absorbed, the burden of entertainment fell upon Captain Plessy. He strove nobly, he told stories, he drank a health to the "Camaraderie of arms," he drew one after the other of his companions into an interchange of words, if not of sympathies. But the strain told on him visibly towards the end of the dinner. His champagne glass had been constantly refilled, his face was now a trifle overflushed, his eyes beyond nature bright, and he loosened the belt about his waist and at a moment when Faversham was not looking the throat buttons of his tunic. Moreover while up till now he had deprecated any allusions to his reputation he now began to talk of it himself; and in a particularly odious way.

"A reputation, Lieutenant, it has its advantages," and he blew a kiss with his fingers into the air to designate the sort of advantages to which he referred. Then he leaned on one side to avoid the candle between Faversham and himself.

"You are English, my Commandant?" he asked.

"My mother was German," replied Faversham.

"But you are English yourself. Now have you ever met in England a certain Miss Marian Beveridge," and his leer was the most disagreeable thing that Faversham ever remembered to have set eyes upon.

"No," he answered shortly.

"And you have not heard of her?"

"No."

"Ah!"

Captain Plessy leaned back in his chair and filled his glass. Lieutenant Faversham's tone was not that of a man inviting confidence. But the Captain's brains were more than a little fuddled, he repeated the name over to himself once or twice with the chuckle which asks for questions, and since the questions did not come, he must needs proceed of his own accord.

"But I must cross to England myself. I must see this Miss Marian Beveridge. Ah, but your English girls are strange, name of Heaven, they are very strange."

Lieutenant Faversham made a movement. The Captain was his guest, he was bound to save him if he could from a breach of manners and saw no way but this of breaking up the party. Captain Plessy, however, was too quick for him, he lifted his hand to his breast.

"You wish for something to smoke. It is true, we have forgotten to smoke, but I have my cigarettes and I beg you to try them, the tobacco I think is good and you will be saved the trouble of moving."

He opened the case and reached it over to Faversham. But as Faversham with a word of thanks took a cigarette, the Captain upset the case as though by inadvertence. There fell out upon the table under Faversham's eyes not merely the cigarettes, but some of the Captain's visiting-cards and a letter. The letter was addressed to Captain Plessy in a firm character but it was plainly the writing of a woman. Faversham picked it up and at once handed it back to Plessy.

"Ah," said Plessy with a start of surprise, "Was the letter indeed in the case?" and he fondled it in his hands and finally kissed it with the upturned eyes of a cheap opera singer. "A pigeon, Sir, flew with it into Paris. Happy pigeon that could be the bearer of such sweet messages."

He took out the letter from the envelope and read a line or two with a sigh, and another line or two with a laugh.

"But your English girls are strange!" he said again. "Here is an instance, an example, fallen by accident from my cigarette-case. M. le Commandant, I will read it to you, that you may see how strange they are."

One of Plessy's subalterns extended his hand and laid it on his sleeve. Plessy turned upon him angrily, and the subaltern withdrew his hand.

"I will read it to you," he said again to Faversham. Faversham did not protest nor did he now make any effort to move. But his face grew pale, he shivered once or twice, his eyes seemed to be taking the measure of Plessy's strength, his brain to be calculating upon his prowess; the sweat began to gather upon his forehead.

Of these signs, however, Plessy took no note. He had reached however inartistically the point at which he had been aiming.

He was no longer to be baulked of reading his letter. He read it through to the end, and Faversham listened to the end. It told its own story. It was the letter of a girl who wrote in a frank impulse of admiration to a man whom she did not know. There was nowhere a trace of coquetry, nowhere the expression of a single sentimentality. Its tone was pure friendliness, it was the work of a quite innocent girl who because she knew the man to whom she wrote to be brave, therefore believed him to be honourable. She expressed her trust in the very last words. "You will not of course show this letter to any one in the world. But I wrong you even by mentioning such an impossibility."

"But you have shown it," said Faversham.

His face was now grown of an extraordinary pallor, his lips twitched as he spoke and his fingers worked in a nervous uneasy manner upon the table-cloth. Captain Plessy was in far too complacent a mood to notice such trifles. His vanity was satisfied, the world was a rosy mist with a sparkle of champagne, and he answered lightly as he unfastened another button of his tunic.

"No, my friend, I have not shown it. I keep the lady's wish."

"You have read it aloud. It is the same thing."

"Pardon me. Had I shown the letter I should have shown the name. And that would have been a dishonour of which a gallant man is incapable, is it not so? I read it and I did not read the name."

"But you took pains, Captain Plessy, that we should know the name before you read the letter."

"I? Did I mention a name?" exclaimed Plessy with an air of concern and a smile upon his mouth which gave the lie to the concern. "Ah, yes, a long while ago. But did I say it was the name of the lady who had written the letter? Indeed, no. You make a slight mistake, my friend. I bear no malice for it— believe me, upon my heart, no! After a dinner and a little bottle of champagne, there is nothing more pardonable. But I will tell you why I read the letter."

"If you please," said Faversham, and the gravity of his tone struck upon his companion suddenly as something unexpected and noteworthy. Plessy drew himself together and for the first time took stock of his host as of a possible adversary. He remarked the agitation of his face, the beads of perspiration upon his forehead, the restless fingers, and beyond all these a certain hunted look in the eyes with which his experience had made him familiar. He nodded his head once or twice slowly as though he were coming to a definite conclusion about Faversham. Then he sat bolt upright.

"Ah," said he with a laugh. "I can answer a question which puzzled me a little this afternoon," and he sank back again in his chair with an easy confidence and puffed the smoke of his cigarette from his mouth. Faversham was not sufficiently composed to consider the meaning of Plessy's remark. He put it aside from his thoughts as an evasion.

"You were to tell me, I think, why you read the letter."

"Certainly," answered Plessy. He twirled his moustache, his voice had lost its suavity and had taken on an accent of almost contemptuous raillery. He even winked at his two brother officers, he was beginning to play with Faversham. "I read the letter to illustrate how strange, how very strange, are your English girls. Here is one of them who writes to me. I am grateful—oh, beyond words, but I think to myself what a different thing the letter would be if it had been written by a Frenchwoman. There would have been some hints, nothing definite you understand, but a suggestion, a delicate, provoking suggestion of herself, like a perfume to sting one into a desire for a nearer acquaintance. She would delicately and without any appearance of intention have permitted me to know her colour, perhaps her height, perhaps even to catch an elusive glimpse of her face. Very likely a silk thread of hair would have been left inadvertently clinging to a sheet of the paper. She would sketch perhaps her home and speak remorsefully of her boldness in writing. Oh, but I can imagine the letter, full of pretty subtleties, alluring from its omissions, a vexation and a delight from end to end. But this, my friend!" He tossed the letter carelessly upon the table-cloth. "I am grateful from the bottom of my heart, but it has no art."

At once Geoffrey Faversham's hand reached out and closed upon the letter.

A. E. W. Mason

"You have told me why you have read it aloud."

"Yes," said Plessy, a little disconcerted by the quickness of Faversham's movement.

"Now I will tell you why I allowed you to read it to the end. I was of the same mind as that English girl whose name we both know. I could not believe that a man, brave as I knew you to be, could outside his bravery be so contemptible."

The words were brought out with a distinct effort. None the less they were distinctly spoken.

A startled exclamation broke from the two subalterns. Plessy commenced to bluster.

"Sir, do I understand you?" and he saw Faversham standing above him, in a quiver of excitement.

"You will hold your tongue, Captain Plessy, until I have finished. I allowed you to read the letter, never thinking but that some pang of forgotten honour would paralyse your tongue. You read it to the end. You complain there is no art in it, that it has no delicate provocations, such as your own countrywomen would not fail to use. It should be the more sacred on that account, and I am glad to believe that you misjudge your country women. Captain Plessy, I acknowledge that as you read out that letter with its simple, friendly expression of gratitude for the spectacle of a brave man, I envied you heartily, I would have been very proud to have received it. I would have much liked to know that some deed which I had done had made the world for a moment brighter to some one a long way off with whom I was not acquainted. Captain Plessy, I shall not allow you to keep this letter. You shall not read it aloud again."

Faversham thrust the letter into the flame of the candle which stood between Plessy and himself. Plessy sprang up and blew the candle out; but little colourless flames were already licking along the envelope. Faversham held the letter downwards by a corner and the colourless flame flickered up into a tongue of yellow, the paper charred and curled in the track of the flames, the flames leapt to Faversham's fingers; he dropped the burning letter on the floor and crushed it with his foot. Then he looked at Plessy and waited. He was as white as the table-cloth, his dark eyes seemed to have sunk into his head and burned unnaturally bright, every nerve in his body seemed to be twitching; he looked very like the young boy who used to sit at the dinner-table on Crimean nights and listen in a quiver to the appalling stories of his father's guests. As he had been silent then, so he was silent now. He waited for Captain Plessy to speak. Captain Plessy, however, was in no hurry to begin. He had completely lost his air of contemptuous raillery, he was measuring Faversham warily with the eyes of a connoisseur.

"You have insulted me," he said abruptly, and he heard again that indrawing of the breath which he had remarked that afternoon in the cellar. He also heard Faversham speak immediately after he had drawn the breath.

"There are reparations for insults," said Faversham.

Captain Plessy bowed. He was now almost as sober as when he had sat down to his dinner.

"We will choose a time and place," said he.

"There can be no better time than now," suddenly cried Faversham, "no better place than this. You have two friends of whom with your leave I will borrow one. We have a large room and a candle apiece to fight by. To-morrow my duties

A. E. W. Mason

begin again. We will fight to-night, Captain Plessy, to-night," and he leaned forward almost feverishly, his words had almost the accent of a prayer. The two subalterns rose from their chairs, but Plessy motioned them to keep still. Then he seized the candle which he had himself blown out, lighted it from the candle at the far end of the table and held it up above his head so that the light fell clearly upon Faversham's face. He stood looking at Faversham for an appreciable time. Then he said quietly,

"I will not fight you to-night."

One of the subalterns started up, the other merely turned his head towards Plessy, but both stared at their Captain with an unfeigned astonishment and an unfeigned disappointment. Faversham continued to plead.

"But you must to-night, for to-morrow you cannot. To-night I am alone here, to-night I give orders, to-morrow I receive them. You have your sword at your side to-night. Will you be wearing it to-morrow? I pray you gentlemen to help me," he said turning to the subalterns, and he began to push the heavy table from the centre of the room.

"I will not fight you to-night, Lieutenant," Captain Plessy replied.

"And why?" asked Faversham ceasing from his work. He made a gesture which had more of despair than of impatience.

Captain Plessy gave his reason. It rang false to every man in the room and indeed he made no attempt to give to it any appearance of sincerity. It was a deliberate excuse and not his reason.

"Because you are the Prussian officer in command and the

Prussian troops march into St. Denis to-morrow. Suppose that I kill you, what sort of penalty should I suffer at their hands?"

"None," exclaimed Faversham. "We can draw up an account of the quarrel, here now. Look here is paper and ink and as luck will have it a pen that will write. I will write an account with my own hand, and the four of us can sign it. Besides if you kill me, you can escape into Paris."

"I will not fight you to-night," said Captain Plessy and he set down the candle upon the table. Then with an elaborate correctness he drew his sword from its scabbard and offered the handle of it to Faversham.

"Lieutenant, you are in command of St. Denis. I am your prisoner of war."

Faversham stood for a moment or two with his hands clenched. The light had gone out of his face.

"I have no authority to make prisoners," he said. He took up one of the candles, gazed at his guest in perplexity.

"You have not given me your real reason, Captain Plessy," he said. Captain Plessy did not answer a word.

"Good-night, gentlemen," said Faversham and Captain Plessy bowed deeply as Faversham left the room.

A silence of some duration followed upon the closing of the door. The two subalterns were as perplexed as Faversham to account for their hero's conduct. They sat dumb and displeased. Plessy stood for a moment thoughtfully, then he made a gesture with his hands as though to brush the whole incident from his mind and taking a cigarette from his case

A. E. W. Mason

proceeded to light it at the candle. As he stooped to the flame he noticed the glum countenances of his brother-officers, and laughed carelessly.

"You are not pleased with me, my friends," said he as he threw himself on to a couch which stood against the wall opposite to his companions. "You think I did not speak the truth when I gave the reason of my refusal? Well you are right. I will give you the real reason why I would not fight. It is very simple. I do not wish to be killed. I know these white-faced, trembling men—there are no men more terrible. They may run away but if they do not, if they string themselves to the point of action—take the word of a soldier older than yourselves—then is the time to climb trees. To-morrow I would very likely kill our young friend, he would have had time to think, to picture to himself the little point of steel glittering towards his heart—but to-night he would assuredly have killed me. But as I say I do not wish to be killed. You are satisfied?"

It appeared that they were not. They sat with all the appearances of discontent. They had no words for Captain Plessy. Captain Plessy accordingly rose lightly from his seat.

"Ah," said he, "my good friend the Lieutenant has after all left me my sword. The table too is already pushed sufficiently on one side. There is only one candle to be sure, but it will serve. You are not satisfied, gentlemen? Then—" But both subalterns now hastened to assure Captain Plessy that they considered his conduct had been entirely justified.

THE DESERTER

Lieutenant Fevrier of the 69th regiment, which belonged to the first brigade of the first division of the army of the Rhine, was summoned to the Belletonge farm just as it was getting dusk. The Lieutenant hurried thither, for the Belletonge farm opposite the woods of Colombey was the headquarters of the General of his division.

"I have been instructed," said General Montaudon, "to select an officer for a special duty. I have selected you."

Now for days Lieutenant Fevrier's duties had begun and ended with him driving the soldiers of his company from eating unripe fruit; and here, unexpectedly, he was chosen from all the officers of his division for a particular exploit. The Lieutenant trembled with emotion.

"My General!" he cried.

The General himself was moved.

"What your task will be," he continued, "I do not known. You will go at once to the Mareschal's headquarters when the chief of the staff, General Jarras, will inform you."

Lieutenant Fevrier went immediately up to Metz. His division

A. E. W. Mason

was entrenched on the right bank of the Mosel and beyond the forts, so that it was dark before he passed through the gates. He had never once been in Metz before; he had grown used to the monotony of camps; he had expected shuttered windows and deserted roads, and so the aspect of the town amazed him beyond measure. Instead of a town besieged, it seemed a town during a fairing. There were railway carriages, it is true, in the Place Royale doing duty as hospitals; the provision shops, too, were bare, and there were no horses visible.

But on the other hand, everywhere was a blaze of light and a bustle of people coming and going upon the footpaths. The cafes glittered and rang with noise. Here one little fat burgher was shouting that the town-guard was worth all the red-legs in the trenches; another as loudly was criticising the tactics of Bazaine and comparing him for his invisibility to a pasha in his seraglio; while a third sprang upon a table and announced fresh victories. An army was already on the way from Paris to relieve Metz. Only yesterday MacMahon had defeated the Prussians, any moment he might be expected from the Ardennes. Nor were they only civilians who shouted and complained. Lieutenant Fevrier saw captains, majors, and even generals who had left their entrenchments to fight the siege their own way with dominoes upon the marble tables of the cabarets.

"My poor France," he said to himself, and a passer-by overhearing him answered:

"True, monsieur. Ah, but if we had a man at Metz!"

Lieutenant Fevrier turned his back upon the speaker and walked on. He at all events would not join in the criticisms. It was just, he reflected, because he had avoided the cafes of Metz that he was singled out for special distinction, and he fell to wondering what work it was he had to do that night.

Was it to surprise a field-watch? Or to spike a battery? Or to capture a convoy? Lieutenant Fevrier raised his head. For any exploit in the world he was ready.

General Jarras was writing at a table when Fevrier was admitted to his office. The Chief of the Staff inclined his lamp-shade so that the light fell full upon Fevrier's face, and the action caused the lieutenant to rejoice. So much care in the choice of the officer meant so much more important a duty.

"The General Montaudon tells me," said Jarras, "that you are an obedient soldier."

"Obedience, my General, is the soldier's first lesson."

"That explains to me why it is first forgotten," answered Jarras, drily. Then his voice became sharp and curt. "You will choose fifty men. You will pick them carefully."

"They shall be the best soldiers in the regiment," said Fevrier.

"No, the worst."

Lieutenant Fevrier was puzzled. When dangers were to be encountered, when audacity was needed, one requires the best soldiers. That was obvious, unless the mission meant annihilation. That thought came to Fevrier, and remembering the cafes and the officers dishonouring their uniforms, he drew himself up proudly and saluted. Already he saw his dead body recovered from the enemy, and borne to the grave beneath a tricolour. He heard the lamentations of his friends, and the firing of the platoon. He saw General Montaudon in tears. He was shaken with emotion. But Jarras's next words fell upon him like cold water.

A. E. W. Mason

"You will parade your fifty men unarmed. You will march out of the lines, and to-morrow morning as soon as it is light enough for the Prussians to see you come unarmed you will desert to them. There are too many mouths to feed in Metz[A]."

[Footnote A: See the Daily News War Correspondence, 1870.]

The Lieutenant had it on his lips to shout, "Then why not lead us out to die?" But he kept silence. He could have flung his kepi in the General's face; but he saluted. He went out again into the streets and among the lighted cafes and reeled like a drunken man, thinking confusedly of many things; that he had a mother in Paris who might hear of his desertion before she heard of its explanation; that it was right to claim obedience but *lache* to exact dishonour—but chiefly and above all that if he had been wise, and had made light of his duty, and had come up to Metz to re-arrange the campaign with dominoes on the marble-tables, he would not have been specially selected for ignominy. It was true, it needed an obedient officer to desert! And so laughing aloud he reeled blindly down to the gates of Metz. And it happened that just by the gates a civilian looked after him, and shrugging his shoulders, remarked, "Ah! But if we had a *Man* at Metz!"

From Metz Lieutenant Fevrier ran. The night air struck cool upon him. And he ran and stumbled and fell and picked himself up and ran again until he reached the Belletonge farm.

"The General," he cried, and so to the General a mud-plastered figure with a white, tormented face was admitted.

"What is it?" asked Montaudon. "What will this say?"

Lieutenant Fevrier stood with the palms of his hands extended, speechless like an animal in pain. Then he suddenly burst into tears and wept, and told of the fine plan to diminish the demands upon the commissariat.

"Courage, my old one!" said the General. "I had a fear of this. You are not alone—other officers in other divisions have the same hard duty," and there was no inflection in the voice to tell Fevrier what his General thought of the duty. But a hand was laid soothingly upon his shoulder, and that told him. He took heart to whisper that he had a mother in Paris.

"I will write to her," said Montaudon. "She will be proud when she receives the letter."

Then Lieutenant Fevrier, being French, took the General's hand and kissed it, and the General, being French, felt his throat fill with tears.

Fevrier left the headquarters, paraded his men, laid his sword and revolver on the ground, and ordered his fifty to pile their arms. Then he made them a speech—a very short speech, but it cost him much to make it in an even voice.

"My braves," said he, "my fellow-soldiers, it is easy to fight for one's country, it is not difficult to die for it. But the supreme test of patriotism is willingly to suffer shame for it. That test your country now claims of you. Attention! March!"

For the last time he exchanged a password with a French sentinel, and tramped out into the belt of ground between the French outposts and the Prussian field-watch. Now in this belt there stood a little village which Fevrier had held with skill and honour all the two days of the battle of Noisseville.

A. E. W. Mason

Doubtless that recollection had something to do with his choice of the village. For in his martyrdom of shame he had fallen to wonder whether after all he had not deserved it, and any reassurance such as the gaping house-walls of Vaudere would bring to him, was eagerly welcomed. There was another reason, however, in the position of the village.

It stood in an abrupt valley at the foot of a steep vine-hill on the summit, and which was the Prussian forepost. The Prussian field-watch would be even nearer to Vaudere and dispersed amongst the vines. So he could get his ignominious work over quickly in the morning. The village would provide, too, safe quarters for the night, since it was well within range of the heavy guns in Fort St. Julien, and the Prussians on that account were unable to hold it.

He led his fifty soldiers then northwestward from his camp, skirted the Bois de Grimont, and marched into the village. The night was dark, and the sky so overhung with clouds that not a star was visible. The one street of Vaudere was absolutely silent. The glimmering white cottages showed their black rents on either side, but never the light of a candle behind any shutter. Lieutenant Fevrier left his men at the western or Frenchward end of the street, and went forward alone.

The doors of the houses stood open. The path was encumbered with the wreckage of their contents, and every now and then he smelt a whiff of paraffin, as though lamps had been broken or cans overset. Vaudere had been looted, but there were no Prussians now in the village.

He made sure of this by walking as far as the large house at the head of the village. Then he went back to his men and led them forward until he reached the general shop which every village has.

"It is not likely," he said, "that we shall find even the makeshift of a supper. But courage, my friends, let us try!"

He could not have eaten a crust himself, but it had become an instinct with him to anticipate the needs of his privates, and he acted from habit. They crowded into the shop; one man shut the door, Fevrier lighted a match and disclosed by its light staved-in barrels, empty cannisters, broken boxes, fragments of lemonade bottles, but of food not so much as a stale biscuit.

"Go upstairs and search."

They went and returned empty-handed.

"We have found nothing, monsieur," said they.

"But I have," replied Fevrier, and striking another match he held up what he had found, dirty and crumpled, in a corner of the shop. It was a little tricolour flag of painted linen upon a bamboo stick, a child's cheap and gaudy toy. But Fevrier held it up solemnly, and of the fifty deserters no one laughed.

"The flag of the Patrie," said Fevrier, and with one accord the deserters uncovered.

The match burned down to Fevrier's fingers, he dropped it and trod upon it and there was a moment's absolute stillness. Then in the darkness a ringing voice leapt out.

"Vive la France!"

It was not the lieutenant's voice, but the voice of a peasant from the south of the Loire, one of the deserters.

"Ah, but that is fine, that cry," said Fevrier.

He could have embraced that private on both cheeks. There was love in that cry, pain as well—it could not be otherwise—but above all a very passion of confidence.

"Again!" said Fevrier; and this time all his men took it up, shouting it out, exultantly. The little ruined shop, in itself a contradiction of the cry, rang out and clattered with the noise until it seemed to Fevrier that it must surely pierce across the country into Metz and pluck the Mareschal in his head-quarters from his diffidence. But they were only fifty deserters in a deserted village, lost in the darkness, and more likely to be overheard by the Prussian sentries than by any of their own blood.

It was Fevrier who first saw the danger of their ebullition. He cut it short by ordering them to seek quarters where they could sleep until daybreak. For himself, he thrust the little toy flag in his breast and walked forward to the larger house at the end of the village beneath the vine-hill; and as he walked, again the smell of paraffin was forced upon his nostrils.

He walked more slowly. That odour of paraffin began to seem remarkable. The looting of the village had not occurred to-day, for there had been thick dust about the general shop. But the paraffin had surely been freshly spilt, or the odour would have evaporated.

Lieutenant Fevrier walked on thinking this over. He found the broken door of his house, and still thinking it over, mounted the stairs. There was a door fronting the stairs. He felt for the handle and opened it, and from a corner of the room a voice challenged him in German.

Fevrier was fairly startled. There were Germans in the village after all. He explained to himself now the smell of paraffin. Meanwhile he did not answer; neither did he move; neither did he hear any movement. He had forgotten for the moment that he was a deserter, and he stood holding his breath and listening. There was a tiny window opposite to the door, but it only declared itself a window, it gave no light. And illusions came to Lieutenant Fevrier, such as will come to the bravest man so long as he listens hard enough in the dark—illusions of stealthy footsteps on the floor, of hands scraping and feeling along the walls, of a man's breathing upon his neck, of many infinitesimal noises and movements close by.

The challenge was repeated and Fevrier remembered his orders.

"I am Lieutenant Fevrier of Montaudon's division."

"You are alone."

Fevrier now distinguished that the voice came from the right-hand corner of the room, and that it was faint.

"I have fifty men with me. We are deserters," he blurted out, "and unarmed."

There followed silence, and a long silence. Then the voice spoke again, but in French, and the French of a native.

"My friend, your voice is not the voice of a deserter. There is too much humiliation in it. Come to my bedside here. I spoke in German, expecting Germans. But I am the cure of Vaudere. Why are you deserters?"

Fevrier had expected a scornful order to marshal his men as prisoners. The extraordinary gentleness of the cure's voice almost overcame him. He walked across to the bedside and told his story. The cure basely heard him out.

"It is right to obey," said he, "but here you can obey and disobey. You can relieve Metz of your appetites, my friend, but you need not desert." The cure reached up, and drawing Fevrier down, laid a hand upon his head. "I consecrate you to the service of your country. Do you understand?"

Fevrier leaned his mouth towards the cure's ear.

"The Prussians are coming to-night to burn the village."

"Yes, they came at dusk."

Just at the moment, in fact, when Fevrier had been summoned to Metz, the Prussians had crept down into Vaudere and had been scared back to their repli by a false alarm.

"But they will come back you may be sure," said the cure, and raising himself upon his elbow he said in a voice of suspense "Listen!"

Fevrier went to the window and opened it. It faced the hill-side, but no sounds came through it beyond the natural murmurs of the night. The cure sank back.

"After the fight here, there were dead soldiers in the streets—French soldiers and so French chassepots. Ah, my friend, the Prussians have found out which is the better rifle—the chassepot or the needle gun. After your retreat they came down the hill for those chassepots. They could not find one. They searched every house, they came here and questioned me. Finally they caught one of the villagers hiding in a field, and he was afraid and he told where the rifles had been buried. The Prussians dug for them and the hole was empty. They believe they are still hidden somewhere in the village;

they fancy, too, that there are secret stores of food; so they mean to burn the houses to the ground. They did not know that I was here this afternoon. I would have come into the French lines had it been possible, but I am tied here to my bed. No doubt God had sent you to me—you and your fifty men. You need not desert. You can make your last stand here for France."

"And perish," cried Fevrier, caught up from the depths of his humiliation, "as Frenchmen should, arms in hand." Then his voice dropped again. "But we have no arms."

The cure shook the lieutenant's arm gently.

"Did I not tell you the chassepots were not found? And why? Because too many knew where they were hidden. Because out of that many I feared there might be one to betray. There is always a Judas. So I got one man whom I knew, and he dug them up and hid them afresh."

"Where, father?"

The question was put with a feverish eagerness—it seemed to the cure with an eagerness too feverish. He drew his hand, his whole body away.

"You have matches? Light one!" he said, in a startled voice.

"But the window—!"

"Light one!"

Every moment of time was now of value. Fevrier took the risk and lit the match, shading it from the window so far as he could with his hand.

"That will do."

Fevrier blew out the light. The cure had seen him, his uniform and his features. He, too, had seen the cure, had noticed his thin emaciated face, and the eyes staring out of it feverishly bright and preternaturally large.

"Shall I tell you your malady, father?" he said gently. "It is starvation."

"What will you, my son? I am alone. There is not a crust from one end of Vaudere to the other. You cannot help me. Help France! Go to the church, stand with your back to the door, turn left, and advance straight to the churchyard wall. You will find a new grave there, the rifles in the grave. Quick! There is a spade in the tower. Quick! The rifles are wrapped from the damp, the cartridges too. Quick! Quick!"

Fevrier hurried downstairs, roused three of his soldiers, bade one of them go from house to house and bring the soldiers in silence to the churchyard, and with the others he went thither himself. In groups of two and three the men crept through the street, and gathered about the grave. It was already open. The spade was driven hard and quick, deeper and deeper, and at last rang upon metal. There were seventy chassepots, complete with bayonets and ammunition. Fifty-one were handed out, the remaining nineteen were hastily covered in again. Fevrier was immeasurably cheered to notice his men clutch at their weapons and fondle them, hold them to their shoulders taking aim, and work the breech-blocks.

"It is like meeting old friends, is it not, my children, or rather new sweethearts?" said he. "Come! The Prussians may advance from the Brasserie at Lanvallier, from Servigny, from Montay, or from Noisseville, straight down the hill. The last direction is the most likely, but we must make no mistake. Ten men will watch on the Lanvallier road, ten on the Servigny, ten on the Montay, twenty will follow me. March!"

An hour ago Lieutenant Fevrier was in command of fifty men who slouched along with their hands in their pockets, robbed even of self-respect. Now he had fifty armed and disciplined soldiers, men alert and inspired. So much difference a chassepot apiece had made. Lieutenant Fevrier was moved to the conception of another plan; and to prepare the way for its execution, he left his twenty men in a house at the Prussian end of Vaudere, and himself crept in among the vines and up the hill.

Somewhere near to him would be the sentries of the field-watch. He went down upon his hands and knees and crawled, parting the vine leaves, that the swish of them might not betray him. In a little knoll high above his head he heard the cracking of wood, the sound of men stumbling. The Prussians were coming down to Vaudere. He lay flat upon the ground waiting and waiting; and the sounds grew louder and approached. At last he heard that for which he waited— the challenge of the field-watch, the answer of the burning-party. It came down to him quite clearly through the windless air. "Sadowa."

Lieutenant Fevrier turned about chuckling. It seemed that in some respects the world after all was not going so ill with him that night. He crawled downwards as quickly as he could. But it was now more than even inspiration that he should not be detected. He dared not stand up and run; he must still keep upon his hands and knees. His arms so ached that he was forced now and then to stop and lie prone to give them ease; he was soaked through and through with perspiration; his blood hammered at his temples; he felt his spine weaken as though the marrow had melted into water;

and his heart throbbed until the effort to breathe was a pain. But he reached the bottom of the hill, he got refuge amongst his men, he even had time to give his orders before the tread of the first Prussian was heard in the street.

"They will make for the other end of Vaudere. They will give the village first as near to the French lines as it reaches and light the rest as they retreat. Let them go forward! We will cut them off. And remember, the bayonet! A shot will bring the Prussians down in force. It will bring the French too, so there is just the chance we may find the enemy as silent as ourselves."

But the plan was to undergo alteration. For as Lieutenant Fevrier ended, the Prussians marched in single file into the street and halted. Fevrier from the corner within his doorway counted them; there were twenty-three in all. Well, he had twenty besides himself, and the advantage of the surprise; and thirty more upon the other roads, for whom, however, he had other work in mind. The officer in command of the Prussians carried a dark lantern, and he now turned the slide, so that the light shone out.

His men fell out of their rank, some to make a cursory search, others to sprinkle yet more paraffin. One man came close to Fevrier's doorway, and even looked in, but he saw nothing, though Fevrier was within six feet of him, holding his breath. Then the officer closed his lantern, the men re-formed and marched on. But they left behind with Lieutenant Fevrier—an idea.

He thought it quickly over. It pleased him, it was feasible, and there was comedy in it. Lieutenant Fevrier laughed again, his spirits were rising, and the world was not after all going so ill with him.

He had noticed by the lantern light that the Prussians had not re-formed in the same order. They were in single file again, but the man who marched last before the halt, did not march last after it. Each soldier, as he came up, fell in in the rear of the file. Now Fevrier had in the darkness experienced some difficulty in counting the number of Prussians, although he had strained his eyes to that end.

He whispered accordingly some brief instructions to his men; he sent a message to the ten on the Servigny road, and when the Prussians marched on after their second halt, Lieutenant Fevrier and two Frenchmen fell in behind them. The same procedure was followed at the next halt and at the next; so that when the Prussians reached the Frenchward end of Vaudere there were twenty-three Prussians and ten Frenchmen in the file. To Fevrier's thinking it was sufficiently comic. There was something artistic about it too.

Fevrier was pleased, but he had not counted on the quick Prussian step to which his soldiers were unaccustomed. At the fourth halt, the officer moved unsuspiciously first on one side of the street, then on the other, but gave no order to his men to fall out. It seemed that he had forgotten, until he came suddenly running down the file and flashed his lantern into Fevrier's face. He had been secretly counting his men.

"The French," he cried. "Load!"

The one word quite compensated Fevrier for the detection. The Germans had come down into Vaudere with their rifles unloaded, lest an accidental discharge should betray their neighbourhood to the French.

"Load!" cried the German. And slipping back he tugged at the revolver in his belt. But before he could draw it out, Fevrier dashed his bayonet through the lantern and hung it

A. E. W. Mason

on the officer's heart. He whistled, and his other ten men came running down the street.

"Vorwarts," shouted Fevrier, derisively. "Immer Vorwarts."

The Prussians surprised, and ignorant how many they had to face, fell back in disorder against a house-wall. The French soldiers dashed at them in the darkness, engaging them so that not a man had the chance to load.

That little fight in the dark street between the white-ruined cottages made Fevrier's blood dance.

"Courage!" he cried. "The paraffin!"

The combatants were well matched, and it was hand-to-hand and bayonet-to-bayonet. Fevrier loved his enemies at that moment. It even occurred to him that it was worth while to have deserted. After the sense of disgrace, the prospect of imprisonment and dishonour, it was all wonderful to him— the feel of the thick coat yielding to the bayonet point, the fatigue of the beaten opponent, the vigour of the new one, the feeling of injury and unfairness when a Prussian he had wounded dropped in falling the butt of a rifle upon his toes.

Once he cried, "*Voila pour la patrie*!" but for the rest he fought in silence, as did the others, having other uses for their breath. All that could be heard was a loud and laborious panting, as of wrestlers in a match, the clang of rifle crossing rifle, the rattle of bayonet guarding bayonet, and now and then a groan and a heavy fall. One Prussian escaped and ran; but the ten who had been stationed on the Servigny road were now guarding the entrance from Noisseville. Fevrier had no fears of him. He pressed upon a new man, drove him against the wall, and the man shouted in despair:

"*A moi!*"

"You, Philippe?" exclaimed Fevrier.

"That was a timely cry," and he sprang back. There were six men standing, and the six saluted Fevrier; they were all Frenchmen. Fevrier mopped his forehead.

"But that was fine," said he, "though what's to come will be still better. Oh, but we will make this night memorable to our friends. They shall talk of us by their firesides when they are grown old and France has had many years of peace—we shall not hear, but they will talk of us, the deserters from Metz."

Lieutenant Fevrier in a word was exalted, and had lost his sense of proportion. He did not, however, relax his activity. He sent off the six to gather the rest of his contingent. He made an examination of the Prussians, and found that sixteen had been killed outright, and eight were lying wounded. He removed their rifles and ammunition out of reach, and from dead and wounded alike took the coats and caps. To the wounded he gave instead French uniforms; and then, bidding twenty-three of his soldiers don the Prussian caps and coats, he snatched a moment wherein to run to the cure.

"It is over," said he. "The Prussians will not burn Vaudere tonight." And he jumped down the stairs again without waiting for any response. In the street he put on the cap and coat of the Prussian officer, buckled the sword about his waist, and thrust the revolver into his belt. He had now twenty-three men who at night might pass for Prussians, and thirteen others.

To these thirteen he gave general instructions. They were to spread out on the right and left, and make their way singly up

A. E. W. Mason

through the vines, and past the field-watch if they could without risk of detection. They were to join him high up on the slope, and opposite to the bonfire which would be burning at the repli. His twenty-three he led boldly, following as nearly as possible the track by which the Prussians had descended. The party trampled down the vine-poles, brushed through the leaves, and in a little while were challenged.

"Sadowa," said Fevrier, in his best imitation of the German accent.

"Pass Sadowa," returned the sentry.

Fevrier and his men filed upwards. He halted some two hundred yards farther on, and went down upon his knees. The soldiers behind him copied his example. They crept slowly and cautiously forward until the flames of the bonfire were visible through the screen of leaves, until the faces of the officers about the bonfire could be read.

Then Fevrier stopped and whispered to the soldier next to him. That soldier passed the whisper on, and from a file the Frenchmen crept into line. Fevrier had now nothing to do but to wait; and he waited without trepidation or excitement. The night from first to last had gone very well with him. He could even think of Mareschal Bazaine without anger.

He waited for perhaps an hour, watching the faces round the fire increase in number and grow troubled with anxiety. The German officers talked in low tones staring through their night-glasses down the hill, to catch the first leaping flame from the roofs of Vaudere, pushing forward their heads to listen for any alarm. Fevrier watched them with the amusement of a spectator in a play house. He was fully aware that he was shortly to step upon the stage himself. He was aware too that the play was to have a tragic ending. Meanwhile, however, here was very good comedy! He had a Frenchman's appreciation of the picturesque. The dark night, the glowing fire on the one broad level of grass, the French soldiers hidden in the vines, within a stone's throw of the Germans, the Germans looking unconsciously on over their heads for the return of those comrades who never would return.—Lieutenant Fevrier was the dramatist who had created this striking and artistic situation. Lieutenant Fevrier could not but be pleased. Moreover there were better effects to follow. One occurred to him at this very moment, an admirable one. He fumbled in his breast and took out the flag. A minute later he saw the Colonel of the forepost join the group, hack nervously with his naked sword at a burning log, and dispatch a subaltern down the hill to the field-watch.

The subaltern came crashing back through the vines. Fevrier did not need to hear his words in order to guess at his report. It could only be that the Prussian party had given the password and come safely back an hour since. Besides, the Colonel's act was significant.

He sent four men at once in different directions, and the rest of his soldiers he withdrew into the darkness behind the bonfire. He did not follow them himself until he had picked up and tossed a fusee into the fire. The fusee flared and spat and spurted, and immediately it seemed to Fevrier—so short an interval of time was there—that the country-side was alive with the hum of a stirring camp, and the rattle of harness-chains, as horses were yoked to guns.

For a third time that evening Fevrier laughed softly. The deserters had roused the Prussian army round Metz to the expectation of an attack in force. He touched his neighbour on the shoulder.

A. E. W. Mason

"One volley when I give the word. Then charge. Pass the order on!" and the word went along the line like a ripple across a pond.

He had hardly given it, the fusee had barely ceased to sputter, before a company doubled out on the open space behind the bonfire. That company had barely formed up, before another arrived to support it.

"Load!"

As the Prussian command was uttered, Fevrier was aware of a movement at his side. The soldier next to him was taking aim. Fevrier reached out his hand and stopped the man. Fevrier was going to die in five minutes, and meant to die chivalrously like a gentleman. He waited until the German companies had loaded, until they were ordered to advance, and then he shouted,

"Fire!"

The little flames shot out and crackled among the vines. He saw gaps in the Prussian ranks, he saw the men waver, surprised at the proximity of the attack.

"Charge," he shouted, and crashing through the few yards of shelter, they burst out upon the repli, and across the open space to the Prussian bayonets. But not one of the number reached the bayonets.

"Fire!" shouted the Prussian officer, in his turn.

The volley flashed out, the smoke cleared away, and showed a little heap of men silent between the bonfire and the Prussian ranks.

The Prussians loaded again and stood ready, waiting for the main attack. The morning was just breaking. They stood silent and motionless till the sky was flooded with light and the hills one after another came into view, and the files of poplars were seen marching on the plains. Then the Colonel approached the little heap. A rifle caught his eye, and he picked it up.

"They are all mad," said he. Forced to the point of the bayonet was a gaudy little linen tri-colour flag.

THE CROSSED GLOVES

"Although you have not been near Ronda for five years," said the Spanish Commandant severely to Dennis Shere, "the face of the country has not changed. You are certainly the most suitable officer I can select, since I am told you are well acquainted with the neighbourhood. You will ride therefore to-day to Olvera and deliver this sealed letter to the officer commanding the temporary garrison there. But it is not necessary that it should reach him before eleven at night, so that you will still have an hour or two before you start in which you can renew your acquaintanceships, as I can very well understand you are anxious to do."

Dennis Shere's reluctance, however, was now changed into alacrity. For the road to Olvera ran past the gates of that white-walled, straggling residencia where he had planned to spend this first evening that he was stationed at Ronda. On his way back from his colonel's quarters he even avoided those squares and streets where he would be likely to meet with old acquaintances, foreseeing their questions as to why he was now a Spanish subject and wore the uniform of a captain of Spanish cavalry and by seven o'clock he was already riding through the Plaza de Toros upon his mission. There, however, a familiar voice hailed him, and turning about in his saddle he saw an old padre who had once gained a small prize for logic at the University of Barcelona, and who had since made his inferences and deductions an excuse for a great deal of inquisitiveness. Shere had no option but to stop. He broke in, however, at once on the inevitable questions as to his uniform with the statement that he must be at Olvera by eleven.

"Fifteen miles," said the padre. "Does it need four hours and a fresh horse to journey fifteen miles?"

"But I have friends to visit on the way," and to give convincing details to an excuse which was plainly disbelieved, Shere added, "Just this side of Setenil I have friends."

The padre was still dissatisfied. "There is only one house just this side of Setenil, and Esteban Silvela I saw with my own eyes to-day in Ronda."

"He may well be home by now, and it is not Esteban whom I go to see."

"Not Esteban," exclaimed the padre. "Then it will be—"

"His sister, the Senora Christina," said Shere with a laugh at his companion's persistency. "Since the brother and sister live alone, and it is not the brother, why it will be the sister. You argue still very closely, padre."

The padre stood back a little from Shere and stared. Then he said slyly, and with the air of one who quotes:

"All women are born tricksters."

"Those were rank words," said Shere composedly.

"Yet they were often spoken when you grew vines in the Ronda Valley."

A. E. W. Mason

"Then a crowd of men must know me for a fool. A young man may make a mistake, padre, and exaggerate a disappointment. Besides, I had not then seen the senora. Esteban I knew, but she was a child, and known to me only by name." And then, warmed by the pleasure in his old friend's face, he said, "I will tell you about it."

They walked on slowly side by side, while Shere, who now that he had begun to confide was quite swept away, bent over his saddle and told how after inheriting a modest fortune, after wandering for three years from city to city, he had at last come to Paris, and there, at a Carlist conversazione, had heard the familiar name called from a doorway, and had seen the unfamiliar face appear. Shere described Christina. She walked with the grace of a deer, as though the floor beneath her foot had the spring of turf. The blood was bright in her face; her brown hair shone; she was sweet with youth; the suppleness of her body showed it and the steadiness of her great clear eyes.

"She passed me," he went on, "and the arrogance of what I used to think and say came sharp home to me like a pain. I suppose that I stared—it was an accident, of course— perhaps my face showed something of my trouble; but just as she was opposite me her fan slipped through her fingers and clattered on the floor."

The padre was at a loss to understand Shere's embarrassment in relating so small a matter.

"Well," said he, "you picked up the fan and so—"

"No," interrupted Shere. His embarrassment increased, and he stammered out awkwardly, "Just for the moment, you see, I began to wonder whether after all I had not been right before; whether after all any woman would or could baulk herself of a fraction of any man's admiration, supposing that it would only cost a trick to extort it. And while I was wondering she herself stooped, picked up the fan, and good-humouredly dropped me a curtsey for my lack of manners. Esteban presented me to her that evening. There followed two magical months in Paris and a June in London."

"But, Esteban?" said the padre, doubtfully. "I do not understand. I know something of Esteban Silvela. A lean man of plots and devices. My friend, do you know that Esteban has not a groat? The Silvela fortunes and estate came from the mother and went to the daughter. Esteban is the Senora Christina's steward, and her marriage would alter his position at the least. Did he not spoil the magic of the months in Paris?"

Shere laughed aloud in assured confidence.

"No, indeed," said he. "I did not know Esteban was dependent on his sister, but what difference would her marriage make? Esteban is my best friend. For instance, you questioned me about my uniform. It is by Esteban's advice and help that I wear it."

"Indeed!" said the padre, quickly. "Tell me."

"That June, in London, two years ago—it was by the way the last time I saw the senora—we three dined at the same house. As the ladies rose from the table I said to Christina quietly, 'I want to speak to you to-night,' and she answered very simply and quietly, 'With all my heart.' She was not so quiet, however, but that Esteban overheard her. He hitched his chair up to mine; I asked him what my chances were, and whether he would second them? He was most cordial, but he thought with his Spaniard's pride that I ought—I use my words, not his—in some way to repair my insufficiency in station and the rest; and he pointed out this way of the uniform. I could not resist his argument; I did not speak that night. I took out my papers and became a Spaniard; with Esteban's help I secured a commission. That was two years ago. I have not seen her since, nor have I written, but I ride to her to-night with my two years' silence and my two years' service to prove the truth of what I say. So you see I have reason to thank Esteban." And since they were now come to the edge of the town they parted company. Shere rode smartly down the slope of the hill, the padre stood and watched him with a feeling of melancholy.

It was not merely that he distrusted Esteban, but he knew Shere, the cadet of an impoverished family, who had come out from England to a small estate in the Ronda valley, which had belonged to his house since the days of the Duke of Wellington in Spain. He knew him for a man of tempests and extremes, and as he thought of his ardent words and tones, of his ready acceptance of Esteban's good faith, of his description of Christina, he fell to wondering whether so sudden and violent a conversion from passionate cynic to passionate believer would not lack permanence. There was that little instructive accident of the dropped fan. Even in the moment of conversion so small a thing had almost sufficed to dissuade Shere.

Shere, however, was quite untroubled—so untroubled, indeed, that he even rode slowly that he might not waste the luxury of anticipating the welcome which his unexpected appearance would surely provoke. He rode into the groves of almond and walnut trees and out again into a wild and stony country. It was just growing dusk when he saw ahead of him the square white walls of the enclosure, and the cluster of buildings within, glimmering at the foot of a rugged hill. The lights began to move in the windows as he approached, and then a man suddenly appeared at his side on the roadway and whistled twice loudly as though he were calling his dog. Shere rode past the man and through the open gates into the courtyard. There were three men lounging there, and they came forward almost as if they had expected Shere. He gave his horse into their charge and impetuously mounted the flight of stone steps to the house. A servant in readiness came forward at once and preceded Shere along a gallery towards a door. Shere's impetuosity led him to outstep the servant, he opened the door, and so entered the room unannounced.

It was a long, low room with a wainscot of dark walnut, and a single lamp upon the table gave it shadows rather than light. He had just time to notice that a girl and a man were bending over the table in the lamplight, to recognise with a throb of the heart the play of the light upon the girl's brown hair, to understand that she was explaining something which she held in her hands, and then Esteban came quickly to him with a certain air of perplexity and a glance of inquiry towards the servant. Then he said:—

"Of course, of course, you stopped and came in of your own accord."

"Of my own accord, indeed," said Shere, who was looking at Christina instead of heeding Esteban's words. His unexpected coming had certainly not missed its effect, although it was not the effect which Shere had desired. There was, to be sure, a great deal of astonishment in her looks, but there was also consternation; and when she spoke it was in a numbed and absent way.

"You are well? We have not seen you this long while. Two years is it? More than two years."

"There have been changes," said Esteban. "We have had war

and, alas, defeats."

"Yes, I was in Cuba," said Shere, and the conversation dragged on impersonal and dull. Esteban talked continually with a forced heartiness, Christina barely spoke at all, and then absently. Shere noticed that she had but lately come in, for she still wore her hat, and her gloves lay crossed on the table in the light of the lamp; she moved restlessly about the room, stopping now and then to give an ear to any chance noise in the courtyard, and to glance alertly at the door; so that Shere understood that she was expecting another visitor, and that he himself was in the way. An inopportune intrusion, it seemed, was the sole outcome of the two years' anticipations, and utterly discouraged he rose from his chair. On the instant, however, Esteban signed to Shere to remain, and with a friendly smile himself made an excuse and left the room.

Christina was now walking up and down one particular seam in the floor with as much care as if the seam was a tight-rope, and this exercise she continued. Shere moved over to the table and quite absently played with the gloves which lay there, disarranging their position, so that they no longer made a cross.

"You remember that night in London," said he, and Christina stopped for a second to say simply and without any suggestion that she was offended, "You should have spoken that night," and then resumed her walk.

"Yes," returned Shere. "But I was always aware that I could not offer you your match, and I found, I thought, quite suddenly that evening a way to make my insufficiency less insufficient."

"Less insufficient by a strip of brass upon your shoulder,"

she exclaimed passionately. She came and stood opposite to him. "Well, that strip of brass stops us both. It stops my ears, it must stop your lips too. Where did we meet first?"

"In Paris."

"Go on!"

"At a Carlist—" and Shere broke off and took a step towards her. "Oh!" he exclaimed, "I never thought of it. I imagined you went there to laugh as I did."

"Does one laugh at one's creed?" she cried violently; and Shere with a helpless gesture of the hands sat down in a chair. Esteban had fooled him, and why, the padre had shown Shere that afternoon, Esteban had fooled him irreparably; it did not need a glance at Christina, as she stood facing him, to convince him of that. There was no anger against him, he noticed, in her face, but on the contrary a great friendliness and pity. But he knew her at that moment. Her looks might soften, but not her resolve. She was heart-whole a Carlist. Carlism was her creed, and her creed would be more than a creed, it would be a passion too. So it was not to persuade her but rather in acknowledgment that he said:

"And one does not change one's creed?"

"No," she answered, and suggested, but in a doubtful voice, "but one can put off one's uniform."

Shere stood up. "Neither can one do that," he said simply. "It is quite true that I sought my commission upon your account. I would just as readily have become a Carlist had I known. I had no inclination one way or the other, only a great hope and longing for you. But I have made the mistake, and I cannot retrieve it. The strip of brass obliges me to good faith.

Already you will understand the uniform has had its inconvenience. It sent me to Cuba, and set me armed against men almost of my own blood. There was no escape then; there is no escape now."

Christina moved closer to him. The reticence with which Shere spoke, and the fact that he made no claim upon her made her voice very gentle.

"No," she agreed. "I thought that you would make that answer. And in my heart I do not think that I should like to have heard from you any other."

"Thank you," said Shere. He drew out his watch. "I have still some way to go. I have to reach Olvera by eleven;" and he was aware that Christina at his side became at once very still, so that even her breathing was arrested. For her sigh of emotion at the abrupt mention of parting he was thankful, but it made him keep his eyes turned from her lest a sight of any distress of hers might lead him to falter from his purpose.

"You are riding to Olvera?" she asked, after a pause, and in a queer muffled voice.

"Yes. So I must say good-bye," and now he turned to her. But she was too quick for him to catch a glimpse of her face. She had already turned from him and was walking towards the door.

"You must also say good-bye to Esteban," said she, as though to gain time. With her fingers on the door-handle she stopped. "Tell me," she exclaimed. "It was Esteban who advised the army, who helped you to your commission? You need not deny it! It was Esteban," she stood silent, turning over this revelation in her mind. Then she added, "Did you see Esteban in Ronda this afternoon?"

"No, but I heard that he was there. I must go."

He took up his hat, and turning again towards the door saw that Christina stood with her back against the panels and her arms outstretched across them like a barrier.

"You need not fear," he said to reassure her. "I shall not quarrel with Esteban. He is your brother, and the harm is done. Besides, I do not know that it is all harm when I look back in the years before I wore the uniform. In those times it was all one's own dissatisfactions and trivial dislikes and trivial ambitions. Now I find a repose in losing them, in becoming a little necessary part of a big machine, even though it is not the best machine of its kind and works creakily. I find a dignity in it too."

It was the man of extremes who spoke, and he spoke quite sincerely. Christina, however, neither answered him nor heard. Her eyes were fixed with a strange intentness upon him; her breath came and went as if she had run a race, and in the silence seemed unnaturally audible.

"You carry orders to Olvera?" she said at length. Shere fetched the sealed letter out of his pocket.

"So I must go, or fail in my duty," said he.

"Give me the letter," said Christina.

Shere stared at her in amazement. The amazement changed to suspicion. His whole face seemed to narrow and sharpen out of his own likeness into something foxy and mean.

"I will not," he said, and slowly replaced the letter. "There was a man in the road," he continued slowly, "who whistled as I passed—a signal, no doubt. You are Carlist. This is a trap."

"A trap not laid for you," said Christina. "Be sure of that! Until you spoke of Olvera I did not know."

"No," admitted Shere, "not laid for me to your knowledge, but to Esteban's. You were surprised at my coming—Esteban only at the manner of my coming. He asked if I had ridden into the gates of my own accord I remember. He was in Ronda this afternoon. Very likely it was he who told my colonel of my knowledge of the neighbourhood. It would suit his purposes well to present me to you suddenly, not merely as an enemy, but an active enemy. Yes, I understand that. But," and his voice hardened again, "even to your knowledge the trap was laid for the man who carries the letter. You have your share in the trick." He repeated the word with a sharp laugh, savouring it, dwelling upon it as upon something long forgotten, and now suddenly remembered. "A murderous trick, too, it seems! I wonder what would have happened if I had not turned in at the gates of my own accord. How much farther should I have ridden towards Olvera, and by what gentle means should I have been stopped?"

"By nothing more dangerous than a hand upon your bridle and an excuse that you might do me some small service at Olvera."

"An excuse, a falsity! To be sure," said Shere bitterly. "Yet you still stand before the door though you know the letter will not be yours. Is the trick after all so harmless? Is there no one—Esteban, for instance—in the dark passage outside the door or on the dark road outside the gates?"

"I will prove to you you are wrong."

Christina dropped her arms to her side, moved altogether from the door, and rang a bell. "Esteban shall come here; he will see you outside the gates; he will set you safely on your road to Olvera." She spoke now quite quietly; all the panic and agitation had gone in a moment from her face, her manner, and her words. But the very suddenness of the change in her increased Shere's suspicions. A moment ago Christina was standing before the door with every nerve astrain, her face white, and her eyes bewildered with horror. Now she stood easily by the table with the lighted lamp, speaking easily, playing easily with the gloves upon the table. Shere watched for the secret of this sudden change.

A servant answered the bell and was bidden to find Esteban. No look of significance passed between them; by no gesture was any signal given. "No harm was intended to any man," Christina continued as soon as the door again was closed; "I insisted—I mean there was no need to insist; for I promised to get the letter from the bearer once he had come into this room."

"How?" Shere asked with a blunt contempt. "By tricks?"

Christina raised her head quickly, stung to a moment's anger; but she did not answer him, and again her head drooped.

"At all events," she said quietly, "I have not tried to trick you," and Shere noticed that she arranged with an absent carelessness the gloves in the form of a cross beneath the lamp; and at once he felt that her action contradicted her words. It was merely an instinct at first. Then he began to reason. Those gloves had been so arranged when first he entered the room. Christina and Esteban were bending over the table. Christina was explaining something. Was she explaining that arrangement of the gloves? Was that arrangement the reason of her ready acceptance of his refusal to part with his orders? Was it, in a word, a signal for Esteban—a signal which should tell him whether or not she had secured the letter? Shere saw a way to answer that question. He was now filled with distrust of Christina as half an hour back he had been filled with faith in her; so that he paid no heed to her apology, or to the passionate and pleading voice in which she spoke it.

"So much was at stake for us," she said. "It seemed a necessity that we must have that letter, that no sudden orders must reach Olvera to-night. For there is some one at Olvera—I must trust you, you see, though you are our pledged enemy—some one of great consequence to us, some one we love, some one to whom we look to revive this Spain of ours. No, it is not our King, but his son—his young and gallant son. He will be gone to-morrow, but he is at Olvera to-night. And so when Esteban found out to-day that orders were to be sent to the commandant there it seemed we had no choice. It seemed those orders must not reach him, and it seemed therefore—just so that no hurt might be done, which otherwise would surely have been done, whatever I might order or forbid—that I must use a woman's way and secure the letter."

"And the bearer?" asked Shere, advancing to the table. "What of him? He, I suppose, might creep back to Ronda, broken in honour and with a lie to tell? The best lie he could invent. Or would you have helped him to the lie?"

Christina shrank away from the table as though she had been struck.

"You had not thought of his plight," continued Shere. "He rides out from Ronda an honest soldier and returns—what? No more a soldier than this glove of yours is your hand," and taking up one of the gloves he held it for a moment, and then tossed it down at a distance from its fellow. He deliberately turned his back to the table as Christina replied:

"The bearer would be just our pledged enemy—pledged to outwit us, as we to outwit him. But when you came there was no effort made to outwit you. Own that at all events? You carry your orders safely, with your honour safe, though the consequence may be disaster for us, and disgrace for that we did not prevent you. Own that! You and I, I suppose, will meet no more. So you might own this that I have used no tricks with you?"

The appeal coming as an answer to his insult and contempt, and coming from one whose pride he knew to be a real and dominant quality, touched Shere against his expectation. He faced Christina on an impulse to give her the assurance she claimed, but he changed his mind.

"Are you sure of that?" he asked slowly, for he saw that the gloves while his back was turned had again been crossed. He at all events was now sure. He was sure that those crossed gloves were a signal for Esteban, a signal that the letter had not changed hands. "You have used no tricks with me?" he repeated. "Are you sure of that?"

The handle of the door rattled; Christina quickly crossed towards it. Shere followed her, but stopped for the fraction of a second at the table and deliberately and unmistakably placed the gloves in parallel lines. As the door opened, he was standing between Christina and the table, blocking it from her view.

It was not she, however, who looked to the table, but Esteban. She kept her eyes upon her brother, and when he in his turn looked to her Shere noticed a glance of comprehension swiftly interchanged. So Shere was confident that he had spoiled this trick of the gloves, and when he took a polite leave of Christina and followed Esteban from the room it was not without an air of triumph.

A. E. W. Mason

Christina stood without changing her attitude, except that perhaps she pushed her head a little forward that she might the better hear the last of her lover's receding steps. When they ceased to sound she ran quickly to the window, opened it, and leaned out that she might the better hear his horse's hoofs on the flagged courtyard. She heard besides Esteban's voice speaking amiably and Shere's making amiable replies. The sharp hard clatter upon the stones softened into the duller thud upon the road; the voices became fainter and lost their character. Then one clear "good-night" rang out loudly, and was followed by the quick beats of a horse trotting. Christina slowly closed the window and turned her eyes upon the room. She saw the lamp upon the table and the gloves in parallel lines beneath it.

Now Shere was so far right in that the gloves were intended as a signal for Esteban; only owing to that complete revulsion of which the padre had seen the possibility, Shere had mistaken the signal. The passionate believer had again become the passionate cynic. He saw the trick, and setting no trust in the girl who played it, heeding neither her looks nor words nor the sincerity of her voice, had no doubt that it was aimed against him; whereas it was aimed to protect him. Shere had no doubt that the gloves crossed meant that he still had the sealed letter in his keeping, and therefore he disarranged them. But in truth the gloves crossed meant that Christina had it, and that the messenger might go unhindered upon his way.

Christina uttered no cry. She simply did not believe what her eyes saw. She needed to touch the gloves before she was convinced, and when she had done that she was at once not sure but that she herself in touching them had ranged them in these lines. In the end, however, she understood, not the how or why, but the mere fact. She ran to the door, along the gallery, down the steps into the courtyard. She met no one.

The house might have been a deserted ruin from its silence. She crossed the courtyard to the glimmering white walls, and passed through the gates on to the road. The night was clear; and ahead of her far away in the middle of the road a lantern shone very red. Christina ran towards it, and as she approached she saw faces like miniatures grouped above it. They did not heed her until she was close upon them, until she had noticed one man holding a riderless horse apart from the group and another coiling up a stout rope. Then Esteban, who was holding the lantern, raised his hand to keep her back.

"There has been an accident," said he. "He fell, and fell awkwardly, the horse with him."

"An accident," said Christina, and she pointed to the coil of rope. It was no use for her now to say that she had forbidden violence. Indeed, at no time, as she told Shere, would it have been of any use. She pushed through the group to where Dennis Shere lay on the ground, his face white and shiny and tortured with pain. She knelt down on the ground and took his head in her hands as though she would raise it on to her lap, but one man stopped her, saying, "It is his back, senora." Shere opened his eyes and saw who it was that bent over him, and Christina, reading their look, was appalled. It was surely impossible that human eyes could carry so much hate. His lips moved, and she leaned her ear close to his mouth to catch the words. But it was only one word he spoke and repeated:—

"Tricks! Tricks!"

There was no time to disprove or explain. Christina had but one argument. She kissed him on the lips.

"This is no trick," she cried, and Esteban, laying a hand upon

A. E. W. Mason

her shoulder, said, "He does not hear, nor can his lips answer;" and Esteban spoke the truth. Shere had not heard, and never would hear, as Christina knew.

"He still has the letter," said Esteban. Christina thrust him back with her hand and crouched over the dead man, protecting him. In a little she said, "True, there is the letter." She unbuttoned Shere's jacket and gently took the letter from his breast. Then she knelt back and looked at the superscription without speaking. Esteban opened the door of the lantern and held the flame towards her. "No," said she. "It had better go to Olvera."

She rode to Olvera that night. They let her go, deceived by her composure and thinking that she meant to carry it to "the man of great consequence."

But Christina's composure meant nothing more than that her mind and her feelings were numbed. She was conscious of only one conviction, that Shere must not fail in his duty, since he had staked his honour upon its fulfilment. And so she rode straight to the commandant's quarters at Olvera, and telling of an accident to the bearer, handed him the letter. The commandant read it, and was most politely distressed that Christina should have put herself to so much trouble, for the orders merely recalled his contingent to Ronda in the morning. It was about this time that Christina began to understand precisely what had happened.

THE SHUTTERED HOUSE

If ever a man's pleasures jumped with his duties mine did in the year 1744, when, as a clerk in the service of the Royal African Company of Adventurers, I was despatched to the remote islands of Scilly in search of certain information which, it was believed, Mr. Robert Lovyes alone could impart. For even a clerk that sits all day conning his ledgers may now and again chance upon a record or name which will tickle his dull fancies with the suggestion of a story. Such a suggestion I had derived from the circumstances of Mr. Lovyes. He had passed an adventurous youth, during which he had for eight years been held to slavery by a negro tribe on the Gambia river; he had afterwards amassed a considerable fortune, and embarked it in the ventures of the Company; he had thereupon withdrawn himself to Tresco, where he had lived for twenty years: so much any man might know without provocation to his curiosity. The strange feature of Mr. Lovyes' conduct was revealed to me by the ledgers. For during all those years he had drawn neither upon his capital nor his interest, so that his stake in the Company grew larger and larger, with no profit to himself that any one could discover. It seemed to me, in fact, clean against nature that a man so rich should so disregard his wealth; and I busied myself upon the journey with discovering strange reasons for his seclusion, of which none, I may say, came near the mark, by so much did the truth exceed them all.

A. E. W. Mason

I landed at the harbour of New Grimsey, on Tresco, in the grey twilight of a September evening; and asking for Mr. Lovyes, was directed across a little ridge of heather to Dolphin Town, which lies on the eastward side of Tresco, and looks across Old Grimsey Sound to the island of St. Helen's. Dolphin Town, you should know, for all its grand name, boasts but a poor half-score of houses dotted about the ferns and bracken, with no semblance of order. One of the houses, however, attracted my notice—first, because it was built in two storeys, and was, therefore, by a storey taller than the rest; and, secondly, because all its windows were closely shuttered, and it wore in that falling light a drooping, melancholy aspect, like a derelict ship upon the seas. It stood in the middle of this scanty village, and had a little unkempt garden about it inclosed within a wooden paling. There was a wicket-gate in the paling, and a rough path from the gate to the house door, and a few steps to the right of this path a well was sunk and rigged with a winch and bucket. I was both tired and thirsty, so I turned into the garden and drew up some water in the bucket. A narrow track was beaten in the grass between the well and the house, and I saw with surprise that the stones about the mouth of the well were splashed and still wet. The house, then, had an inmate. I looked at it again, but the shutters kept their secret: there was no glimmer of light visible through any chink. I approached the house, and from that nearer vantage discovered that the shutters were common planks fitted into the windows and nailed fast to the woodwork from without. Growing yet more curious, I marched to the door and knocked, with an inquiry upon my tongue as to where Mr. Lovyes lived. But the excuse was not needed; the sound of my blows echoed through the house in a desolate, solitary fashion, and no step answered them. I knocked again, and louder. Then I leaned my ear to the panel, and I distinctly heard the rustling of a woman's dress. I held my breath to hear the more surely. The sound was repeated, but more faintly, and it was followed by a noise like the closing of a door. I drew back from the house, keeping an eye upon the upper storey, for I thought it possible the woman might reconnoitre me thence. But the windows stared at me blind, unresponsive. To the right and left lights twinkled in the scattered dwellings, and I found something very ghostly in the thought of this woman entombed as it were in the midst of them and moving alone in the shuttered gloom. The twilight deepened, and suddenly the gate behind me whined on its hinges. At once I dropped to my full length on the grass—the gloom was now so thick there was little fear I should be discovered—and a man went past me to the house. He walked, so far as I could judge, with a heavy stoop, but was yet uncommon tall, and he carried a basket upon his arm. He laid the basket upon the doorstep, and, to my utter disappointment, turned at once, and so down the path and out at the gate. I heard the gate rattle once, twice, and then a click as its latch caught. I was sufficiently curious to desire a nearer view of the basket, and discovered that it contained food. Then, remembering me that all this while my own business waited, I continued on my way to Mr. Lovyes' house. It was a long building of a brownish granite, under Merchant's Point, at the northern extremity of Old Grimsey Harbour. Mr. Lovyes was sitting over his walnuts in the cheerless solitude of his dining-room—a frail old gentleman, older than his years, which I took to be sixty or thereabouts, and with the air of a man in a decline. I unfolded my business forthwith, but I had not got far before he interrupted me.

"There is a mistake," he said. "It is doubtless my brother Robert you are in search of. I am John Lovyes, and was, it is true, captured with my brother in Africa, but I escaped six years before he did, and traded no more in those parts. We fled together from the negroes, but we were pursued. My brother was pierced by an arrow, and I left him, believing him to be dead."

A. E. W. Mason

I had, indeed, heard something of a brother, though I little expected to find him in Tresco too. He pressed upon me the hospitality of his house, but my business was with Mr. Robert, and I asked him to direct me on my path, which he did with some hesitation and reluctance. I had once more to pass through Dolphin Town, and an impulse prompted me to take another look at the shuttered house. I found that the basket of food had been removed, and an empty bucket stood in its place. But there was still no light visible, and I went on to the dwelling of Mr. Robert Lovyes. When I came to it, I comprehended his brother's hesitation. It was a rough, mean little cottage standing on the edge of the bracken close to the sea—a dwelling fit for the poorest fisherman, but for no one above that station, and a large open boat was drawn up on the hard beside it as though the tenant fished for his bread. I knocked at the door, and a man with a candle in his hand opened it.

"Mr. Robert Lovyes?" I asked.

"Yes, I am he." And he led the way into a kitchen, poor and mean as the outside warranted, but scrupulously clean and bright with a fire. He led the way, as I say, and I was still more mystified to observe from his gait, his height, and the stoop of his shoulders that he was the man whom I had seen carrying the basket through the garden. I had now an opportunity of noticing his face, wherein I could detect no resemblance to his brother's. For it was broader and more vigorous, with a great, white beard valancing it; and whereas Mr. John's hair was neatly powdered and tied with a ribbon, as a gentleman's should be, Mr. Robert's, which was of a black colour with a little sprinkling of grey, hung about his head in a tangled mane. There was but a two-years difference between the ages of the brothers, but there might have been a decade. I explained my business, and we sat down to a supper of fish, freshly caught, which he served himself. And during supper he gave me the information I was come after. But I lent only an inattentive ear to his talk. For my knowledge of his wealth, the picture of him as he sat in his great sea-boots and coarse seaman's vest, as though it was the most natural garb in the world, and his easy discourse about those far African rivers, made a veritable jumble of my mind. To add to it all, there was the mystery of the shuttered house. More than once I was inclined to question him upon this last account, but his manner did not promise confidences, and I said nothing. At last he perceived my inattention.

"I will repeat all this to-morrow," he said grimly. "You are, no doubt, tired. I cannot, I am afraid, house you, for, as you see, I have no room; but I have a young friend who happens by good luck to stay this night on Tresco, and no doubt he will oblige me." Thereupon he led me to a cottage on the outskirts of Dolphin Town, and of all in that village nearest to the sea.

"My friend," said he, "is named Ginver Wyeth, and, though he comes from these parts, he does not live here, being a school-master on the mainland. His mother has died lately, and he is come on that account."

Mr. Wyeth received me hospitably, but with a certain pedantry of speech which somewhat surprised me, seeing that his parents were common fisherfolk. He readily explained the matter, however, over a pipe, when Mr. Lovyes had left us. "I owe everything to Mrs. Lovyes," he said. "She took me when a boy, taught me something herself, and sent me thereafter, at her own charges, to a school in Falmouth."

"Mrs. Lovyes!" I exclaimed.

"Yes," he continued, and, bending forward, lowered his

A. E. W. Mason

voice. "You went up to Merchant's Point, you say? Then you passed Crudge's Folly—a house of two storeys with a well in the garden."

"Yes, yes!" I said.

"She lives there," said he.

"Behind those shutters!" I cried.

"For twenty years she has lived in the midst of us, and no one has seen her during all that time. Not even Robert Lovyes. Aye, she has lived behind the shutters."

There he stopped. I waited, thinking that in a little he would take up his tale, but he did not, and I had to break the silence.

"I had not heard that Mr. Robert was ever married," I said as carelessly as I might.

"Nor was he," replied Mr. Wyeth. "Mrs. Lovyes is the wife of John. The house at Merchant's Point is hers, and there twenty years ago she lived."

His words caught my breath away, so little did I expect them.

"The wife of John Lovyes!" I stammered, "but—" And I told him how I had seen Robert Lovyes carry his basket up the path.

"Yes," said Wyeth. "Twice a day Robert draws water for her at the well, and once a day he brings her food. It is in his house, too, that she lives—Crudge's Folly, that was his name for it, and the name clings. But, none the less, she is the wife of John;" and with little more persuasion Mr. Wyeth told me the story.

"It is the story of a sacrifice," he began, "mad or great, as you please; but, mark you, it achieved its end. As a boy, I witnessed it from its beginnings. For it was at this very door that Robert Lovyes rapped when he first landed on Tresco on the night of the seventh of May twenty-two years ago, and I was here on my holidays at the time. I had been out that day in my father's lugger to the Poul, which is the best fishing-ground anywhere near Scilly, and the fog took us, I remember, at three of the afternoon. So what with that and the wind failing, it was late when we cast anchor in Grimsey Sound. The night had fallen in a brown mirk, and so still that the sound of our feet brushing through the ferns was loud, like the sweep of scythes. We sat down to supper in this kitchen about nine, my mother, my father, two men from the boat, and myself, and after supper we gathered about the fire here and talked. The talk in these parts, however it may begin, slides insensibly to that one element of which the noise is ever in our ears; and so in a little here were we chattering of wrecks and wrecks and wrecks and the bodies of dead men drowned. And then, in the thick of the talk, came the knock on the door—a light rapping of the knuckles, such as one hears twenty times a day; but our minds were so primed with old wives' tales that it fairly shook us all. No one stirred, and the knocking was repeated.

"Then the latch was lifted, and Robert Lovyes stepped in. His beard was black then—coal black, like his hair—and his face looked out from it pale as a ghost and shining wet from the sea. The water dripped from his clothes and made a puddle about his feet.

"'How often did I knock?' he asked pleasantly. 'Twice, I think. Yes, twice.'"

"Then he sat down on the settle, very deliberately pulled off his great sea-boots, and emptied the water out of them."

A. E. W. Mason

"'What island is this?' he asked."

"'Tresco.'"

"'Tresco!' he exclaimed, in a quick, agitated whisper, as though he dreaded yet expected to hear the name. 'We were wrecked, then, on the Golden Ball.'"

"'Wrecked?' cried my father; but the man went on pursuing his own thoughts."

"'I swam to an islet.'"

"'It would be Norwithel,' said my father."

"'Yes,' said he, 'it would be Norwithel.' And my mother asked curiously—

"'You know these islands?' For his speech was leisurely and delicate, such as we heard neither from Scillonians nor from the sailors who visit St. Mary's."

"'Yes,' he answered, his face breaking into a smile of unexpected softness, 'I know these islands. From Rosevean to Ganilly, from Peninnis Head to Maiden Bower: I know them well.'"

*   *   *   *   *

At this point Mr. Wyeth broke off his story, and crossing to the window, opened it. "Listen!" he said. I heard as it were the sound of innumerable voices chattering and murmuring and whispering in some mysterious language, and at times the voices blended and the murmurs became a single moan.

"It is the tide making on the Golden Ball," said Mr. Wyeth.

"The reef stretches seawards from St. Helen's island and half way across the Sound. You may see it at low tide, a ledge level as a paved causeway, and God help the ship that strikes on it!"

Even while he spoke, from these undertones of sound there swelled suddenly a great booming like a battery of cannon.

"It is the ledge cracking," said Mr. Wyeth, "and it cracks in the calmest weather." With that, he closed the window, and, lighting his pipe, resumed his story.

*　　*　　*　　*　　*

"It was on that reef that Mr. Robert Lovyes was wrecked. The ship, he told us, was the schooner *Waking Dawn*, bound from Cardiff to Africa, and she had run into the fog about half-past three, when they were a mile short of the Seven Stones. She bumped twice on the reef, and sank immediately, with, so far as he knew, all her crew.

"'So now,' Robert continued, tapping his belt, 'since I have the means to pay, I will make bold to ask for a lodging, and for this night I will hang up here my dripping garments to Neptune.'"

"'Me tabula sacer Votiva paries—'"

"I began in the pride of my schooling, for I had learned that verse of Horace but a week before."

"'This, no doubt, is the Cornish tongue,' he interrupted gravely, 'and will you please to carry my boots outside?'"

"What followed seemed to me then the strangest part of all this business, though, indeed, our sea-fogs come and go as often as not with a like abruptness. But the time of this fog's dispersion shocked the mind as something pitiless and arbitrary. For had the air cleared an hour before, the *Waking Dawn* would not have struck. I opened the door, and it was as though a panel of brilliant white was of a sudden painted on the floor. Robert Lovyes sprang up from the settle, ran past me into the open, and stood on the bracken in his stockinged feet. A little patch of fog still smoked on the shining beach of Tean; a scarf of it was twisted about the granite bosses of St. Helen's; and for the rest the moonlight sparkled upon the headlands and was spilled across miles of placid sea. There was a froth of water upon the Golden Ball, but no sign of the schooner sunk among its weeds.

"My father, however, and the two boatmen hurried down to the shore, while I was despatched with the news to Merchant's Point. My mother asked Mr. Lovyes his name, that I might carry it with me. But he spoke in a dreamy voice, as though he had not heard her.

"'There were eight of the crew. Four were below, and I doubt if the four on deck could swim.'"

"I ran off on my errand, and, coming back a little later with a bottle of cordial waters, found Mr. Lovyes still standing in the moonlight. He seemed not to have moved a finger. I gave him the bottle, with a message that any who were rescued should be carried to Merchant's Point forthwith, and that he himself should go down there in the morning.

"'Who taught you Latin?' he asked suddenly."

"'Mrs. Lovyes taught me the rudiments,' I began; and with that he led me on to talk of her, but with some cunning. For now he would divert me to another topic and again bring me back to her, so that it all seemed the vagrancies of a boy's inconsequent chatter.

"Mrs. Lovyes, who was remotely akin to the Lord Proprietor, had come to Tresco three years before, immediately after her marriage, and, it was understood, at her husband's wish. I talked of her readily, for, apart from what I owed to her bounty, she was a woman most sure to engage the affections of any boy. For one thing she was past her youth, being thirty years of age, tall, with eyes of the kindliest grey, and she bore herself in everything with a tender toleration, like a woman that has suffered much.

"Of the other topics of this conversation there was one which later I had good reason to remember. We had caught a shark twelve feet long at the Poul that day, and the shark fairly divided my thoughts with Mrs. Lovyes.

"'You bleed a fish first into the sea,' I explained. 'Then you bait with a chad's head, and let your line down a couple of fathoms. You can see your bait quite clearly, and you wait.'"

"'No doubt,' said Robert; 'you wait.'"

"'In a while,' said I, 'a dim lilac shadow floats through the clear water, and after a little you catch a glimpse of a forked tail and waving fins and an evil devil's head. The fish smells at the bait and sinks again to a lilac shadow—perhaps out of sight; and again it rises. The shadow becomes a fish, the fish goes circling round your boat, and it may be a long while before he turns on his back and rushes at the bait.'"

"'And as like as not, he carries the bait and line away.'"

"'That depends upon how quick you are with the gaff,' said I.' Here comes my father.'"

A. E. W. Mason

"My father returned empty-handed. Not one of the crew had been saved."

"'You asked my name,' said Robert Lovyes, turning to my mother. 'It is Crudge—Jarvis Crudge.' With that he went to his bed, but all night long I heard him pacing his room.

"The next morning he complained of his long immersion in the sea, and certainly when he told his story to Mr. and Mrs. Lovyes as they sat over their breakfast in the parlour at Merchant's Point, he spoke with such huskiness as I never heard the like of. Mr. Lovyes took little heed to us, but went on eating his breakfast with only a sour comment here and there. I noticed, however, that Mrs. Lovyes, who sat over against us, bent her head forward and once or twice shook it as though she would unseat some ridiculous conviction. And after the story was told, she sat with no word of kindness for Mr. Crudge, and, what was yet more unlike her, no word of pity for the sailors who were lost. Then she rose and stood, steadying herself with the tips of her fingers upon the table. Finally she came swiftly across the room and peered into Mr. Crudge's face.

"'If you need help,' she said, 'I will gladly furnish it. No doubt you will be anxious to go from Tresco at the earliest. No doubt, no doubt you will,' she repeated anxiously.

"'Madame,' he said, 'I need no help, being by God's leave a man'—and he laid some stress upon the 'man,' but not boastfully—rather as though all *women* did, or might need help, by the mere circumstance of their sex—'and as for going hence, why yesterday I was bound for Africa. I sailed unexpectedly into a fog off Scilly. I was wrecked in a calm sea on the Golden Ball—I was thrown up on Tresco—no one on that ship escaped but myself. No sooner was I safe than the fog lifted—'

"'You will stay?' Mrs. Lovyes interrupted. 'No?'"

"'Yes,' said he, 'Jarvis Grudge will stay.'"

"And she turned thoughtfully away. But I caught a glimpse of her face as we went out, and it wore the saddest smile a man could see.

"Mr. Grudge and I walked for a while in silence."

"'And what sort of a name has Mr. John Lovyes in these parts?' he asked."

"'An honest sort,' said I emphatically—'the name of a man who loves his wife.'"

"'Or her money,' he sneered. 'Bah! a surly ill-conditioned dog, I'll warrant, the curmudgeon!'"

"'You are marvellously recovered of your cold,' said I."

"He stopped, and looked across the Sound. Then he said in a soft, musing voice: 'I once knew just such another clever boy. He was so clever that men beat him with sticks and put on great sea-boots to kick him with, so that he lived a miserable life, and was subsequently hanged in great agony at Tyburn.'"

"Mr. Grudge, as he styled himself, stayed with us for a week, during which time he sailed much with me about these islands; and I made a discovery. Though he knew these islands so well, he had never visited them before, and his knowledge was all hearsay. I did not mention my discovery to him, lest I should meet with another rebuff. But I was none the less sure of its truth, for he mistook Hanjague for Nornor, and Priglis Bay for Beady Pool, and made a number of suchlike mistakes. After a week he hired the cottage in which he now lives, bought his boat, leased from the steward the patch of ground in Dolphin Town, and set about building his house. He undertook the work, I am sure, for pure employment and distraction. He picked up the granite stones, fitted them together, panelled them, made the floors from the deck of a brigantine which came ashore on Annet, pegged down the thatch roof—in a word, he built the house from first to last with his own hands and he took fifteen months over the business, during which time he did not exchange a single word with Mrs. Lovyes, nor anything more than a short 'Good-day' with Mr. John. He worked, however, with no great regularity. For while now he laboured in a feverish haste, now he would sit a whole day idle on the headlands; or, again, he would of a sudden throw down his tools as though the work overtaxed him, and, leaping into his boat, set all sail and run with the wind. All that night you might see him sailing in the moonlight, and he would come home in the flush of the dawn.

"After he had built the house, he furnished it, crossing for that purpose backwards and forwards between Tresco and St. Mary's. I remember that one day he brought back with him a large chest, and I offered to lend him a hand in carrying it. But he hoisted it on his back and took it no farther than the cottage in which he lived, where it remained locked with a padlock.

"Towards Christmas-time, then, the house was ready, but to our surprise he did not move into it. He seemed, indeed, of a sudden, to have lost all liking for it, and whether it was that he had no longer any work upon his hands, he took to following Mrs. Lovyes about, but in a way that was unnoticeable unless you had other reasons to suspect that his thoughts were following her.

"His conduct in this respect was particularly brought home to me on Christmas Day. The afternoon was warm and sunny, and I walked over the hill at Merchant's Point, meaning to bathe in the little sequestered bay beyond. From the top of the hill I saw Mrs. Lovyes walking along the strip of beach alone, and as I descended the hill-side, which is very deep in fern and heather, I came plump upon Jarvis Grudge, stretched full-length on the ground. He was watching Mrs. Lovyes with so greedy a concentration of his senses that he did not remark my approach. I asked him when he meant to enter his new house.

"'I do not know that I ever shall,' he replied."

"'Then why did you build it?' I asked."

"'Because I was a fool!' and then he burst out in a passionate whisper. 'But a fool I was to stay here, and a fool's trick it was to build that house!' He shook his fist in its direction. 'Call it Grudge's Folly, and there's the name for it!' and with that he turned him again to spying upon Mrs. Lovyes."

"After a while he spoke again, but slowly and with his eyes fixed upon the figure moving upon the beach."

"'Do you remember the night I came ashore? You had caught a shark that day, and you told me of it. The great lilac shadow which rises from the depths and circles about the bait, and sinks again and rises again and takes—how long?— two years maybe before he snaps it.'"

"'But he does not carry it away,' said I, taking his meaning."

"'Sometimes—sometimes," he snarled.

"'That depends on how quick we are with the gaff.'"

A. E. W. Mason

"'You!' he laughed, and taking me by the elbows, he shook me till I was giddy."

"'I owe Mrs. Lovyes everything,' I said. At that he let me go. The ferocity of his manner, however, confirmed me in my fears, and, with a boy's extravagance, I carried from that day a big knife in my belt.

"'The gaff, I suppose,' said Mr. Grudge with a polite smile when first he remarked it. During the next week, however, he showed more contentment with his lot, and once I caught him rubbing his hands and chuckling, like a man well pleased; so that by New Year's Eve I was wellnigh relieved of my anxiety on Mrs. Lovyes' account.

"On that night, however, I went down to Grudge's cottage, and peeping through the window on my way to the door, I saw a strange man in the room. His face was clean-shaven, his hair tied back and powdered; he was in his shirt-sleeves, with a satin waistcoat, a sword at his side, and shining buckles to his shoes. Then I saw that the big chest stood open. I opened the door and entered.

"'Come in!' said the man, and from his voice I knew him to be Mr. Crudge. He took a candle in his hand and held it above his head.

"'Tell me my name,' he said. His face, shaved of its beard and no longer hidden by his hair, stood out distinct, unmistakable.

"'Lovyes,' I answered."

"'Good boy,' said he. 'Robert Lovyes, brother to John.'"

"'Yet he did not know you,' said I, though, indeed, I could

not wonder."

"'But she did,' he cried, with a savage exultation. 'At the first glance, at the first word, she knew me.' Then, quietly, 'My coat is on the chair beside you.'"

"I took it up. 'What do you mean to do?' I asked.

"'It is New Year's Eve,' he said grimly. 'The season of good wishes. It is only meet that I should wish my brother, who stole my wife, much happiness for the next twelve months.'"

"He took the coat from my hands."

"'You admire the coat? Ah! true, the colour is lilac.' He held it out at arm's length. Doubtless I had been staring at the coat, but I had not even given it a thought. 'The lilac shadow!' he went on, with a sneer. 'Believe me, it is the purest coincidence.' And as he prepared to slip his arm into the sleeve I flashed the knife out of my belt. He was too quick for me, however. He flung the coat over my head. I felt the knife twisted out of my hand; he stumbled over the chair; we both fell to the ground, and the next thing I know I was running over the bracken towards Merchant's Point with Robert Lovyes hot upon my heels. He was of a heavy build, and forty years of age. I had the double advantage, and I ran till my chest cracked and the stars danced above me. I clanged at the bell and stumbled into the hall.

"'Mrs. Lovyes!' I choked the name out as she stepped from the parlour."

"'Well?' she asked. 'What is it?'"

"'He is following—Robert Lovyes!'"

"She sprang rigid, as though I had whipped her across the face. Then, 'I knew it would come to this at the last,' she said; and even as she spoke Robert Lovyes crossed the threshold.

"'Molly,' he said, and looked at her curiously. She stood singularly passive, twisting her fingers. 'I hardly know you,' he continued. 'In the old days you were the wilfullest girl I ever clapped eyes on.'"

"'That was thirteen years ago,' she said, with a queer little laugh at the recollection."

"He took her by the hand and led her into the parlour. I followed. Neither Mrs. Lovyes nor Robert remarked my presence, and as for John Lovyes, he rose from his chair as the pair approached him, stretched out a trembling hand, drew it in, stretched it out again, all without a word, and his face purple and ridged with the veins.

"'Brother,' said Robert, taking between his fingers half a gold coin, which was threaded on a chain about Mrs. Lovyes' wrist, 'where is the fellow to this? I gave it to you on the Gambia river, bidding you carry it to Molly as a sign that I would return.'"

"I saw John's face harden and set at the sound of his brother's voice. He looked at his wife, and, since she now knew the truth, he took the bold course.

"'I gave it to her,' said he, 'as a token of your death; and, by God! she was worth the lie!'"

"The two men faced one another—Robert smoothing his chin, John with his arms folded, and each as white and ugly with passion as the other. Robert turned to Mrs. Lovyes, who stood like a stone.

"'You promised to wait,' he said in a constrained voice. 'I escaped six years after my noble brother.'"

"'Six years?' she asked. 'Had you come back then you would have found me waiting.'"

"'I could not,' he said. 'A fortune equal to your own—that was what I promised to myself before I returned to marry you.'"

"'And much good it has done you,' said John, and I think that he meant by the provocation to bring the matter to an immediate issue. 'Pride, pride!' and he wagged his head. 'Sinful pride!'

"Robert sprang forward with an oath, and then, as though the movement had awakened her, Mrs. Lovyes stepped in between the two men, with an arm outstretched on either side to keep them apart."

"'Wait!' she said. 'For what is it that you fight? Not, indeed, for me. To you, my husband, I will no more belong; to you, my lover, I cannot. My woman's pride, my woman's honour—those two things are mine to keep.'"

"So she stood casting about for an issue, while the brothers glowered at one another across her. It was evident that if she left them alone they would fight, and fight to the death. She turned to Robert.

"'You meant to live on Tresco here at my gates, unknown to me; but you could not.'"

"'I could not,' he answered. 'In the old days you had spoken so much of Scilly—every island reminded me—and I saw you every day.'"

"I could read the thought passing through her mind. It would not serve for her to live beside them, visible to them each day. Sooner or later they would come to grips. And then her face flushed as the notion of her great sacrifice came to her.

"'I see but the one way,' she said. 'I will go into the house that you, Robert, have built. Neither you nor John shall see me, but none the less, I shall live between you, holding you apart, as my hands do now. I give my life to you so truly that from this night no one shall see my face. You, John, shall live on here at Merchant's Point. Robert, you at your cottage, and every day you will bring me food and water and leave it at my door.'"

"The two men fell back shamefaced. They protested they would part and put the world between them; but she would not trust them. I think, too, the notion of her sacrifice grew on her as she thought of it. For women are tenacious of sacrifice even as men are of revenge. And in the end she had her way. That night Robert Lovyes nailed the boards across the windows, and brought the door-key back to her; and that night, twenty years ago, she crossed the threshold. No man has seen her since. But, none the less, for twenty years she has lived between the brothers, keeping them apart."

This was the story which Mr. Wyeth told me as we sat over our pipes, and the next day I set off on my journey back to London. The conclusion of the affair I witnessed myself. For a year later we received a letter from Mr. Robert, asking that a large sum of money should be forwarded to him. Being curious to learn the reason for his demand, I carried the sum to Tresco myself. Mr. John Lovyes had died a month before, and I reached the island on Mr. Robert's wedding-day. I was present at the ceremony. He was now dressed in a manner which befitted his station—an old man bent and bowed, but still handsome, and he bore upon his arm a tall woman, grey-haired and very pale, yet with the traces of great beauty. As the parson laid her hand in her husband's, I heard her whisper to him, "Dust to Dust."

A. E. W. Mason

KEEPER OF THE BISHOP

For a fortnight out of every six weeks the little white faced man walked the garrison on St. Mary's Island in a broadcloth frock-coat, a low waistcoat and a black riband of a tie fastened in a bow; and it gave him great pleasure to be mistaken for a commercial traveller. But during the other four weeks he was head-keeper of the lighthouse on the Bishop's Rock, with thirty years of exemplary service to his credit. By what circumstances he had been brought to enlist under the Trinity flag I never knew. But now, at the age of forty-eight he was entirely occupied with a great horror of the sea and its hunger for the bodies of men; the frock-coat which he wore during his spells on shore was a protest against the sea; and he hated not only the sea but all things that were in the sea, especially rock lighthouses, and of all rock lighthouses especially the Bishop.

"The Atlantic's as smooth as a ballroom floor," said he. It was a clear, still day and we were sitting among the gorse on the top of the garrison, looking down the sea towards the west. Five miles from the Scillies, the thin column of the Bishop showed like a cord strung tight in the sky. "But out there all round the lighthouse there are eddies twisting and twisting, without any noise, and extraordinary quick, and every other second, now here, now there, you'll notice the sea dimple, and you'll hear a sound like a man hiccoughing, and all at once, there's a wicked black whirlpool. The tide runs seven miles an hour past the Bishop. But in another year I have done with her." To her Garstin nodded across from St. Mary's to that grey finger post of the Atlantic. "One more winter, well, very likely during this one more winter the Bishop will go—on some night when a storm blows from west or west-nor'west and the Irish coast takes none of its strength."

He was only uttering the current belief of the islands. The first Bishop lighthouse had been swept away before its building was finished, and though the second stood, a fog bell weighing no less than a ton, and fixed ninety feet above the water, had been lifted from its fittings by a single wave, and tossed like a tennis-ball into the sea. I asked Garstin whether he had been stationed on the rock at the time.

"People talk of lightships plunging and tugging at their cables," he returned. "Well, I've tried lightships, and what I say is, ships are built to plunge and tug at their cables. That's their business. But it isn't the business of one hundred and twenty upright feet of granite to quiver and tremble like a steel spring. No, I wasn't on the Bishop when the bell went. But I was there when a wave climbed up from the base of the rock and smashed in the glass wall of the lantern, and put the light out. That was last spring at four o'clock in the morning. The day was breaking very cold and wild, and one could just see the waves below, a lashing tumble of grey and white water as far as the eye could reach. I was in the lantern reading 'It's never too late to mend.' I had come to where the chaplain knocks down the warder, and I was thinking how I'd like to have a go at that warder myself, when all the guns in the world went off together in my ears. And there I was dripping wet, and fairly sliced with splinters of glass, and the wind blowing wet in my face, and the lamp out, and a bitter grey light of morning, as though there never, never had been

A. E. W. Mason

any sun, and all the dead men in the sea shouting out for me one hundred feet below," and Garstin shivered, and rose to his feet. "Well, I have only one more winter of it."

"And then?" I asked.

"Then I get the North Foreland, and the trippers come out from Margate, and I live on shore with my wife and—By the way, I wanted to speak to you about my boy. He's getting up in years. What shall I make of him? A linen-draper, eh? In the Midlands, what? or something in a Free Library, handing out Charles Reade's books? He's at home now. Come and see him!"

In Garstin's quarters, within the coastguard enclosure, I was introduced to his wife and the lad, Leopold. "What shall we call him?" Mrs. Garstin had asked, some fifteen years before. "I don't know any seafaring man by the name of Leopold," Garstin had replied, after a moment of reflection. So Leopold he was named.

Mrs. Garstin was a buxom, unimaginative woman, but she shared to the full her husband's horror of the sea. She told me of nights when she lay alone listening to the moan of the wind overhead, and seeing the column of the Bishop rock upon its base, and of mornings when she climbed from the sheltered barracks up the gorse, with her heart tugging in her breast, certain, certain that this morning, at least, there would be no Bishop lighthouse visible from the top of the garrison.

"It seems a sort of insult to the works of God," said she, in a hushed voice. "It seems as if it stood up there in God's face and cried, 'You can't hurt me!'"

"Yes, most presumptuous and provoking," said Garstin; and so they fell to talking of the boy, who, at all events, should fulfil his destiny very far inland from the sea. Mrs. Garstin leaned to the linen-drapery; Garstin inclined to the free library.

"Well, I will come down to the North Foreland," said I, "and you shall tell me which way it is."

"Yes, if—" said Garstin, and stopped.

"Yes, if—" repeated his wife, with a nod of the head.

"Oh! it won't go this winter," said I.

And it didn't. But, on the other hand, Garstin did not go to the North Foreland, nor for two years did I hear any more of him. But two years later I returned to St. Mary's and walked across the beach of the island to the little graveyard by the sea. A new tablet upon the outer wall of the church caught and held my eye. I read the inscription and remained incredulous. For the Bishop still stood. But the letters were there engraved upon the plate, and as I read them again, the futility of Garstin's fears was enforced upon me with a singular pathos.

For the Bishop still stood and Garstin had died on the Christmas Eve of that last year which he was to spend upon rock lighthouses. Of how he died the tablet gave a hint, but no more than a hint. There were four words inscribed underneath his name:

"And he was not."

I walked back to Hugh Town, wondering at the tragedy which those four words half hid and half revealed, and remembering that the tide runs seven miles an hour past the Bishop, with many eddies and whirlpools. Almost

A. E. W. Mason

unconsciously I went up the hill above Hugh Town and came to the signal station on the top of the garrison. And so occupied was I with my recollections of Garstin that it did not strike me as strange that I should find Mrs. Garstin standing now where he had stood and looking out to the Bishop as he was used to look.

"I had not heard," I said to her.

"No?" she returned simply, and again turned her eyes seawards. It was late on a midsummer afternoon. The sun hung a foot or so above the water, a huge ball of dull red fire, and from St. Mary's out to the horizon's rim the sea stretched a rippling lagoon of the colour of claret. Over the whole expanse there was but one boat visible, a lugger, between Sennen and St. Agnes, beating homewards against a light wind.

"It was a storm, I suppose," said I. "A storm out of the west?"

"No. There was no wind, but—there was a haze, and it was growing dark." Mrs. Garstin spoke in a peculiar tone of resignation, with a yearning glance towards the Bishop as I thought, towards the lugger as I know. But even then I was sure that those last words: "There was a haze and it was growing dark," concealed the heart of her distress. She explained the inscription upon the tablet, while the lugger tacked towards St. Mary's, and while I gradually began to wonder what still kept her on the island.

At four o'clock on the afternoon of that Christmas Eve, the lighthouse on St. Agnes' Island showed its lamps; five minutes later the red beams struck out from Round Island to the north; but to the west on the Bishop all was dark. The haze thickened, and night came on; still there was no flash from the Bishop, and the islands wondered. Half an hour passed; there was still darkness in the west, and the islands became alarmed. The Trinity Brethren subsidise a St. Agnes' lugger to serve the Bishop, and this boat was got ready. At a quarter to five suddenly the Bishop light shot through the gloom, but immediately after a shutter was interposed quickly some half-a-dozen times. It was the signal of distress, and the lugger worked out to the Bishop with the tide. Of the three keepers there were now only two.

It appeared from their account that Garstin took the middle day watch, that they themselves were asleep, and that Garstin should have roused them to light the lamps at a quarter to four. They woke of their own accord in the dark, and at once believed they had slept into the night. The clock showed them it was half-past four. They mounted to the lantern room, and nowhere was there any sign of Garstin. They lit the lamps. The first thing they saw was the log. It was open and the last entry was written in Garstin's hand and was timed 3.40 P.M. It mentioned a ketch reaching northwards. The two men descended the winding-stairs, and the cold air breathed upon their faces. The brass door at the foot of the stairs stood open. From that door thirty feet of gun-metal rungs let in to the outside of the lighthouse lead down to the set-off, which is a granite rim less than a yard wide, and unprotected by any rail. They shouted downwards from the doorway, and received no answer. They descended to the set-off, and again no Garstin, not even his cap. He was not.

Garstin had entered up the log, had climbed down to the set-off for five minutes of fresh air, and somehow had slipped, though the wind was light and the sea whispering. But the whispering sea ran seven miles an hour past the Bishop.

This was Mrs. Garstin's story and it left me still wondering why she lived on at St. Mary's. I asked after her son.

A. E. W. Mason

"How is Leopold? What is he—a linen-draper?" She shaded her eyes with her hand and said:

"That's the St. Agnes' lugger from the Bishop, and if we go down to the pier now we shall meet it."

We walked down to the pier. The first person to step on shore was Leopold, with the Trinity House buttons on his pilot coat.

"He's the third hand on the Bishop now," said Mrs. Garstin. "You are surprised?" She sent Leopold into Hugh Town upon an errand, and as we walked back up the hill she said: "Did you notice a grave underneath John's tablet?"

"No," said I.

"I told you there was a mention in the log of a ketch."

"Yes."

"The ketch went ashore on the Crebinachs at half-past four on that Christmas Eve. One man jumped for the rocks when the ketch struck, and was drowned. The rest were brought off by the lugger. But one man was drowned."

"He drowned because he jumped," said I.

"He drowned because my man hadn't lit the Bishop light," said she, brushing my sophistry aside. "So I gave my boy in his place."

And now I knew why those words—"There was a haze and it was growing dark"—held the heart of her distress.

"And if the Bishop goes next winter," she continued, "why, it will just be a life for a life;" and she choked down a sob as a young voice hailed us from behind.

But the Bishop still stands in the Atlantic, and Leopold, now the second hand, explains to the Margate trippers the wonders of the North Foreland lights.

A. E. W. Mason

THE CRUISE OF THE "WILLING MIND"

The cruise happened before the steam-trawler ousted the smack from the North Sea. A few newspapers recorded it in half-a-dozen lines of small print which nobody read. But it became and—though nowadays the *Willing Mind* rots from month to month by the quay—remains staple talk at Gorleston ale-houses on winter nights.

The crew consisted of Weeks, three fairly competent hands, and a baker's assistant, when the *Willing Mind* slipped out of Yarmouth. Alexander Duncan, the photographer from Derby, joined the smack afterwards under peculiar circumstances. Duncan was a timid person, but aware of his timidity. He was quite clear that his paramount business was to be a man; and he was equally clear that he was not successful in his paramount business. Meanwhile he pretended to be, hoping that on some miraculous day a sudden test would prove the straw man he was to have become real flesh and blood. A visit to a surgeon and the flick of a knife quite shattered that illusion. He went down to Yarmouth afterwards, fairly disheartened. The test had been applied, and he had failed.

Now, Weeks was a particular friend of Duncan's. They had chummed together on Gorleston Quay some years before, perhaps because they were so dissimilar. Weeks had taught Duncan to sail a boat, and had once or twice taken him for a short trip on his smack; so that the first thing that Duncan did on his arrival at Yarmouth was to take the tram to Gorleston and to make inquiries.

A fisherman lounging against a winch replied to them—

"If Weeks is a friend o' yours I should get used to missin' 'im, as I tell his wife."

There was at that time an ingenious system by which the skipper might buy his smack from the owner on the instalment plan—as people buy their furniture—only with a difference: for people sometimes get their furniture. The instalments had to be completed within a certain period. The skipper could do it—he could just do it; but he couldn't do it without running up one little bill here for stores, and another little bill there for sail-mending. The owner worked in with the sail-maker, and just as the skipper was putting out to earn his last instalment, he would find the bailiffs on board, his cruise would be delayed, he would be, consequently, behindhand with his instalment and back would go the smack to the owner with a present of four-fifths of its price. Weeks had to pay two hundred pounds, and had eight weeks to earn it in. But he got the straight tip that his sail-maker would stop him; and getting together any sort of crew he could, he slipped out at night with half his stores.

"Now the No'th Sea," concluded the fisherman, "in November and December ain't a bobby's job."

Duncan walked forward to the pier-head. He looked out at a grey tumbled sky shutting down on a grey tumbled sea. There were flecks of white cloud in the sky, flecks of white breakers on the sea, and it was all most dreary. He stood at the end of the jetty, and his great possibility came out of the grey to him. Weeks was shorthanded. Cribbed within a few

A. E. W. Mason

feet of the smack's deck, there would be no chance for any man to shirk. Duncan acted on the impulse. He bought a fisherman's outfit at Gorleston, travelled up to London, got a passage the next morning on a Billingsgate fish-carrier, and that night went throbbing down the great water street of the Swim, past the green globes of the Mouse. The four flashes of the Outer Gabbard winked him good-bye away on the starboard, and at eleven o'clock the next night far out in the North Sea he saw the little city of lights swinging on the Dogger.

The *Willing Mind's* boat came aboard the next morning and Captain Weeks with it, who smiled grimly while Duncan explained how he had learnt that the smack was shorthanded.

"I can't put you ashore in Denmark," said Weeks knowingly. "There'll be seven weeks, it's true, for things to blow over; but I'll have to take you back to Yarmouth. And I can't afford a passenger. If you come, you come as a hand. I mean to own my smack at the end of this voyage."

Duncan climbed after him into the boat. The *Willing Mind* had now six for her crew, Weeks; his son Willie, a lad of sixteen; Upton, the first hand; Deakin, the decky; Rall, the baker's assistant, and Alexander Duncan. And of these six four were almost competent. Deakin, it is true, was making his second voyage; but Willie Weeks, though young, had begun early; and Upton, a man of forty, knew the banks and currents of the North Sea as well as Weeks.

"It's all right," said the skipper, "if the weather holds." And for a month the weather did hold, and the catches were good, and Duncan learned a great deal. He learnt how to keep a night-watch from midnight till eight in the morning, and then stay on deck till noon; how to put his tiller up and down when his tiller was a wheel, and how to vary the order according as his skipper stood to windward or to lee; he learnt to box a compass and to steer by it; to gauge the leeway he was making by the angle of his wake and the black line in the compass; above all, he learnt to love the boat like a live thing, as a man loves his horse, and to want every scanty inch of brass on her to shine.

But it was not for this that Duncan had come out to sea. He gazed out at night across the rippling starlit water, and the smacks nestling upon it, and asked of his God: "Is this all?" And his God answered him.

The beginning of it was the sudden looming of ships upon the horizon, very clear, till they looked like carved toys. The skipper got out his accounts and totted up his catches, and the prices they had fetched in Billingsgate Market. Then he went on deck and watched the sun set. There were no cloud-banks in the west, and he shook his head.

"It'll blow a bit from the east before morning," said he, and he tapped on the barometer. Then he returned to his accounts and added them up again. After a little he looked up, and saw the first hand watching him with comprehension.

"Two or three really good hauls would do the trick," suggested Weeks.

The first hand nodded. "If it was my boat I should chance it to-morrow before the weather blows up."

Weeks drummed his fists on the table and agreed.

On the morrow the Admiral headed north for the Great Fisher Bank, and the fleet followed, with the exception of the *Willing Mind*. The *Willing Mind* lagged along in the rear without her topsails till about half-past two in the afternoon, when Captain Weeks became suddenly alert. He bore away till he was right before the wind, hoisted every scrap of sail he could carry, rigged out a spinnaker with his balloon fore-sail, and made a clean run for the coast of Denmark. Deakin explained the manoeuvre to Duncan. "The old man's goin' poachin'. He's after soles."

"Keep a look-out, lads!" cried Weeks. "It's not the Danish gun-boat I'm afraid of; it's the fatherly English cruiser a-turning of us back."

Darkness, however, found them unmolested. They crossed the three-mile limit at eight o'clock, and crept close in under the Danish headlands without a glimmer of light showing.

"I want all hands all night," said Weeks; "and there's a couple of pounds for him as first see the bogey-man."

"Meaning the Danish gun-boat," explained Deakin.

The trawl was down before nine. The skipper stood by his lead. Upton took the wheel, and all night they trawled in the shallows, bumping on the grounds, with a sharp eye for the Danish gun-boat. They hauled in at twelve and again at three and again at six, and they had just got their last catch on deck when Duncan saw by the first grey of the morning a dun-coloured trail of smoke hanging over a projecting knoll.

"There she is!" he cried.

"Yes, that's the gun-boat," answered Weeks. "We can laugh at her with this wind."

He put his smack about, and before the gun-boat puffed round the headland, three miles away, was reaching northwards with his sails free. He rejoined the fleet that afternoon. "Fifty-two boxes of soles!" said Weeks. "And every one of them worth two-pound-ten in Billingsgate Market. This smack's mine!" and he stamped on the deck in all the pride of ownership. "We'll take a reef in," he added. "There's a no'th-easterly gale blowin' up and I don't know anything worse in the No'th Sea. The sea piles in upon you from Newfoundland, piles in till it strikes the banks. Then it breaks. You were right, Upton; we'll be lying hove-to in the morning."

They were lying hove-to before the morning. Duncan, tossing about in his canvas cot, heard the skipper stamping overhead, and in an interval of the wind caught a snatch of song bawled out in a high voice. The song was not reassuring, for the two lines which Duncan caught ran as follows—

You never can tell when your death-bells are ringing,
Your never can know when you're going to die.

Duncan tumbled on to the floor, fell about the cabin as he pulled on his sea-boots and climbed up the companion. He clung to the mizzen-runners in a night of extraordinary blackness. To port and to starboard the lights of the smacks rose on the crests and sank in the troughs, with such violence they had the air of being tossed up into the sky and then extinguished in the water; while all round him there flashed little points of white which suddenly lengthened out into a horizontal line. There was one quite close to the quarter of the *Willing Mind*. It stretched about the height of the gaff in a line of white. The line suddenly descended towards him and became a sheet; and then a voice bawled, "Water! Jump! Down the companion! Jump!"

There was a scamper of heavy boots, and a roar of water plunging over the bulwarks, as though so many loads of

A. E. W. Mason

wood had been dropped on the deck. Duncan jumped for the cabin. Weeks and the mate jumped the next second and the water sluiced down after them, put out the fire, and washed them, choking and wrestling, about on the cabin floor. Weeks was the first to disentangle himself, and he turned fiercely on Duncan.

"What were you doing on deck? Upton and I keep the watch to-night. You stay below, and, by God, I'll see you do it! I have fifty-two boxes of soles to put aboard the fish-cutter in the morning, and I'm not going to lose lives before I do that! This smack's mine!"

Captain Weeks was transformed into a savage animal fighting for his own. All night he and the mate stood on the deck and plunged down the open companion with a torrent of water to hurry them. All night Duncan lay in his bunk listening to the bellowing of the wind, the great thuds of solid green wave on the deck, the horrid rush and roaring of the seas as they broke loose to leeward from under the smack's keel. And he listened to something more—the whimpering of the baker's assistant in the next bunk. "Three inches of deck! What's the use of it! Lord ha' mercy on me, what's the use of it? No more than an eggshell! We'll be broken in afore morning, broken in like a man's skull under a bludgeon.... I'm no sailor, I'm not; I'm a baker. It isn't right I should die at sea!"

Duncan stopped his ears, and thought of the journey some one would have to make to the fish-cutter in the morning. There were fifty-two boxes of soles to be put aboard.

He remembered the waves and the swirl of foam upon their crests and the wind. Two men would be needed to row the boat, and the boat must make three trips. The skipper and the first hand had been on deck all night. There remained four, or rather three, for the baker's assistant had ceased to count—Willie Weeks, Deakin, and himself, not a great number to choose from. He felt that he was within an ace of a panic, and not so far, after all, from that whimperer his neighbour. Two men to row the boat—two men! His hands clutched at the iron bar of his hammock; he closed his eyes tight; but the words were thundered out at him overhead, in the whistle of the wind, and slashed at him by the water against the planks at his side. He found that his lips were framing excuses.

Duncan was on deck when the morning broke. It broke extraordinarily slowly, a niggardly filtering of grey, sad light from the under edge of the sea. The bare topmasts of the smacks showed one after the other. Duncan watched each boat as it came into view with a keen suspense. This was a ketch, and that, and that other, for there was the peak of its reefed mainsail just visible, like a bird's wing, and at last he saw it—the fish-cutter—lurching and rolling in the very middle of the fleet, whither she had crept up in the night. He stared at it; his belly was pinched with fear as a starveling's with hunger; and yet he was conscious that, in a way, he would have been disappointed if it had not been there.

"No other smack is shipping its fish," quavered a voice at his elbow. It was the voice of the baker's assistant.

"But this smack is," replied Weeks, and he set his mouth hard. "And, what's more, my Willie is taking it aboard. Now, who'll go with Willie?"

"I will."

Weeks swung round on Duncan and stared at him. Then he stared out to sea. Then he stared again at Duncan.

"You?"

A. E. W. Mason

"When I shipped as a hand on the *Willing Mind*, I took all a hand's risks."

"And brought the willing mind," said Weeks with a smile, "Go, then! Some one must go. Get the boat tackle ready, forward. Here, Willie, put your life-belt on. You, too, Duncan, though God knows life-belts won't be of no manner of use; but they'll save your insurance. Steady with the punt there! If it slips inboard off the rail there will be a broken back! And, Willie, don't get under the cutter's counter. She'll come atop of you and smash you like an egg. I'll drop you as close as I can to windward, and pick you up as close as I can to leeward."

The boat was dropped into the water and loaded up with fish-boxes. Duncan and Willie Weeks took their places, and the boat slid away into a furrow. Duncan sat in the boat and rowed. Willie Weeks stood in the stern, facing him, and rowed and steered.

"Water!" said Willie every now and then, and a wave curled over the bows and hit Duncan a stunning blow on the back.

"Row," said Willie, and Duncan rowed and rowed. His hands were ice, he sat in water ice-cold, and his body perspired beneath his oil-skins, but he rowed. Once, on the crest of a wave, Duncan looked out and saw below them the deck of a smack, and the crew looking upwards at them as though they were a horserace. "Row!" said Willie Weeks. Once, too, at the bottom of a slope down which they had bumped dizzily, Duncan again looked out, and saw the spar of a mainmast tossing just over the edge of a grey roller. "Row," said Weeks, and a moment later, "Ship your oar!" and a rope caught him across the chest.

They were alongside the cutter.

Duncan made fast the rope.

"Push her off!" suddenly cried Willie, and grasped an oar. But he was too late. The cutter's bulwarks swung down towards him, disappeared under water, caught the punt fairly beneath the keel and scooped it clean on to the deck, cargo and crew.

"And this is only the first trip!" said Willie.

The two following trips, however, were made without accident.

"Fifty-two boxes at two-pound-ten," said Weeks, as the boat was swung inboard. "That's a hundred and four, and ten two's are twenty, and carry two, and ten fives are fifty, and two carried, and twenties into that makes twenty-six. One hundred and thirty pounds—this smack's mine, every rope on her. I tell you what, Duncan: you've done me a good turn to-day, and I'll do you another. I'll land you at Helsund, in Denmark, and you can get clear away. All we can do now is to lie out this gale."

Before the afternoon the air was dark with a swither of foam and spray blown off the waves in the thickness of a fog. The heavy bows of the smack beat into the seas with a thud and a hiss—the thud of a steam-hammer, the hiss of molten iron plunged into water; the waves raced exultingly up to the bows from windward, and roared angrily away in a spume of foam from the ship's keel to lee; and the thrumming and screaming of the storm in the rigging exceeded all that Duncan had ever imagined. He clung to the stays appalled. This storm was surely the perfect expression of anger, too persistent for mere fury. There seemed to be a definite aim of destruction, a deliberate attempt to wear the boat down, in the steady follow of wave upon wave, and in the steady volume of the wind.

Captain Weeks, too, had lost all of a sudden all his exhilaration. He stood moodily by Duncan's side, his mind evidently labouring like his ship. He told Duncan stories which Duncan would rather not have listened to, the story of the man who slipped as he stepped from the deck into the punt, and weighted by his boots, had sunk down and down and down through the clearest, calmest water without a struggle; the story of the punt which got its painter under its keel and drowned three men; the story of the full-rigged ship which got driven across the seven-fathom part of the Dogger—the part that looks like a man's leg in the chart—and which was turned upside-down through the bank breaking. The skipper and the mate got outside and clung to her bottom, and a steam-cutter tried to get them off, but smashed them both with her iron counter instead.

"Look!" said Weeks, gloomily pointing his finger. "I don't know why that breaker didn't hit us. I don't know what we should have done if it had. I can't think why it didn't hit us! Are you saved?"

Duncan was taken aback, and answered vaguely—"I hope so."

"But you must know," said Weeks, perplexed. The wind made a theological discussion difficult. Weeks curved his hand into a trumpet, and bawled into Duncan's ear: "You are either saved or not saved! It's a thing one knows. You must know if you are saved, if you've felt the glow and illumination of it." He suddenly broke off into a shout of triumph: "But I got my fish on board the cutter. The *Willing Mind's* the on'y boat that did." Then he relapsed again into melancholy: "But I'm troubled about the poachin'. The temptation was great, but it wasn't right; and I'm not sure but what this storm ain't a judgment."

He was silent for a little, and then cheered up. "I tell you what. Since we're hove-to, we'll have a prayer-meeting in the cabin to-night and smooth things over."

The meeting was held after tea, by the light of a smoking paraffin-lamp with a broken chimney. The crew sat round and smoked, the companion was open, so that the swish of the water and the man on deck alike joined in the hymns. Rail, the baker's assistant, who had once been a steady attendant at Revivalist meetings, led off with a Moody and Sankey hymn, and the crew followed, bawling at the top pitch of their lungs, with now and then some suggestion of a tune. The little stuffy cabin rang with the noise. It burst upwards through the companion-way, loud and earnest and plaintive, and the winds caught it and carried it over the water, a thin and appealing cry. After the hymn Weeks prayed aloud, and extempore and most seriously. He prayed for each member of the crew by name, one by one, taking the opportunity to mention in detail each fault which he had had to complain of, and begging that the offender's chastisement might be light. Of Duncan he spoke in ambiguous terms.

"O Lord!" he prayed, "a strange gentleman, Mr. Duncan, has come amongst us. O Lord! we do not know as much about Mr. Duncan as You do, but still bless him, O Lord!" and so he came to himself.

"O Lord! this smack's mine, this little smack labouring in the North Sea is mine. Through my poachin' and your lovin' kindness it's mine; and, O Lord, see that it don't cost me dear!" And the crew solemnly and fervently said "Amen!"

But the smack was to cost him dear. For in the morning Duncan woke to find himself alone in the cabin. He thrust his head up the companion, and saw Weeks with a very grey face standing by the lashed wheel.

A. E. W. Mason

"Halloa!" said Duncan. "Where's the binnacle?"

"Overboard," said Weeks.

Duncan looked round the deck.

"Where's Willie and the crew?"

"Overboard," said Weeks. "All except Rail! He's below deck forward and clean daft. Listen and you'll hear 'im. He's singing hymns for those in peril on the sea."

Duncan stared in disbelief. The skipper's face drove the disbelief out of him.

"Why didn't you wake me?" he asked.

"What's the use? You want all the sleep you can get, because you an' me have got to sail my smack into Yarmouth. But I was minded to call you, lad," he said, with a sort of cry leaping from his throat. "The wave struck us at about twelve, and it's been mighty lonesome on deck since with Willie callin' out of the sea. All night he's been callin' out of the welter of the sea. Funny that I haven't heard Upton or Deakin, but on'y Willie! All night until daybreak he called, first on one side of the smack and then on t'other, I don't think I'll tell his mother that. An' I don't see how I'm to put you on shore in Denmark, after all."

What had happened Duncan put together from the curt utterances of Captain Weeks and the crazy lamentations of Rail. Weeks had roused all hands except Duncan to take the last reef in. They were forward by the mainmast at the time the wave struck them. Weeks himself was on the boom, threading the reefing-rope through the eye of the sail. He shouted "Water!" and the water came on board, carrying the three men aft. Upton was washed over the taffrail. Weeks threw one end of the rope down, and Rail and Willie caught it and were swept overboard, dragging Weeks from the boom on to the deck and jamming him against the bulwarks.

The captain held on to the rope, setting his feet against the side. The smack lifted and dropped and tossed, and each movement wrenched his arms. He could not reach a cleat. Had he moved he would have been jerked overboard.

"I can't hold you both!" he cried, and then, setting his teeth and hardening his heart, he addressed his words to his son: "Willie! I can't hold you both!" and immediately the weight upon the rope was less. With each drop of the stern the rope slackened, and Weeks gathered the slack in. He could now afford to move. He made the rope fast and hauled the one survivor on deck. He looked at him for a moment. "Thank God, it's not my son!" he had the courage to say.

"And my heart's broke!" had gasped Rail. "Fair broke." And he had gone forward and sung hymns.

They saw little more of Rall. He came aft and fetched his meals away; but he was crazed and made a sort of kennel for himself forward, and the two men left on the smack had enough upon their hands to hinder them from waiting on him. The gale showed no sign of abatement; the fleet was scattered; no glimpse of the sun was visible at any time; and the compass was somewhere at the bottom of the sea.

"We may be making a bit of headway no'th, or a bit of leeway west," said Weeks, "or we may be doing a sternboard. All that I'm sure of is that you and me are one day going to open Gorleston Harbour. This smack's cost me too dear for me to lose her now. Lucky there's the tell-tale compass in the cabin to show us the wind hasn't shifted."

All the energy of the man was concentrated upon this wrestle with the gale for the ownership of the *Willing Mind*; and he imparted his energy to his companion. They lived upon deck, wet and starved and perishing with the cold—the cold of December in the North Sea, when the spray cuts the face like a whip-cord. They ate by snatches when they could, which was seldom; and they slept by snatches when they could, which was even less often. And at the end of the fourth day there came a blinding fall of snow and sleet, which drifted down the companion, sheeted the ropes with ice, and hung the yards with icicles, and which made every inch of brass a searing-iron and every yard of the deck a danger to the foot.

It was when this storm began to fall that Weeks grasped Duncan fiercely by the shoulder.

"What is it you did on land?" he cried. "Confess it, man! There may be some chance for us if you go down on your knees and confess it."

Duncan turned as fiercely upon Weeks. Both men were overstrained with want of food and sleep.

"I'm not your Jonah—don't fancy it! I did nothing on land!"

"Then what did you come out for?"

"What did you? To fight and wrestle for your ship, eh? Well, I came out to fight and wrestle for my immortal soul, and let it go at that!"

Weeks turned away, and as he turned, slipped on the frozen deck. A lurch of the smack sent him sliding into the rudder-chains, where he lay. Once he tried to rise, and fell back. Duncan hauled himself along the bulwarks to him.

"Hurt?"

"Leg broke. Get me down into the cabin. Lucky there's the tell-tale. We'll get the *Willing Mind* berthed by the quay, see if we don't." That was still his one thought, his one belief.

Duncan hitched a rope round Weeks, underneath his arms, and lowered him as gently as he could down the companion.

"Lift me on to the table so that my head's just beneath the compass! Right! Now take a turn with the rope underneath the table, or I'll roll off. Push an oily under my head, and then go for'ard and see if you can find a fish-box. Take a look that the wheel's fast."

It seemed to Duncan that the last chance was gone. There was just one inexperienced amateur to change the sails and steer a seventy-ton ketch across the North Sea into Yarmouth Roads. He said nothing, however, of his despair to the indomitable man upon the table, and went forward in search of a fish-box. He split up the sides into rough splints and came aft with them.

"Thank 'ee, lad," said Weeks. "Just cut my boot away, and fix it up best you can."

The tossing of the smack made the operation difficult and long. Weeks, however, never uttered a groan. Only Duncan once looked up, and said—"Halloa! You've hurt your face too. There's blood on your chin!"

"That's all right!" said Weeks, with an effort. "I reckon I've just bit through my lip."

Duncan stopped his work.

A. E. W. Mason

"You've got a medicine-chest, skipper, with some laudanum in it—?"

"Daren't!" replied Weeks. "There's on'y you and me to work the ship. Fix up the job quick as you can, and I'll have a drink of Friar's Balsam afterwards. Seems to me the gale's blowing itself out, and if on'y the wind holds in the same quarter—" And thereupon he fainted.

Duncan bandaged up the leg, got Weeks round, gave him a drink of Friar's Balsam, set the teapot within his reach, and went on deck. The wind was going down; the air was clearer of foam. He tallowed the lead and heaved it, and brought it down to Weeks. Weeks looked at the sand stuck on the tallow and tasted it, and seemed pleased.

"This gives me my longitude," said he, "but not my latitude, worse luck. Still, we'll manage it. You'd better get our dinner now; any odd thing in the way of biscuits or a bit of cold fish will do, and then I think we'll be able to run."

After dinner Duncan said: "I'll put her about now."

"No; wear her and let her jibe," said Weeks, "then you'll on'y have to ease your sheets."

Duncan stood at the wheel, while Weeks, with the compass swinging above his head, shouted directions through the companion. They sailed the boat all that night with the wind on her quarter, and at daybreak Duncan brought her to and heaved his lead again. There was rough sand with blackish specks upon the tallow, and Weeks, when he saw it, forgot his broken leg.

"My word," he cried, "we've hit the Fisher Bank! You'd best lash the wheel, get our breakfast, and take a spell of sleep on deck. Tie a string to your finger and pass it down to me, so that I can wake you up."

Weeks waked him up at ten o'clock, and they ran southwest with a steady wind till six, when Weeks shouted—

"Take another cast with your lead."

The sand upon the tallow was white like salt.

"Yes," said Weeks; "I thought we was hereabouts. We're on the edge of the Dogger, and we'll be in Yarmouth by the morning." And all through the night the orders came thick and fast from the cabin. Weeks was on his own ground; he had no longer any need of the lead; he seemed no longer to need his eyes; he felt his way across the currents from the Dogger to the English coast; and at daybreak he shouted—

"Can you see land?"

"There's a mist."

"Lie to, then, till the sun's up."

Duncan lay the boat to for a couple of hours, till the mist was tinged with gold and the ball of the sun showed red on his starboard quarter. The mist sank, the brown sails of a smack thrust upwards through it; coastwards it shifted and thinned and thickened, as though cunningly to excite expectation as to what it hid. Again Weeks called out—

"See anything?"

"Yes," said Duncan, in a perplexed voice. "I see something. Looks like a sort of mediaeval castle on a rock."

A. E. W. Mason

A shout of laughter answered him.

"That's the Gorleston Hotel. The harbour-mouth's just beneath. We've hit it fine," and while he spoke the mist swept clear, and the long, treeless esplanade of Yarmouth lay there a couple of miles from Duncan's eyes, glistening and gilded in the sun like a row of dolls' houses.

"Haul in your sheets a bit," said Weeks. "Keep no'th of the hotel, for the tide'll set you up and we'll sail her in without dawdlin' behind a tug. Get your mainsail down as best you can before you make the entrance."

Half an hour afterwards the smack sailed between the pier-heads.

"Who are you?" cried the harbour-master.

"The *Willing Mind*."

"The *Willing Mind's* reported lost with all hands."

"Well, here's the *Willing Mind*," said Duncan, "and here's one of the hands."

The irrepressible voice bawled up the companion to complete the sentence—

"And the owner's reposin' in his cabin." But in a lower key he added words for his own ears. "There's the old woman to meet. Lord! but the *Willing Mind* has cost me dear."

HOW BARRINGTON RETURNED TO
JOHANNESBURG

Norris wanted a holiday. He stood in the marketplace looking southwards to the chimney-stacks, and dilating upon the subject to three of his friends. He was sick of the Stock Exchange, the men, the women, the drinks, the dances—everything. He was as indifferent to the price of shares as to the rise and fall of the quicksilver in his barometer; he neither desired to go in on the ground floor nor to come out in the attics. He simply wanted to get clean away. Besides he foresaw a slump, and he would be actually saving money on the veld. At this point Teddy Isaacs strolled up and interrupted the oration.

"Where are you off to, then?"

"Manicaland," answered Norris.

"Oh! You had better bring Barrington back."

Teddy Isaacs was a fresh comer to the Rand, and knew no better. Barrington meant to him nothing more than the name of a man who had been lost twelve months before on the eastern borders of Mashonaland. But he saw three pairs of eyebrows lift simultaneously, and heard three simultaneous outbursts on the latest Uitlander grievance. However, Norris

A. E. W. Mason

answered him quietly enough.

"Yes, if I come across Barrington, I'll bring him back." He nodded his head once or twice and smiled. "You may make sure of that," he added, and turned away from the group.

Isaacs gathered that there had been trouble between Barrington and Morris, and applied to his companions for information. The commencement of the trouble, he was told, dated back to the time when the two men were ostrich-farming side by side, close to Port Elizabeth in the Cape Colony. Norris owned a wife; Barrington did not. The story was sufficiently ugly as Johannesburg was accustomed to relate it, but upon this occasion Teddy Isaacs was allowed to infer the details. He was merely put in possession of the more immediate facts. Barrington had left the Cape Colony in a hurry, and coming north to the Transvaal when Johannesburg was as yet in its brief infancy, had prospered exceedingly. Meanwhile, Norris, as the ostrich industry declined, had gone from worse to worse, and finally he too drifted to Johannesburg with the rest of the flotsam of South Africa. He came to the town alone, and met Barrington one morning eye to eye on the Stock Exchange. A certain amount of natural disappointment was expressed when the pair were seen to separate without hostilities; but it was subsequently remarked that they were fighting out their duel, though not in the conventional way. They fought with shares, and Barrington won. He had the clearer head, and besides, Norris didn't need much ruining; Barrington could see to that in his spare time. It was, in fact, as though Norris stood up with a derringer to face a machine gun. His turn, however, had come after Barrington's disappearance, and he was now able to contemplate an expedition into Manicaland without reckoning up his pass-book.

He bought a buck-wagon with a tent covering over the

hinder part, provisions sufficient for six months, a span of oxen, a couple of horses salted for the thickhead sickness, hired a Griqua lad as wagon-driver, and half a dozen Matabele boys who were waiting for a chance to return, and started northeastward.

From Johannesburg he travelled to Makoni's town, near the Zimbabwe ruins, and with half a dozen brass rings and an empty cartridge case hired a Ma-ongwi boy, who had been up to the Mashonaland plateau before. The lad guided him to the head waters of the Inyazuri, and there Norris fenced in his camp, in a grass country fairly wooded, and studded with gigantic blocks of granite.

The Ma-ongwi boy chose the site, fifty yards west of an ant-heap, and about a quarter of a mile from a forest of machabel. He had camped on the spot before, he said.

"When?" asked Norris.

"Twice," replied the boy. "Three years ago and last year."

"Last year?" Norris looked up with a start of surprise. "You were up here last year?"

"Yes!"

For a moment or two Norris puffed at his pipe, then he asked slowly—

"Who with?"

"Mr. Barrington," the boy told him, and added, "It is his wagon-track which we have been following."

Norris rose from the ground, and walked straight ahead for

the distance of a hundred yards until he reached a jasmine bush, which stood in a bee-line with the opening of his camp fence. Thence he moved round in a semicircle until he came upon a wagon-track in the rear of the camp, and, after pausing there, he went forward again, and completed the circle. He returned to his wagon chuckling. Barrington, he remembered, had been lost while travelling northwards to the Zambesie; but the track stopped here. There was not a trace of it to the north or the east or the west. It was evident that the boy had chosen Barrington's last camping-ground as the site for his own, and he discovered a comforting irony in the fact. He felt that he was standing in Barrington's shoes.

That night, as he was smoking by the fire, he called out to the Ma-ongwi boy. The lad came forward from his hut behind the wagon.

"Tell me how you lost him," said Norris.

"He rode that way alone after a sable antelope." The boy pointed an arm to the southwest. "The beast was wounded, and we followed its blood-spoor. We found Mr. Barrington's horse gored by the antelope's horns. He himself had gone forward on foot. We tracked him to a little stream, but the opposite bank was trampled, and we lost all sign of him." This is what the boy said though his language is translated.

Norris remained upon this encampment for a fortnight. Blue wildebeests, koodoos, elands, and gems-bok were plentiful, and once he got a shot at a wart-hog boar. At the end of the fortnight he walked round the ant-heap early one morning, and of a sudden plumped down full length in the grass. Straight in front of him he saw a herd of buffaloes moving in his direction down a glade of the forest a quarter of a mile away. Norris cast a glance backwards; the camp was hidden from the herd by the intervening ant-heap. He looked again towards the forest; the buffaloes advanced slowly, pasturing as they moved. Norris crawled behind the ant-heap on his hands and knees, ran thence into the camp, buckled on a belt of cartridges, snatched up a 450-bore Metford rifle, and got back to his position just as the first of the herd stepped into the open. It turned to the right along the edge of the wood, and the others followed in file. Norris wriggled forward through the grass, and selecting a fat bull in the centre of the line, aimed behind its shoulder and fired. The herd stampeded into the forest, the bull fell in its tracks.

Norris sprang forward with a shout; but he had not run more than thirty yards before the bull began to kick. It kneeled upon its forelegs, rose thence on to its hind legs, and finally stood up. Norris guessed what had happened. He had hit the bull in the neck instead of behind the shoulders, and had broken no bones. He fired his second barrel as the brute streamed away in an oblique line southeastwards from the wood, and missed. Then he ran back to camp, slapped a bridle on to his swiftest horse, and without waiting to saddle it, sprang on its back and galloped in pursuit. He rode as it were along the base of a triangle, whereas the bull galloped from the apex, and since his breakfast was getting hot behind him, he wished to make that triangle an isosceles. So he jammed his heels into his horse's ribs, and was fast drawing within easy range, when the buffalo got his wind and swerved on the instant into a diagonal course due southwest.

The manoeuvre left Norris directly behind his quarry, and with a long, stern chase in prospect. However, his blood was up, and he held on to wear the beast down. He forgot his breakfast; he took no more than a casual notice of the direction he was following; he simply braced his knees in a closer grip, while the distorted shadows of himself and the horse lengthened and thinned along the ground as the sun rose over his right shoulder.

A. E. W. Mason

Suddenly the buffalo disappeared in a dip of the veld, and a few moments later came again into view a good hundred yards further to the south. Norris pulled his left rein, and made for the exact spot at which the bull had reappeared. He found himself on the edge of a tiny cliff which dropped twenty feet in a sheer fall to a little stream, and he was compelled to ride along the bank until he reached the incline which the buffalo had descended. He forded the stream, galloped under the opposite bank across a patch of ground which had been trampled into mud by the hoofs of beasts coming here to water, and mounted again to the open. The bull had gained a quarter of a mile's grace from his mistake, and was heading straight for a huge cone of granite.

Norris recognised the cone. It towered up from the veld, its cliffs seamed into gullies by the rain-wash of ages, and he had used it more than once as a landmark during the last fortnight, for it rose due southwest of his camp.

He watched the bull approach the cone and vanish into one of the gullies. It did not reappear, and he rode forward, keeping a close eye upon the gully. As he came opposite to it, however, he saw through the opening a vista of green trees flashing in the sunlight. He turned his horse through the passage, and reined up in a granite amphitheatre. The floor seemed about half a mile in diameter; it was broken into hillocks, and strewn with patches of a dense undergrowth, while here and there a big tree grew. The walls, which converged slightly towards an open top, were robed from summit to base with wild flowers, so that the whole circumference of the cone was one blaze of colour.

Norris hitched forward and reloaded the rifle. Then he advanced slowly between the bushes on the alert for a charge from the wounded bull; but nothing stirred. No sound came to his ears except the soft padding noise of his horse's hoofs upon the turf. There was not a crackle of the brushwood, and the trees seemed carved out of metal. He rode through absolute silence in a suspension of all movement. Once his horse trod upon a bough, and the snapping of the twigs sounded like so many cracks of a pistol. At first the silence struck Norris as merely curious, a little later as very lonesome. Once or twice he stopped his horse with a sudden jerk of the reins, and sat crouched forwards with his neck outstretched, listening. Once or twice he cast a quick, furtive glance over his shoulder to make certain that no one stood between himself and the entrance to the hollow. He forgot the buffalo; he caught himself labouring his breath, and found it necessary to elaborately explain the circumstance in his thoughts on the ground of heat.

The next moment he began to plead this heat not merely as an excuse for his uneasiness, but as a reason for returning to camp. The heat was intense, he argued. Above him the light of an African midday sun poured out of a brassy sky into a sort of inverted funnel, and lay in blinding pools upon the scattered slabs of rock. Within the hollow, every cup of the innumerable flowers which tapestried the cliffs seemed a mouth breathing heat. He became possessed with a parching thirst, and he felt his tongue heavy and fibrous like a dried fig. There was, however, one obstacle which prevented him from acting upon his impulse, and that obstacle was his sense of shame. It was not so much that he thought it cowardly to give up the chase and quietly return, but he knew that the second after he had given way, he would be galloping madly towards the entrance in no child's panic of terror. He finally compromised matters by dropping the reins upon his horse's neck in the unformulated hope that the animal would turn of its own accord; but the horse kept straight on.

As Norris drew towards the innermost wall of granite, there was a quick rustle all across its face as though the screen of

A. E. W. Mason

shrubs and flowers had been fluttered by a draught of wind. Norris drew himself erect with a distinct appearance of relief, loosened the clench of his fingers upon his rifle, and began once more to search the bushes for the buffalo.

For a moment his attention was arrested by a queer object lying upon the ground to his left. It was in shape something like a melon, but bigger, and it seemed to be plastered over with a black mould. Norris rode by it, turned a corner, and then with a gasp reined back his horse upon its haunches. Straight in front of him a broken rifle lay across the path.

Norris stood still, and stared at it stupidly. Some vague recollection floated elusively through his brain. He tried to grasp and fix it clearly in his mind. It was a recollection of something which had happened a long while ago, in England, when he was at school. Suddenly, he remembered. It was not something which had happened, but something he had read under the great elm trees in the close. It was that passage in *Robinson Crusoe* which tells of the naked footprint in the sand.

Norris dismounted, and stooped to lift the rifle; but all at once he straightened himself, and swung round with his arms guarding his head. There was no one, however, behind him, and he gave a little quavering laugh, and picked up the rifle. It was a heavy lo-bore Holland, a Holland with a single barrel, and that barrel was twisted like a corkscrew. The lock had been wrenched off, and there were marks upon the stock—marks of teeth, and other queer, unintelligible marks as well.

Norris held the rifle in his hands, gazing vacantly straight ahead. He was thinking of the direction in which he had come, southwest, and of the stream which he had crossed, and of the patch of trampled mud, where track obliterated track. He dropped the rifle. It rang upon a stone, and again the screen of foliage shivered and rustled. Norris, however, paid no attention to the movement, but ran back to that object which he had passed, and took it in his hands.

It was oval in shape, being slightly broader at one end than the other. Norris drew his knife and cleaned the mould from one side of it. To the touch of the blade it seemed softer than stone, and smoother than wood. "More like bone," he said to himself. In the side which he had cleaned, there was a little round hole filled up with mould. Norris dug his knife in and scraped round the hole as one cleans a caked pipe. He drew out a little cube of mud. There was a second corresponding hole on the other side. He turned the narrower end of the thing upwards. It was hollow, he saw, but packed full of mould, and more deliberately packed, for there were finger-marks in the mould. "What an aimless trick!" he muttered vaguely.

He carried the thing back to the rifle, and, comparing them, understood those queer marks upon the stock. They were the mark of fingers, of human fingers, impressed faintly upon the wood with superhuman strength. He was holding the rifle in his hands and looking down at it; but he saw below the rifle, and he saw that his knees were shaking in a palsy.

On an instant he tossed the rifle away, and laughed to reassure himself—laughed out boldly, once, twice; and then he stopped with his eyes riveted upon the granite wall. At each laugh that he gave the shrubs and flowers rippled, and shook the sunlight from their leaves. For the first time he remarked the coincidence as something strange. He lifted up his face, but not a breath of air fanned it; he looked across the hollow, the trees and bushes stood immobile. He laughed a third time, louder than before, and all at once his laughter got hold of him; he sent it pealing out hysterically, burst after

A. E. W. Mason

burst, until the hollow seemed brimming with the din of it. His body began to twist; he beat time to his laughter with his feet, and then he danced. He danced there alone in the African sunlight faster and faster, with a mad tossing of his limbs, and with his laughter grown to a yell. And as though to keep pace with him, each moment the shiver of the foliage increased. Up and down, crosswise and breadthwise, the flowers were tossed and flung, while their petals rained down the cliff's face in a purple storm. It appeared, indeed, to Norris that the very granite walls were moving.

In the midst of his dance he kicked something and stumbled. He stopped dead when he saw what that something was. It was the queer, mud-plastered object which he had compared with the broken rifle, and the sight of it recalled him to his wits. He tucked it hastily beneath his jacket, and looked about him for his horse. The horse was standing behind him some distance away, and nearer to the cliff. Norris snatched up his own rifle, and ran towards it. His hand was on the horse's mane, when just above its head he noticed a clean patch of granite, and across that space he saw a huge grey baboon leap, and then another, and another. He turned about, and looked across to the opposite wall, straining his eyes, and a second later to the wall on his right. Then he understood; the twisted rifle, the finger marks, this thing which he held under his coat, he understood them all. The walls of the hollow were alive with baboons, and the baboons were making along the cliffs for the entrance.

Norris sprang on to his horse, and kicked and beat it into a gallop. He had only to traverse the length of a diameter, he told himself, the baboons the circumference of a circle. He had covered three-quarters of the distance when he heard a grunt, and from a bush fifty yards ahead the buffalo sprang out and came charging down at him.

Norris gave one scream of terror, and with that his nerves steadied themselves. He knew that it was no use firing at the front of a buffalo's head when the beast was charging. He pulled a rein and swerved to the left; the bull made a corresponding turn. A moment afterwards Norris swerved back into his former course, and shot just past the bull's flanks. He made no attempt to shoot them; he held his rifle ready in his hands, and looked forwards. When he was fifty yards from the passage he saw the first baboon perched upon a shoulder of rock above the entrance. He lifted his rifle, and fired at a venture. He saw the brute's arms wave in the air, and heard a dull thud on the ground behind him as he drove through the gully and out on to the open veld.

The next morning Norris broke up his camp, and started homewards for Johannesburg. He went down to the Stock Exchange on the day of his arrival, and chanced upon Teddy Isaacs.

"What's that?" asked Isaacs, touching a bulge of his coat.

"That?" replied Norris, unfastening the buttons. "I told you I would bring back Barrington if I found him," and he trundled a scoured and polished skull across the floor of the Stock Exchange.

A. E. W. Mason

HATTERAS

The story was told to us by James Walker in the cabin of a seven-ton cutter one night when we lay anchored in Helford river. It was towards the end of September; during this last week the air had grown chilly with the dusk, and the sea when it lost the sun took on a leaden and a dreary look. There was no other boat in the wooded creek and the swish of the tide against the planks had a very lonesome sound. All the circumstances I think provoked Walker to tell the story but most of all the lonely swish of the tide against the planks. For it is the story of a man's loneliness and the strange ways into which loneliness misled him. However, let the story speak for itself.

Hatteras and Walker had been schoolfellows, though never schoolmates. Hatteras indeed was the head of the school and prophecy vaguely sketched out for him a brilliant career in some service of importance. The definite law, however, that the sins of the fathers shall be visited upon the children, overbore the prophecy. Hatteras, the father, disorganised his son's future by dropping unexpectedly through one of the trap ways of speculation into the bankruptcy court beneath just two months before Hatteras, the son, was to have gone up to Oxford. The lad was therefore compelled to start life in a stony world with a stock in trade which consisted of a school boy's command of the classics, a real inborn gift of tongues and the friendship of James Walker. The last item proved of the most immediate value. For Walker, whose father was the junior partner in a firm of West African merchants, obtained for Hatteras an employment as the bookkeeper at a branch factory in the Bight of Benin.

Thus the friends parted. Hatteras went out to West Africa alone and met with a strange welcome on the day when he landed. The incident did not come to Walker's ears until some time afterwards, nor when he heard of it did he at once appreciate the effect which it had upon Hatteras. But chronologically it comes into the story at this point, and so may as well be immediately told.

There was no settlement very near to the factory. It stood by itself on the swamps of the Forcados river with the mangrove forest closing in about it. Accordingly the captain of the steamer just put Hatteras ashore in a boat and left him with his traps on the beach. Half-a-dozen Kru boys had come down from the factory to receive him, but they could speak no English, and Hatteras at this time could speak no Kru. So that although there was no lack of conversation there was not much interchange of thought. At last Hatteras pointed to his traps. The Kru boys picked them up and preceded Hatteras to the factory. They mounted the steps to the verandah on the first floor and laid their loads down. Then they proceeded to further conversation. Hatteras gathered from their excited faces and gestures that they wished to impart information, but he could make neither head nor tail of a word they said and at last he retired from the din of their chatter through the windows of a room which gave on the verandah, and sat down to wait for his superior, the agent. It was early in the morning when Hatteras landed and he waited until midday patiently. In the afternoon it occurred to him that the agent would have shown a kindly consideration if he had left a written message or an intelligible Kru boy to receive him. It

A. E. W. Mason

is true that the blacks came in at intervals and chattered and gesticulated, but matters were not thereby appreciably improved. He did not like to go poking about the house, so he contemplated the mud-banks and the mud-river and the mangrove forest, and cursed the agent. The country was very quiet. There are few things in the world quieter than a West African forest in the daytime. It is obtrusively, emphatically quiet. It does not let you forget how singularly quiet it is. And towards sundown the quietude began to jar on Hatteras' nerves. He was besides very hungry. To while away the time he took a stroll round the verandah.

He walked along the side of the house towards the back, and as he neared the back he head a humming sound. The further he went the louder it grew. It was something like the hum of a mill, only not so metallic and not so loud; and it came from the rear of the house.

Hatteras turned the corner and what he saw was this—a shuttered window and a cloud of flies. The flies were not aimlessly swarming outside the window; they streamed in through the lattices of the shutters in a busy practical way; they came in columns from the forest and converged upon the shutters; and the hum sounded from within the room.

Hatteras looked about for a Kru boy just for the sake of company, but, at that moment there was not one to be seen. He felt the cold strike at his spine, he went back to the room in which he had been sitting. He sat again, but he sat shivering. The agent had left no work for him.... The Kru boys had been anxious to explain something. The humming of the flies about that shuttered window seemed to Hatteras to have more explicit language than the Kru boys' chatterings. He penetrated into the interior of the house, and reckoned up the doors. He opened one of them ever so slightly, and the buzzing came through like the hum of a wheel in a factory, revolving in the collar of a strap. He flung the door open and stood upon the threshold. The atmosphere of the room appalled him; he felt the sweat break cold upon his forehead and a deadly sickness in all his body. Then he nerved himself to enter.

At first he saw little because of the gloom. In a moment, however, he made out a bed stretched along the wall and a thing stretched upon the bed. The thing was more or less shapeless because it was covered with a black, furry sort of rug. Hatteras, however, had little trouble in defining it. He knew now for certain what it was that the Kru boys had been so anxious to explain to him. He approached the bed and bent over it, and as he bent over it the horrible thing occurred which left so vivid an impression on Hatteras. The black, furry rug suddenly lifted itself from the bed, beat about Hatteras' face, and dissolved into flies. The Kru boys found Hatteras in a dead swoon on the floor half-an-hour later, and next day, of course, he was down with the fever. The agent had died of it three days before.

Hatteras recovered from the fever, but not from the impression. It left him with a prevailing sense of horror and, at first, with a sense of disgust too. "It's a damned obscene country," he would say. But he stayed in it, for he had no choice. All the money which he could save went to the support of his family, and for six years the firm he served moved him from district to district, from factory to factory.

Now the second item in the stock in trade was a gift of tongues and about this time it began to bring him profit. Wherever Hatteras was posted, he managed to pick up a native dialect and with the dialect inevitably a knowledge of native customs. Dialects are numerous on the west coast, and at the end of six years, Hatteras could speak as many of them as some traders could enumerate. Languages ran in his

A. E. W. Mason

blood; because he acquired a reputation for knowledge and was offered service under the Niger Protectorate, so that when two years later, Walker came out to Africa to open a new branch factory at a settlement on the Bonny river, he found Hatteras stationed in command there.

Hatteras, in fact, went down to Bonny river town to meet the steamer which brought his friend.

"I say, Dick, you look bad," said Walker.

"People aren't, as a rule, offensively robust about these parts."

"I know that; but your the weariest bag of bones I've ever seen."

"Well, look at yourself in a glass a year from now for my double," said Hatteras, and the pair went up river together.

"Your factory's next to the Residency," said Hatteras. "There's a compound to each running down to the river, and there's a palisade between the compounds. I've cut a little gate in the palisade as it will shorten the way from one house to the other."

The wicket gate was frequently used during the next few months—indeed, more frequently than Walker imagined. He was only aware that, when they were both at home, Hatteras would come through it of an evening and smoke on his verandah. Then he would sit for hours cursing the country, raving about the lights in Piccadilly-circus, and offering his immortal soul in exchange for a comic-opera tune played upon a barrel-organ. Walker possessed a big atlas, and one of Hatteras' chief diversions was to trace with his finger a bee-line across the African continent and the Bay of Biscay until he reached London.

More rarely Walker would stroll over to the Residency, but he soon came to notice that Hatteras had a distinct preference for the factory and for the factory verandah. The reason for the preference puzzled Walker considerably. He drew a quite erroneous conclusion that Hatteras was hiding at the Residency—well, some one whom it was prudent, especially in an official, to conceal. He abandoned the conclusion, however, when he discovered that his friend was in the habit of making solitary expeditions. At times Hatteras would be absent for a couple of days, at times for a week, and, so far as Walker could ascertain, he never so much as took a servant with him to keep him company. He would simply announce at night his intended departure, and in the morning he would be gone. Nor on his return did he ever offer to Walker any explanation of his journeys. On one occasion, however, Walker broached the subject. Hatteras had come back the night before, and he sat crouched up in a deck chair, looking intently into the darkness of the forest.

"I say," asked Walker, "isn't it rather dangerous to go slumming about West Africa alone?"

Hatteras did not reply for a moment. He seemed not to have heard the suggestion, and when he did speak it was to ask a quite irrelevant question.

"Have you ever seen the Horse Guards' Parade on a dark, rainy night?" he asked; but he never moved his head, he never took his eyes from the forest. "The wet level of ground looks just like a lagoon and the arches a Venice palace above it."

"But look here, Dick!" said Walker, keeping to his subject. "You never leave word when you are coming back. One never knows that you have come back until you show

A. E. W. Mason

yourself the morning after."

"I think," said Hatteras slowly, "that the finest sight in the world is to be seen from the bridge in St. James's Park when there's a State ball on at Buckingham Palace and the light from the windows reddens the lake and the carriages glance about the Mall like fireflies."

"Even your servants don't know when you come back," said Walker.

"Oh," said Hatteras quietly, "so you have been asking questions of my servants?"

"I had a good reason," replied Walker, "your safety," and with that the conversation dropped.

Walker watched Hatteras. Hatteras watched the forest. A West African mangrove forest at night is full of the eeriest, queerest sounds that ever a man's ears harkened to. And the sounds come not so much from the birds, or the soughing of the branches; they seem to come from the swamp life underneath the branches, at the roots of trees. There's a ceaseless stir as of a myriad of reptiles creeping in the slime. Listen long enough and you will fancy that you hear the whirr and rush of innumerable crabs, the flapping of innumerable fish. Now and again a more distinctive sound emerges from the rest—the croaking of a bull-frog, the whining cough of a crocodile. At such sounds Hatteras would start up in his chair and cock his head like a dog in a room that hears another dog barking in the street.

"Doesn't it sound damned wicked?" he said, with a queer smile of enjoyment.

Walker did not answer. The light from a lamp in the room

behind them struck obliquely upon Hatteras' face and slanted off from it in a narrowing column until it vanished in a yellow thread among the leaves of the trees. It showed that the same enjoyment which ran in Hatteras' voice was alive upon his face. His eyes, his ears, were alert, and he gently opened and shut his mouth with a little clicking of the teeth. In some horrible way he seemed to have something in common with, he appeared almost to participate in, the activity of the swamp. Thus, had Walker often seen him sit, but never with the light so clear upon his face, and the sight gave to him a quite new impression of his friend. He wondered whether all these months his judgment had been wrong. And out of that wonder a new thought sprang into his mind.

"Dick," he said, "this house of mine stands between your house and the forest. It stands on the borders of the trees, on the edge of the swamp. Is that why you always prefer it to your own?"

Hatteras turned his head quickly towards his companion, almost suspiciously. Then he looked back into the darkness, and after a little he said:—

"It's not only the things you care about, old man, which tug at you, it's the things you hate as well. I hate this country. I hate these miles and miles of mangroves, and yet I am fascinated. I can't get the forest and the undergrowth out of my mind. I dream of them at nights. I dream that I am sinking into that black oily batter of mud. Listen," and he suddenly broke off with his head stretched forwards. "Doesn't it sound wicked?"

"But all this talk about London?" cried Walker.

"Oh, don't you understand?" interrupted Hatteras roughly.

A. E. W. Mason

Then he changed his tone and gave his reason. "One has to struggle against a fascination of that sort. It's devil's work. So for all I am worth I talk about London."

"Look here, Dick," said Walker. "You had better get leave and go back to the old country for a spell."

"A very solid piece of advice," said Hatteras, and he went home to the Residency.

II

The next morning he had again disappeared. But Walker discovered upon his table a couple of new volumes. He glanced at the titles. They were Burton's account of his pilgrimage to al-Madinah and Mecca.

Five nights afterwards Walker was smoking a pipe on the verandah when he fancied that he heard a rubbing, scuffling sound as if some one very cautiously was climbing over the fence of his compound. The moon was low in the sky and dipping down toward the forest; indeed the rim of it touched the tree-tops so that while a full half of the enclosure was bare to the yellow light that half which bordered on the forest was inky black in shadow; and it was from the furthest corner of this second half that the sound came. Walker bent forward listening. He heard the sound again, and a moment after another sound, which left him in no doubt. For in that dark corner he knew that a number of palisades for repairing the fence were piled and the second sound which he heard was a rattle as some one stumbled against them. Walker went inside and fetched a rifle.

When he came back he saw a negro creeping across the bright open space towards the Residency. Walker hailed to him to stop. Instead the negro ran. He ran towards the wicket gate in the palisades. Walker shouted again; the figure only ran the faster. He had covered half the distance before Walker fired. He clutched his right forearm with his left hand, but he did not stop. Walker fired again, this time at his legs, and the man dropped to the ground. Walker heard his servants stirring as he ran down the steps. He crossed quickly to the negro and the negro spoke to him, but in English, and with the voice of Hatteras.

A. E. W. Mason

"For God's sake keep your servants off!"

Walker ran to the house, met his servants at the foot of the steps, and ordered them back. He had shot at a monkey he said. Then he returned to Hatteras.

"Dicky, are you hurt?" he whispered.

"You hit me each time you fired, but not very badly I think."

He bandaged Hatteras' arm and thigh with strips of his shirt and waited by his side until the house was quiet. Then he lifted him and carried him across the enclosure to the steps and up the steps into his bedroom. It was a long and fatiguing process. For one thing Walker dared make no noise and must needs tread lightly with his load; for another, the steps were steep and ricketty, with a narrow balustrade on each side waist high. It seemed to Walker that the day would dawn before he reached the top. Once or twice Hatteras stirred in his arms, and he feared the man would die then and there. For all the time his blood dripped and pattered like heavy raindrops on the wooden steps.

Walker laid Hatteras on his bed and examined his wounds. One bullet had passed through the fleshy part of the forearm, the other through the fleshy part of his right thigh. But no bones were broken and no arteries cut. Walker lit a fire, baked some plaintain leaves, and applied them as a poultice. Then he went out with a pail of water and scrubbed down the steps.

Again he dared not make any noise, and it was close on daybreak before he had done. His night's work, however, was not ended. He had still to cleanse the black stain from Hatteras' skin, and the sun was up before he stretched a rug upon the ground and went to sleep with his back against the door.

"Walker," Hatteras called out in a low voice, an hour or so later.

Walker woke up and crossed over to the bed.

"Dicky, I'm frightfully sorry. I couldn't know it was you."

"That's all right, Jim. Don't you worry about that. What I wanted to say was that nobody had better know. It wouldn't do, would it, if it got about?"

"Oh, I am not so sure. People would think it rather a creditable proceeding."

Hatteras shot a puzzled look at his friend. Walker, however, did not notice it, and continued, "I saw Burton's account of his pilgrimage in your room; I might have known that journeys of the kind were just the sort of thing to appeal to you."

"Oh, yes, that's it," said Hatteras, lifting himself up in bed. He spoke eagerly—perhaps a thought too eagerly. "Yes, that's it. I have always been keen on understanding the native thoroughly. It's after all no less than one's duty if one has to rule them, and since I could speak their lingo—" he broke off and returned to the subject which had prompted him to rouse Walker. "But, all the same, it wouldn't do if the natives got to know."

"There's no difficulty about that," said Walker. "I'll give out that you have come back with the fever and that I am nursing you. Fortunately there's no doctor handy to come making inconvenient examinations."

Hatteras knew something of surgery, and under his directions Walker poulticed and bandaged him until he recovered. The

A. E. W. Mason

bandaging, however, was amateurish, and, as a result, the muscles contracted in Hatteras' thigh and he limped—ever so slightly, still he limped—he limped to his dying day. He did not, however, on that account abandon his explorations, and more than once Walker, when his lights were out and he was smoking a pipe on the verandah, would see a black figure with a trailing walk cross his compound and pass stealthily through the wicket in the fence. Walker took occasion to expostulate with his friend.

"It's too dangerous a game for a man to play for any length of time. It is doubly dangerous now that you limp. You ought to give it up."

Hatteras made a strange reply.

"I'll try to," he said.

Walker pondered over the words for some time. He set them side by side in his thoughts with that confession which Hatteras had made to him one evening. He asked himself whether, after all, Hatteras' explanation of his conduct was sincere, whether it was really a desire to know the native thoroughly which prompted these mysterious expeditions; and then he remembered that he himself had first suggested the explanation to Hatteras. Walker began to feel uneasy— more than uneasy, actually afraid on his friend's account. Hatteras had acknowledged that the country fascinated him, and fascinated him through its hideous side. Was this masquerading as a black man a further proof of the fascination? Was it, as it were, a step downwards towards a closer association? Walker sought to laugh the notion from his mind, but it returned and returned, and here and there an incident occurred to give it strength and colour.

For instance, on one occasion after Hatteras had been three

weeks absent, Walker sauntered over to the Residency towards four o'clock in the afternoon. Hatteras was trying cases in the court-house, which formed the ground floor of the Residency. Walker stepped into the room. It was packed with a naked throng of blacks, and the heat was over-powering. At the end of the hall sat Hatteras. His worn face shone out amongst the black heads about him white and waxy like a gardenia in a bouquet of black flowers. Walker invented his simile and realised its appositeness at one and the same moment. Bouquet was not an inappropriate word since there is a penetrating aroma about the native of the Niger delta when he begins to perspire.

Walker, however, thinking that the Court would rise, determined to wait for a little. But, at the last moment, a negro was put up to answer to a charge of participation in Fetish rites. The case seemed sufficiently clear from the outset, but somehow Hatteras delayed its conclusion. There was evidence and unrebutted evidence of the usual details— human sacrifice, mutilations and the like, but Hatteras pressed for more. He sat until it was dusk, and then had candles brought into the Court-house. He seemed indeed not so much to be investigating the negro's guilt as to be adding to his own knowledge of Fetish ceremonials. And Walker could not but perceive that he took more than a merely scientific pleasure in the increase of his knowledge. His face appeared to smooth out, his eyes became quick, interested, almost excited; and Walker again had the queer impression that Hatteras was in spirit participating in the loathsome ceremonies, and participating with an intense enjoyment. In the end the negro was convicted and the Court rose. But he might have been convicted a good three hours before. Walker went home shaking his head. He seemed to be watching a man deliberately divesting himself of his humanity. It seemed as though the white man were ambitious to decline into the black. Hatteras was growing into an

A. E. W. Mason

uncanny creature. His friend began to foresee a time when he should hold him in loathing and horror. And the next morning helped to confirm him in that forecast.

For Walker had to make an early start down river for Bonny town, and as he stood on the landing-stage Hatteras came down to him from the Residency.

"You heard that negro tried yesterday?" he asked with an assumption of carelessness.

"Yes, and condemned. What of him?"

"He escaped last night. It's a bad business, isn't it?"

Walker nodded in reply and his boat pushed off. But it stuck in his mind for the greater part of that day that the prison adjoined the Court-house and so formed part of the ground floor of the Residency. Had Hatteras connived at his escape? Had the judge secretly set free the prisoner whom he had publicly condemned? The question troubled Walker considerably during his month of absence, and stood in the way of his business. He learned for the first time how much he loved his friend and how eagerly he watched for the friend's advancement. Each day added to his load of anxiety. He dreamed continually of a black-painted man slipping among the tree-boles nearer and nearer towards the red glow of a fire in some open space secure amongst the swamps, where hideous mysteries had their celebration. He cut short his business and hurried back from Bonny. He crossed at once to the Residency and found his friend in a great turmoil of affairs. Walker came back from Bonny a month later and hurried across to his friend.

"Jim," said Hatteras, starting up, "I've got a year's leave; I am going home."

"Dicky!" cried Walker, and he nearly wrung Hatteras' hand from his arm. "That's grand news."

"Yes, old man, I thought you would be glad; I sail in a fortnight." And he did.

For the first month Walker was glad. A year's leave would make a new man of Dick Hatteras, he thought, or, at all events, restore the old man, sane and sound, as he had been before he came to the West African coast. During the second month Walker began to feel lonely. In the third he bought a banjo and learnt it during the fourth and fifth. During the sixth he began to say to himself, "What a time poor Dick must have had all those six years with those cursed forests about him. I don't wonder—I don't wonder." He turned disconsolately to his banjo and played for the rest of the year; all through the wet season while the rain came down in a steady roar and only the curlews cried—until Hatteras returned. He returned at the top of his spirits and health. Of course he was hall-marked West African, but no man gets rid of that stamp. Moreover there was more than health in his expression. There was a new look of pride in his eyes and when he spoke of a bachelor it was in terms of sympathetic pity.

"Jim," said he, after five minutes of restraint, "I am engaged to be married."

Jim danced round him in delight. "What an ass I have been," he thought, "why didn't I think of that cure myself?" and he asked, "When is it to be?"

"In eight months. You'll come home and see me through."

Walker agreed and for eight months listened to praises of the lady. There were no more solitary expeditions. In fact, Hatteras seemed absorbed in the diurnal discovery of new perfections in his future wife.

"Yes, she seems a nice girl," Walker commented. He found her upon his arrival in England more human than Hatteras' conversation had led him to expect, and she proved to him that she was a nice girl. For she listened for hours to him lecturing her on the proper way to treat Dick without the slightest irritation and with only a faintly visible amusement. Besides she insisted on returning with her husband to Bonny river, which was a sufficiently courageous thing to undertake.

For a year in spite of the climate the couple were commonplace and happy. For a year Walker clucked about them like a hen after its chickens and slept the sleep of the untroubled. Then he returned to England and from that time made only occasional journeys to West Africa. Thus for awhile he almost lost sight of Hatteras and consequently still slept the sleep of the untroubled. One morning, however, he arrived unexpectedly at the settlement and at once called on Hatteras. He did not wait to be announced, but ran up the steps outside the house and into the dining-room. He found Mrs. Hatteras crying. She dried her eyes, welcomed Walker, and said that she was sorry, but her husband was away.

Walker started, looked at her eyes, and asked hesitatingly whether he could help. Mrs. Hatteras replied with an ill-assumed surprise that she did not understand. Walker suggested that there was trouble. Mrs. Hatteras denied the truth of the suggestion. Walker pressed the point and Mrs. Hatteras yielded so far as to assert that there was no trouble in which Hatteras was concerned. Walker hardly thought it the occasion for a parade of manners, and insisted on pointing out that his knowledge of her husband was intimate and dated from his schooldays. Thereupon Mrs. Hatteras gave way.

"Dick goes away alone," she said. "He stains his skin and goes away at night. He tells me that he must, that it's the only way by which he can know the natives, and that so it's a sort of duty. He says the black tells nothing of himself to the white man—ever. You must go amongst them if you are to know them. So he goes, and I never know when he will come back. I never know whether he will come back."

"But he has done that sort of thing on and off for years, and he has always come back," replied Walker.

"Yes, but one day he will not." Walker comforted her as well as he could, praised Hatteras for his conduct, though his heart was hot against him, spoke of risks that every one must run who serve the Empire. "Never a lotus closes, you know," he said, and went back to the factory with the consciousness that he had been telling lies.

It was no sense of duty that prompted Hatteras, of that he was certain, and he waited—he waited from darkness to daybreak in his compound for three successive nights. On the fourth he heard the scuffling sound at the corner of the fence. The night was black as the inside of a coffin. Half a regiment of men might steal past him and he not have seen them. Accordingly he walked cautiously to the palisade which separated the enclosure of the Residency from his own, felt along it until he reached the little gate and stationed himself in front of it. In a few moments he thought that he heard a man breathing, but whether to the right or the left he could not tell; and then a groping hand lightly touched his face and drew away again. Walker said nothing, but held his breath and did not move. The hand was stretched out again. This time it touched his breast and moved across it until it felt a button of Walker's coat. Then it was snatched away and Walker heard a gasping in-draw of the breath and afterwards a sound as of a man turning in a flurry. Walker sprang

A. E. W. Mason

forward and caught a naked shoulder with one hand, a naked arm with the other.

"Wait a bit, Dick Hatteras," he said.

There was a low cry, and then a husky voice addressed him respectfully as "Daddy" in trade-English.

"That won't do, Dick," said Walker.

The voice babbled more trade-English.

"If you're not Dick Hatteras," continued Walker, tightening his grasp, "You've no manner of right here. I'll give you till I count ten and then I shall shoot."

Walker counted up to nine aloud and then—

"Jim," said Hatteras in his natural voice.

"That's better," said Walker. "Let's go in and talk."

III

He went up the step and lighted the lamp. Hatteras followed him and the two men faced one another. For a little while neither of them spoke. Walker was repeating to himself that this man with the black skin, naked except for a dirty loincloth and a few feathers on his head was a white man married to a white wife who was sleeping—Nay, more likely crying—not thirty yards away.

Hatteras began to mumble out his usual explanation of duty and the rest of it.

"That won't wash," interrupted Walker. "What is it? A woman?"

"Good Heaven, no!" cried Hatteras suddenly. It was plain that that explanation was at all events untrue. "Jim, I've a good mind to tell you all about it."

"You have got to," said Walker. He stood between Hatteras and the steps.

"I told you how this country fascinated me in spite of myself," he began.

"But I thought," interrupted Walker, "that you had got over that since. Why, man, you are married," and he came across to Hatteras and shook him by the shoulder. "Don't you understand? You have a wife!"

"I know," said Hatteras. "But there are things deeper at the heart of me than the love of woman, and one of those things is the love of horror. I tell you it bites as nothing else does in this world. It's like absinthe that turns you sick at the

A. E. W. Mason

beginning and that you can't do without once you have got the taste of it. Do you remember my first landing? It made me sick enough at the beginning, you know. But now—" He sat down in a chair and drew it close to Walker. His voice dropped to a passionate whisper, he locked and unlocked his fingers with feverish movements, and his eyes shifted and glittered in an unnatural excitement.

"It's like going down to Hell and coming up again and wanting to go down again. Oh, you'd want to go down again. You'd find the whole earth pale. You'd count the days until you went down again. Do you remember Orpheus? I think he looked back not to see if Eurydice was coming after him but because he knew it was the last glimpse he would get of Hell." At that he broke off and began to chant in a crazy voice, wagging his head and swaying his body to the rhythm of the lines:—

"Quum subita in cantum dementia cepit amantem Ignoscenda quidem scirent si ignoscere manes; Restilit Eurydicengue suam jam luce sub ipsa Immemor heu victusque animi respexit."

"Oh, stop that!" cried Walker, and Hatteras laughed. "For God's sake, stop it!"

For the words brought back to him in a flash the vision of a class-room with its chipped desks ranged against the varnished walls, the droning sound of the form-master's voice, and the swish of lilac bushes against the lower window panes on summer afternoons. "Go on," he said. "Oh, go on, and let's have done with it."

Hatteras took up his tale again, and it seemed to Walker that the man breathed the very miasma of the swamp and infected the room with it. He spoke of leopard societies, murder clubs, human sacrifices. He had witnessed them at the beginning, he had taken his share in them at the last. He told the whole story without shame, with indeed a growing enjoyment. He spared Walker no details. He related them in their loathsome completeness until Walker felt stunned and sick. "Stop," he said, again, "Stop! That's enough."

Hatteras, however, continued. He appeared to have forgotten Walker's presence. He told the story to himself, for his own amusement, as a child will, and here and there he laughed and the mere sound of his laughter was inhuman. He only came to a stop when he saw Walker hold out to him a cocked and loaded revolver.

"Well?" he asked. "Well?"

Walker still offered him the revolver.

"There are cases, I think, which neither God's law nor man's law seems to have provided for. There's your wife you see to be considered. If you don't take it I shall shoot you myself now, here, and mark you I shall shoot you for the sake of a boy I loved at school in the old country."

Hatteras took the revolver in silence, laid it on the table, fingered it for a little.

"My wife must never know," he said.

"There's the pistol. Outside's the swamp. The swamp will tell no tales, nor shall I. Your wife need never know."

Hatteras picked up the pistol and stood up.

"Good-bye, Jim," he said, and half pushed out his hand. Walker shook his head, and Hatteras went out on to the verandah and down the steps.

Walker heard him climb over the fence; and then followed as far as the verandah. In the still night the rustle and swish of the undergrowth came quite clearly to his ears. The sound ceased, and a few minutes afterwards the muffled crack of a pistol shot broke the silence like the tap of a hammer. The swamp, as Walker prophesied, told no tales. Mrs. Hatteras gave the one explanation of her husband's disappearance that she knew and returned brokenhearted to England. There was some loud talk about the self-sacrificing energy, which makes the English a dominant race, and there you might think is the end of the story.

But some years later Walker went trudging up the Ogowe river in Congo Francais. He travelled as far as Woermann's factory in Njole Island and, having transacted his business there, pushed up stream in the hope of opening the upper reaches for trade purposes. He travelled for a hundred and fifty miles in a little stern-wheel steamer. At that point he stretched an awning over a whale-boat, embarked himself, his banjo and eight blacks from the steamer, and rowed for another fifty miles. There he ran the boat's nose into a clay cliff close to a Fan village and went ashore to negotiate with the chief.

There was a slip of forest between the village and the river bank, and while Walker was still dodging the palm creepers which tapestried it he heard a noise of lamentation. The noise came from the village and was general enough to assure him that a chief was dead. It rose in a chorus of discordant howls, low in note and long-drawn out—wordless, something like the howls of an animal in pain and yet human by reason of their infinite melancholy.

Walker pushed forward, came out upon a hillock, fronting

the palisade which closed the entrance to the single street of huts, and passed down into the village. It seemed as though he had been expected. For from every hut the Fans rushed out towards him, the men dressed in their filthiest rags, the women with their faces chalked and their heads shaved. They stopped, however, on seeing a white man, and Walker knew enough of their tongue to ascertain that they looked for the coming of the witch doctor. The chief, it appeared, had died a natural death, and, since the event is of sufficiently rare occurrence in the Fan country, it had promptly been attributed to witchcraft, and the witch doctor had been sent for to discover the criminal. The village was consequently in a lively state of apprehension, since the end of those who bewitch chiefs to death is not easy. The Fans, however, politely invited Walker to inspect the corpse. It lay in a dark hut, packed with the corpse's relations, who were shouting to it at the top of their voices on the on-chance that its spirit might think better of its conduct and return to the body. They explained to Walker that they had tried all the usual varieties of persuasion. They had put red pepper into the chief's eyes while he was dying. They had propped open his mouth with a stick; they had burned fibres of the oil nut under his nose. In fact, they had made his death as uncomfortable as possible, but none the less he had died.

The witch doctor arrived on the heels of the explanation, and Walker, since he was powerless to interfere, thought it wise to retire for the time being. He went back to the hillock on the edge of the trees. Thence he looked across and over the palisade and had the whole length of the street within his view.

The witch doctor entered it from the opposite end, to the beating of many drums. The first thing Walker noticed was that he wore a square-skirted eighteenth century coat and a tattered pair of brocaded knee breeches on his bare legs; the

A. E. W. Mason

second was that he limped—ever so slightly. Still he limped and—with the right leg. Walker felt a strong desire to see the man's face, and his heart thumped within him as he came nearer and nearer down the street. But his hair was so matted about his cheeks that Walker could not distinguish a feature. "If I was only near enough to see his eyes," he thought. But he was not near enough, nor would it have been prudent for him to have gone nearer.

The witch doctor commenced the proceedings by ringing a handbell in front of every hut. But that method of detection failed to work. The bell rang successively at every door. Walker watched the man's progress, watched his trailing limb, and began to discover familiarities in his manner. "Pure fancy," he argued with himself. "If he had not limped I should have noticed nothing."

Then the doctor took a wicker basket, covered with a rough wooden lid. The Fans gathered in front of him; he repeated their names one after the other and at each name he lifted the lid. But that plan appeared to be no improvement, for the lid never stuck. It came off readily at each name. Walker, meanwhile, calculated the distance a man would have to cover who walked across country from Bonny river to the Ogowe, and he reflected with some relief that the chances were several thousand to one that any man who made the attempt, be he black or white, would be eaten on the way.

The witch doctor turned up the big square cuffs of his sleeves, as a conjurer will do, and again repeated the names. This time, however, at each name, he rubbed the palms of his hands together. Walker was seized with a sudden longing to rush down into the village and examine the man's right forearm for a bullet mark. The longing grew on him. The witch doctor went steadily through the list. Walker rose to his feet and took a step or two down the hillock, when, of a sudden, at one particular name, the doctor's hands flew apart and waved wildly about him. A single cry from a single voice went up out of the group of Fans. The group fell back and left one man standing alone. He made no defence, no resistance. Two men came forward and bound his hands and his feet and his body with tie-tie. Then they carried him within a hut.

"That's sheer murder," thought Walker. He could not rescue the victim, he knew. But—he could get a nearer view of that witch doctor. Already the man was packing up his paraphernalia. Walker stepped back among the trees and, running with all his speed, made the circuit of the village. He reached the further end of the street just as the witch doctor walked out into the open.

Walker ran forward a yard or so until he too stood plain to see on the level ground. The witch doctor did see him and stopped. He stopped only for a moment and gazed earnestly in Walker's direction. Then he went on again towards his own hut in the forest.

Walker made no attempt to follow him. "He has seen me," he thought. "If he knows me he will come down to the river bank to-night." Consequently, he made the black rowers camp a couple of hundred yards down stream. He himself remained alone in his canoe.

The night fell moonless and black, and the enclosing forest made it yet blacker. A few stars burned in the strip of sky above his head like gold spangles on a strip of black velvet. Those stars and the glimmering of the clay bank to which the boat was moored were the only lights which Walker had. It was as dark as the night when Walker waited for Hatteras at the wicket-gate.

A. E. W. Mason

He placed his gun and a pouch of cartridges on one side, an unlighted lantern on the other, and then he took up his banjo and again he waited. He waited for a couple of hours, until a light crackle as of twigs snapping came to him out of the forest. Walker struck a chord on his banjo and played a hymn tune. He played "Abide with me," thinking that some picture of a home, of a Sunday evening in England's summer time, perhaps of a group of girls singing about a piano might flash into the darkened mind of the man upon the bank and draw him as with cords. The music went tinkling up and down the river, but no one spoke, no one moved upon the bank. So Walker changed the tune and played a melody of the barrel organs and Piccadilly circus. He had not played more than a dozen bars before he heard a sob from the bank and then the sound of some one sliding down the clay. The next instant a figure shone black against the clay. The boat lurched under the weight of a foot upon the gunwale, and a man plumped down in front of Walker.

"Well, what is it?" asked Walker, as he laid down his banjo and felt for a match in his pocket.

It seemed as though the words roused the man to a perception that he had made a mistake. He said as much hurriedly in trade-English, and sprang up as though he would leap from the boat. Walker caught hold of his ankle.

"No, you don't," said he, "you must have meant to visit me. This isn't Heally," and he jerked the man back into the bottom of the boat.

The man explained that he had paid a visit out of the purest friendliness.

"You're the witch doctor, I suppose," said Walker. The other replied that he was and proceeded to state that he was willing to give information about much that made white men curious. He would explain why it was of singular advantage to possess a white man's eyeball, and how very advisable it was to kill any one you caught making Itung. The danger of passing near a cotton-tree which had red earth at the roots provided a subject which no prudent man should disregard; and Tando, with his driver ants, was worth conciliating. The witch doctor was prepared to explain to Walker how to conciliate Tando. Walker replied that it was very kind of the witch doctor but Tando didn't really worry him. He was, in fact, very much more worried by an inability to understand how a native so high up the Ogowe River had learned how to speak trade-English.

The witch doctor waved the question aside and remarked that Walker must have enemies. "Pussim bad too much," he called them. "Pussim woh-woh. Berrah well! Ah send grand Krau-Krau and dem pussim die one time." Walker could not recollect for the moment any "pussim" whom he wished to die one time, whether from grand Krau-Krau or any other disease. "Wait a bit," he continued, "there is one man—Dick Hatteras!" and he struck the match suddenly. The witch doctor started forward as though to put it out. Walker, however, had the door of the lantern open. He set the match to the wick of the candle and closed the door fast. The witch doctor drew back. Walker lifted the lantern and threw the light on his face. The witch doctor buried his face in his hands and supported his elbows on his knees. Immediately Walker darted forward a hand, seized the loose sleeve of the witch doctor's coat and slipped it back along his arm to the elbow. It was the sleeve of the right arm and there on the fleshy part of the forearm was the scar of a bullet.

"Yes," said Walker. "By God, it is Dick Hatteras!"

"Well?" cried Hatteras, taking his hands from his face.

A. E. W. Mason

"What the devil made you turn-turn 'Tommy Atkins' on the banjo? Damn you!"

"Dick, I saw you this afternoon."

"I know, I know. Why on earth didn't you kill me that night in your compound?"

"I mean to make up for that mistake to-night!"

Walker took his rifle on to his knees. Hatteras saw the movement, leaned forward quickly, snatched up the rifle, snatched up the cartridges, thrust a couple of cartridges into the breech, and handed the loaded rifle back to his old friend.

"That's right," he said. "I remember. There are some cases neither God's law nor man's law has quite made provision for." And then he stopped, with his finger on his lip. "Listen!" he said.

From the depths of the forest there came faintly, very sweetly the sound of church-bells ringing—a peal of bells ringing at midnight in the heart of West Africa. Walker was startled. The sound seemed fairy work, so faint, so sweet was it.

"It's no fancy, Jim," said Hatteras, "I hear them every night and at matins and at vespers. There was a Jesuit monastery here two hundred years ago. The bells remain and some of the clothes." He touched his coat as he spoke. "The Fans still ring the bells from habit. Just think of it! Every morning, every evening, every midnight, I hear those bells. They talk to me of little churches perched on hillsides in the old country, of hawthorn lanes, and women—English women, English girls, thousands of miles away—going along them to church. God help me! Jim, have you got an English pipe?"

"Yes; an English briarwood and some bird's-eye."

Walker handed Hatteras his briarwood and his pouch of tobacco. Hatteras filled the pipe, lit it at the lantern, and sucked at it avidly for a moment. Then he gave a sigh and drew in the tobacco more slowly, and yet more slowly.

"My wife?" he asked at last, in a low voice.

"She is in England. She thinks you dead."

Hatteras nodded.

"There's a jar of Scotch whiskey in the locker behind you," said Walker. Hatteras turned round, lifted out the jar and a couple of tin cups. He poured whiskey into each and handed one to Walker.

"No thanks," said Walker. "I don't think I will."

Hatteras looked at his companion for an instant. Then he emptied deliberately both cups over the side of the boat. Next he took the pipe from his lips. The tobacco was not half consumed. He poised the pipe for a little in his hand. Then he blew into the bowl and watched the dull red glow kindle into sparks of flame as he blew. Very slowly he tapped the bowl against the thwart of the boat until the burning tobacco fell with a hiss into the water. He laid the pipe gently down and stood up.

"So long, old man," he said, and sprang out on to the clay. Walker turned the lantern until the light made a disc upon the bank.

"Good bye, Jim," said Hatteras, and he climbed up the bank until he stood in the light of the lantern. Twice Walker raised

A. E. W. Mason

the rifle to his shoulder, twice he lowered it. Then he remembered that Hatteras and he had been at school together.

"Good bye, Dicky," he cried, and fired. Hatteras tumbled down to the boat-side. The blacks down-river were roused by the shot. Walker shouted to them to stay where they were, and as soon as their camp was quiet he stepped on shore. He filled up the whiskey jar with water, tied it to Hatteras' feet, shook his hand, and pushed the body into the river. The next morning he started back to Fernan Vaz.

THE PRINCESS JOCELIANDE

The truth concerning the downfall of the Princess Joceliande has never as yet been honestly inscribed. Doubtless there be few alive except myself that know it; for from the beginning many strange and insidious rumours were set about to account for her mishap, whereby great damage was done to the memory of the Sieur Rudel le Malaise and Solita his wife; and afterwards these rumours were so embroidered and painted by rhymesters that the truth has become, as you might say, doubly lost. For minstrels take more thought of tickling the fancies of those to whom they sing with joyous and gallant histories than of their high craft and office, and hence it is that though many and various accounts are told to this day throughout the country-side by grandsires at their winter hearths, not one of them has so much as a grain of verity. They are but rude and homely versions of the chaunts of Troubadours.

And yet the truth is sweet and pitiful enough to furnish forth a song, were our bards so minded. Howbeit, I will set it down here in simple prose; for so my duty to the Sieur Rudel bids me, and, moreover, 'twas from this event his wanderings began wherein for twenty years I bare him company.

And let none gainsay my story, for that I was not my master's servant at the time, and saw not the truth with mine own eyes. I had it from the Sieur Rudel's lips, and more than once when he was vexed at the aspersions thrown upon his name. But he was ever proud, as befitted so knightly a gentleman, and deigned not to argue or plead his honour to the world, but only with his sword. Thus, then, it falls to me to right him as skilfully as I may. Though, alas! I fear my skill is little worth, and calumnies are ever fresh to the palate, while truth needs the sauce of a bright fancy to command it.

These columnies have assuredly gained some credit, because with ladies my lord was ever blithe and *debonnaire*. That he loved many I do not deny; but while he loved, he loved right loyally, and, indeed, it is no small honour to be loved by a man of so much worship, even for a little—the which many women thought also, and those amongst the fairest. And I doubt not that as long as she lived, he loved his wife Solita no less ardently than those with whom he fell in after she had most unfortunately died.

The Sieur Rudel was born within the castle of Princess Joceliande, and there grew to childhood and from childhood to youth, being ever entreated with great amity and love for his own no less than for his father's sake. Though of a slight and delicate figure, he excelled in all manly exercises and sports and in venery and hawking. There was not one about the court that could equal him. Books too he read, and in many languages, labouring at philosophies and logics, so that had you but heard him speak, and not marked the hardihood of his limbs and his open face, you might have believed you were listening to some doxical monk.

In the tenth year of his age came Solita to the castle, whence no man knew, nor could they ever learn more than this, that she sailed out of the grey mists of a November morning to our bleak Brittany coast in a white-painted boat. A fisherman drew the boat to land, perceiving it when he was casting his nets, and found a woman-child therein, cushioned upon white satin; and marvelling much at the richness of her purveyance, for even the sail of the boat was of white silk, he bore her straightway to the castle. And the abbot took her and baptised her and gave her Sola for a name. "For," said he, "she hath come alone and none knoweth her parentage or place." In time she grew to exceeding beauty, with fair hair clustering like finest silk above her temples and curling waywardly about her throat; wondrous fair she was and white, shaming the snowdrops, so that all men stopped and gazed at her as she passed.

And the Princess Joceliande, perceiving her, joined her to the company of her hand-maidens and took great delight in her for her modesty and beauty, so that at last she changed her name. "Sola have you been called till now," she said, "but henceforth shall your name be Solita, as who shall say 'you have become my wont.'"

Meanwhile the Sieur Rudel was advanced from honour to honour, until he stood ever at the right hand of the Princess, and ruled over her kingdom as her chancellor and vicegerent. Her enemies he conquered and added their lands and sovereignties to hers, until of all the kings in those parts, none had such power and dominions as the Princess Joceliande. Many ladies, you may believe, cast fond eyes on him, and dropped their gauntlet that he might bend to them upon his knee and pick it up, but his heart they could not bend, strive how they might, and to each and all he showed the same courtesy and gentleness. For he had seen the maiden Solita, and of an evening when the Court was feasting in the hall and the music of harps rippled sweetly in the ears, he would slip from the table as one that was busied in statecraft, and in company with Solita pace the terrace in the dark, beneath the lighted windows. Yet neither spoke of love, though loving was their intercourse. Solita for that her

A. E. W. Mason

modesty withheld her, and she feared even to hope that so great a lord should give his heart to her keeping; Rudel because he had not achieved enough to merit she should love him. "In a little," he would mutter, "in a little! One more thing must I do, and then will I claim my guerdon of the Princess Joceliande."

Now this one more thing was the highest and most dangerous emprise of all that he had undertaken. Beyond the confines of the kingdom there dwelt a great horde of men that had come to Brittany from the East in many deep ships and had settled upon the coast, whence they would embark and, travelling hard by the land, burn and ravage the sea-borders for many days.

Against these did the Sieur Rudel make war, and gathering the nobles and yeomen he mustered them in boats and prepared to sail forth to what he believed was the last of his adventures, knowing not that it was indeed but the beginning. And to the princess he said: "Lady, I have served you faithfully, as a gentleman should serve his queen. From nothing have I drawn back that could establish or increase you. Therefore when I get me home again, one boon will I ask of you, and I pray you of your mercy grant it me."

"I will well," replied the princess. "For such loyal service hath no queen known before—nay, not even Dame Helen among the Trojans."

So right gladly did the Sieur Rudel depart from her, and down he walked among the sandhills, where he found Solita standing in a hollow in the midst of a cloud of sand which the sharp wind whirled about her. Nothing she said to him, but she stood with downcast head and eyes that stung with tears.

"Solita," said he, "the Princess hath granted me such boon as I may ask on my return. What say you?"

And she answered in a low voice. "Who am I, my lord, that I should oppose the will of the princess? A nameless maiden, meet only to yoke with a nameless yeoman!"

At that the Sieur Rudel laughed and said, "Look you into a mirror, sweet! and your face will gainsay your words."

She lifted her eyes to his and the light came into them again, so that they danced behind the tears, and Rudel clipped her about the waist for all that he had not as yet merited her, and kissed her upon the lips and the forehead and upon her white hands and wrists.

But she, gazing past his head, saw the blowing sands beyond and the armed men in the boats upon the sea, and "O, Rudel, my sweet lord!" she cried, "never till this moment did I know how barren and lonely was the coast. Come back, and that soon—for of a truth I dread to be left alone!"

"In God's good time and if so He will, I will come back, and from the moment of my coming I will never again depart from you."

"Promise me that!" she said, clinging to him with her arms twined about his neck, and he promised her, and so, comforting her a little more, he got him into his boat and sailed away upon his errand.

But of all this, the Princess Joceliande knew nothing. From her balcony in the castle she saw the Sieur Rudel sail forth. He stood upon the poop, the wind blowing the hair back from his face, and as she watched his straight figure, she said, "A boon he shall ask, but a greater will I grant. Surely

A. E. W. Mason

no man ever did such loyal service but for love, and for love's sake, he shall share my throne with me." With that she wept a little for fear he might be slain or ever he should return; but she remembered from how many noble exploits he had come scatheless, and so taking heart once more she fell to thinking of his black locks and clear olive face and darkly shining eyes. For, in truth, these outward qualities did more enthral and delight her than his most loyal services.

But for the maiden Solita, she got her back to her chamber and, remembering her lord's advice, spied about for a mirror. No mirror, however, did she possess, having never used aught else but a basin of clear water, and till now found it all-sufficient, so little curious had she been concerning the whiteness of her beauty. Thereupon she thought for a little, and unbinding her hair so that it fell to her feet in a golden cloud, hied her to Joceliande, who bade her take a book of chivalry and read aloud. But Solita so bent her head that her hair fell ever across the pages and hindered her from reading, and each time she put it roughly back from her forehead with some small word of anger as though she was vexed.

"What ails you, child?" asked the princess.

"It is my hair," replied Solita. But the princess paid no heed. She heard little, indeed, even of what was read, but sat by the window gazing out across the grey hungry sea, and bethinking her of the Sieur Rudel and his gallant men. And again Solita let her hair fall upon the scroll, and again she tossed it back, saying, "Fie! Fie!"

"What ails you, child?" the princess asked.

"It is my hair," she replied, and Joceliande, smiling heed-lessly, bade her read on. So she read until Joceliande bade her stop and called to her, and Solita came over to the window and knelt by the side of the princess, so that her hair fell across the wrist of Joceliande and fettered it. "It *is* ever in the way," said Solita, and she loosed it from the wrist of the princess. But the princess caught the silky coils within her hand and smoothed them tenderly. "That were easily remedied," she replied with a smile, and she sought for the scissors which hung at her girdle.

But Solita bethought her that many men had praised the colour and softness of her hair—why, she could not tell, for dark locks alone were beautiful in her eyes. Howbeit men praised hers, and for Sieur Rudel's sake she would fain be as praiseworthy as might be. Therefore she stayed Joceliande's hand and cried aloud in fear, "Nay, nay, sweet lady, 'tis all the gold I have, and I pray you leave it me who am so poor."

And the Princess Joceliande laughed, and replaced the scissors in her girdle. "I did but make pretence, to try you," she said, "for, in truth, I had begun to think you were some holy angel and no woman, so little share had you in a woman's vanities. But 'tis all unbound, and I wonder not that it hinders you. Let me bind it up!"

And while the princess bound the hair cunningly in a coronal upon her head, Solita spake again hesitatingly, seeking to conceal her craft.

"Madame, it is easy for you to bind my hair, but for myself, I have no mirror and so dress it awkwardly."

Joceliande laughed again merrily at the words. "Dear heart!" she cried. "What man is it? Hast discovered thou art a woman after all? First thou fearest for thy hair, and now thou askest a mirror. But in truth I like thee the better for thy discovery." And she kissed Solita very heartily, who blushed that her secret was so readily found out, and felt no small shame at her lack of subtlety. For many ladies, she knew, had secrets—ay, even from their bosom lords and masters—and kept them without effort in the subterfuge, whereas she, poor fool, betrayed hers at the first word.

"And what man is it?" laughed the princess. "For there is not one that deserves thee, as thou shalt judge for thyself." Whereupon she summoned one of her servants and bade him place a mirror in the bed-chamber of Solita, wherein she might see herself from top to toe.

"Art content?" she asked. "Thus shalt thou see thyself, without blemish or fault even for this crown of hair to the heel of thy foot. But I fear me the sight will change all thy thoughts and incline thee to scorn of thy suitor."

Then she stood for a little watching the sunlight play upon the golden head and pry into the soft shadows of the curls, and her face saddened and her voice faltered.

"But what of me, Solita?" she said. "All men give me reverence, not one knows me for a woman. I crave the bread of love, all day long I hunger for it, but they offer me the polished stones of courtesy and respect, and so I starve slowly to my death. What of me, Solita? What of me?"

But Solita made reply, soothing her:

"Madame," she said, "all your servants love you, but it beseems them not to flaunt it before your face, so high are you placed above them. You order their fortunes and their lives, and surely 'tis nobler work than meddling with this idle love-prattle."

"Nay," replied the princess, laughing in despite of her heaviness, for she noted how the blush on Solita's cheek belied the scorn of her tongue. "There spoke the saint, and I will hear no more from her now that I have found the woman. Tell me, did he kiss you?"

And Solita blushed yet more deeply, so that even her neck down to her shoulders grew rosy, and once or twice she nodded her head, for her lips would not speak the word.

Then Joceliande sighed to herself and said—

"And yet, perchance, he would not die for you, whereas men die for me daily, and from mere obedience. How is he called?"

"Madame," she replied, "I may not tell you, for all my pride in him. 'Twill be for my lord to answer you in his good time. But that he would die for me, if need there were, I have no doubt. For I have looked into his eyes and read his soul."

So she spake with much spirit, upholding Sieur Rudel; but Joceliande was sorely grieved for that Solita would not trust her with her lover's name, and answered bitterly:

"And his soul which you did see was doubtless your own image. And thus it will be with the next maiden who looks into his eyes. Her own image will she see, and she will go away calling it his soul, and not knowing, poor fool, that it has already faded from his eyes."

At this Solita kept silence, deeming it unnecessary to make reply. It might be as the princess said with other men and other women, but the Sieur Rudel had no likeness to other men, and in possessing the Sieur Rudel's love she was far removed from other women. Therefore did she keep silence, but Joceliande fancied that she was troubled by the words which she had spoken, and straightway repented her of them.

"Nay, child," she said, and she laid her hand again upon Solita's head. "Take not the speech to heart. 'Tis but the plaint of a woman whose hair is withered from its brightness and who grows peevish in her loneliness. But open your mind to me, for you have twined about my heart even as your curls did but now twine and coil about my wrist, and the more for this pretty vanity of yours. Therefore tell me his name, that I may advance him."

But once more Solita did fob her off, and the princess would no longer question her, but turned her wearily to the window.

"All day long," she said, "I listen to soft speeches and honeyed tongues, and all night long I listen to the breakers booming upon the sands, and in truth I wot not which sound is the more hollow."

Such was the melancholy and sadness of her voice that the tears sprang into Solita's eyes and ran down her cheeks for very pity of Joceliande.

"Think not I fail in love to you, sweet princess," she cried. "But I may not tell you, though I would be blithe and proud to name him. But 'tis for him to claim me of you, and I must needs wait his time."

But Joceliande would not be comforted, and chiding her roughly, sent her to her chamber. So Solita departed out of her sight, her heart heavy with a great pity, though little she understood of Joceliande's distress. For this she could not know: that at the sight of her white beauty the Princess Joceliande was ashamed.

And coming into her chamber, Solita beheld the mirror

ranged against the wall, and long she stood before it, being much comforted by the image which she saw. From that day ever she watched the ladies of the court, noting jealously if any might be more fair than she whom Sieur Rudel had chosen; and often of a night when she was troubled by the aspect of some fair and delicate new-comer, she would rise from her couch and light a taper, and so gaze at herself until the fear of her unworthiness diminished. For there were none that could compare with her in daintiness and fair looks ever came to the castle of the Princess Joceliande.

But of the Sieur Rudel, though oft she thought, she never spake, biding his good time, and the princess questioned her in vain. For she, whose heart hitherto had lain plain to see, like a pebble in a clear brook of water, had now learnt all the sweet cunning of love's duplicity.

Thus the time drew on towards the Sieur Rudel's home-coming, and ever the twain looked out across the sea for the black boats to round the bluff and take the beach— Joceliande from her balcony, Solita from the window of her little chamber in the tower; and each night the princess gave orders to light a beacon on the highest headland that the wayfarers might steer safely down that red path across the tumbling waters.

So it fell that one night both ladies beheld two ships swim to the shore, and each made dolorous moan, seeing how few of the goodly company that sailed forth had got them home again, and wondering in sore distress whether Rudel had returned with them or no.

But in a little there came a servant to the princess and told of one Sir Broyance de Mille-Faits, a messenger from the neighbouring kingdom of Broye, that implored instant speech with her. And being admitted before all the Court assembled in the great hall, he fell upon his knees at the foot of the princess, and, making his obeisance, said—

"Fair Lady Joceliande, I crave a boon, and I pray you of your gentleness to grant it me."

"But what boon, good Sir Broyance?" replied the princess. "I know you for a true and loyal gentleman who has ever been welcome at my castle. Speak, then, your need, and if so be I may, you shall find me complaisant to your request."

Thereupon, Sir Broyance took heart and said:

"Since our king died, God rest his soul, there has been no peace or quiet in our kingdom of Broye. 'Tis rent with strife and factions, so that no man may dwell in it but he must fight from morn to night, and withal win no rest for the morrow. The king's three sons contend for the throne, and meanwhile is the country eaten up. Therefore am I sent by many, and those our chiefest gentlemen, to ask you to send us Sieur Rudel, that he may quell these conflicts and rule over us as our king."

So Sir Broyance spake and was silent, and a great murmur and acclamation rose about the hall for that the Sieur Rudel was held in such honour and worship even beyond his own country. But for the Princess Joceliande, she sat with downcast head, and for a while vouchsafed no reply. For her heart was sore at the thought that Sieur Rudel should go from her.

"There is much danger in the adventure," she said at length, doubtfully.

"Were there no danger, madame," he replied, "we should not

ask Sieur Rudel of you to be our leader, and great though the danger be, greater far is the honour. For we offer him a kingdom."

Then the princess spake again to Sir Broyance:

"It may not be," she said. "Whatever else you crave, that shall you have, and gladly will I grant it you. But the Sieur Rudel is the flower of our Court, he stands ever at my right hand, and woe is me if I let him go, for I am only a woman."

"But, madame, for his knighthood's sake, I pray you assent to our prayer," said Sir Broyance. "Few enemies have you, but many friends, whereas we are sore pressed on every side."

But the princess repeated: "I am only a woman," and for a long while he made his prayer in vain.

At last, however, the princess said:

"For his knighthood's sake thus far will I yield to you: Bide here within my castle until Sieur Rudel gets him home, and then shall you make your prayer to him, and by his answer will I be bound."

"That I will well," replied Sir Broyance, bethinking him of the Sieur Rudel's valour, and how that he had a kingdom to proffer to him.

But the Princess Joceliande said to herself:

"I, too, will offer him a kingdom. My throne shall he share with me;" and so she entertained Sir Broyance right pleasantly until the Sieur Rudel should get him back from the foray. Meanwhile she would say to Solita, "He shall not go to Broye, for in truth I need him;" and Solita would laugh

A. E. W. Mason

happily, replying, "It is truth: he will not go to Broye," and thinking thereto silently, "but it is not the princess who will keep him, but even I, her poor handmaiden. For I have his promise never to depart from me." So much confidence had her mirror taught her, as it ever is with women.

But despite them both did the Sieur Rudel voyage to Broye and rule over the kingdom as its king, and how that came about ye shall hear.

Now on the fourth day after the coming of Sir Broyance, the Princess Joceliande was leaning over the baluster of her balcony and gazing seawards as was her wont. The hours had drawn towards evening, and the sun stood like a glowing wheel upon the farthest edge of the sea's grey floor, when she beheld a black speck crawl across its globe, and then another and another, to the number of thirty. Thereupon, she knew that the Sieur Rudel had returned, and joyfully she summoned her tirewomen and bade them coif and robe her as befitted a princess. A coronet of gold and rubies they set upon her head, and a robe of purple they hung about her shoulders. With pearls they laced her neck and her arms, and with pearls they shod her feet, and when she saw the ships riding at their anchorage, and the Sieur Rudel step forth amid the shouts of the sailors, then she hied her to the council-chamber and prepared to give him instant audience. Yet for all her jewels and rich attire, she trembled like a common wench at the approach of her lover, and feared that the loud beating of her heart would drown the sound of his footsteps in the passage.

But the Sieur Rudel came not, and she sent a messenger to inquire why he tarried, and the messenger brought word and said:

"He is with the maiden Solita in the tower."

Then the princess stumbled as though she were about to fall, and her women came about her. But she waved them back with her hand, and so stood shivering for a little. "The night blows cold," she said; "I would the lamps were lit." And when her servants had lighted the council-chamber, she sent yet another messenger to Sieur Rudel, bidding him instantly come to her, and waited in great bitterness of spirit. For she remembered how that she had promised to grant him the boon that he should ask, and much she feared that she knew what that boon was.

Now leave we the Princess Joceliande, and hie before her messenger to the chamber of Solita. No pearls or purple robes had she to clad her beauty in, but a simple gown of white wool fastened with a silver girdle about the waist, and her hair she loosed so that it rippled down her shoulders and nestled round her ears and face.

Thither the Sieur Rudel came straight from the sea, and—

"Love," he said, kissing her, "it has been a weary waste of days and nights, and yet more weary for thee than for me. For stern work was there ever to my hand—ay, and well-nigh more than I could do; but for thee nought but to wait."

"Yet, my dear lord," she replied, "the princess did give me this mirror, wherein I could see myself from top to toe, and a great comfort has it been to me."

So she spake, and the messenger from the princess brake in upon them, bidding the Sieur Rudel hasten to the council-chamber, for that the Princess Joceliande waited this long while for his coming.

"Now will I ask for the fulfilment of her promise," said Rudel to Solita, "and to-night, sweet, I will claim thee before

A. E. W. Mason

the whole Court." With that he got him from the chamber and, following the messenger, came to where the princess awaited him.

"Madame," he said, "good tidings! By God's grace we have won the victory over your enemies. Never again will they buzz like wasps about your coasts, but from this day forth they will pay you yearly truage."

"Sir," she replied, rebuking him shrewdly, "indeed you bring me good tidings, but you bring them over-late. For here have I tarried for you this long while, and it beseems neither you nor me."

"Madame," he answered, "I pray you acquit me of the fault and lay the blame on Love. For when sweet Cupid thrones a second queen in one's heart beside the first, what wonder that a man forgets his duty? And now I would that of your gentleness you would grant me your maiden Solita for wife."

"That I may not," returned Joceliande, stricken to the soul at that image of a second queen. "A nameless child, and my handmaiden! Sieur Rudel, it befits a man to look above him for a wife."

"And that, madame," he answered, "in very truth I do. Moreover, though no man knows Solita's parentage and place, yet must she be of gentle nurture, else had there been no silk sail to float her hitherwards; and so much it liketh you to grant my boon, for God's love, I pray you, hold your promise."

Thereupon was the princess sore distressed for that she had given her promise. Howbeit she said: "Since it is so, and since my maiden Solita is the boon you crave, I give her to you;" and so dismissed the Sieur Rudel from her presence, and getting her back to her chamber, made moan out of all measure.

"Lord Jesu," she cried, "of all my kingdom and barony, but one thing did I hunger for and covet, and that one thing this child, whom of my kindness I loved and fostered, hath traitorously robbed me of! Why did I take her from the sea?"

So she wept for a great while, until she bethought her of a remedy. Then she wiped her tears and gave order that Sir Broyance should come to her. To him she said: "To-night at the high feast you shall make your prayer to the Lord Rudel, and I myself will join with you, so that he shall become your leader and rule over you as king."

So she spake, thinking that when the Sieur Rudel had departed, she would privily put Solita to death—openly she dared not do it, for the great love the nobles bore towards Rudel—and when Solita was dead, then would she send again for Rudel and share her siege with him. Sir Broyance, as ye may believe, was right glad at her words, and made him ready for the feast. Hither, when the company was assembled, came the Sieur Rudel, clad in a green tunic edged with fur of a white fox, and a chain set with stones of great virtue about his neck. His hose were green and of the finest silk, and on his feet he wore shoes of white doeskin, and the latchets were of gold. So he came into the hall, and seeing him thus gaily attired with all his harness off, much did all marvel at his knightly prowess. For in truth he looked more like some tender minstrel than a gallant warrior. Then up rose Sir Broyance and said;

"From the kingdom of Broye the nobles send greeting to the Sieur Rudel, and a message."

And with that he set forth his errand and request; but the

A. E. W. Mason

Sieur Rudel laughed and answered:

"Sir Broyance, great honour you do me, and so, I pray, tell your countrymen of Broye. But never more will I draw sword or feuter spear, for this day hath the Princess Joceliande granted me her maiden Solita for wife, and by her side I will bide till death."

Thereupon rose a great murmur of astonishment within the hall, the men lamenting that the Sieur Rudel would lead them no more to battle, and the women marvelling to each other that he should choose so mean a thing as Solita for wife. But Sir Broyance said never a word, but got him from the table and out of the hall, so that the company marvelled yet more for that he had not sought to persuade the Sieur Rudel. Then said the Princess Joceliande, and greatly was she angered both against Solita and Rudel:

"Fie, my lord! shame on you; you forget your knighthood!"

And he replied, "My knighthood, your highness, had but one use, and that to win my sweet Solita."

Wherefore was Joceliande's heart yet hotter against the twain, and she cried aloud:

"Nay, but it is on us that the shame of your cowardice will fall. Even now Sir Broyance left our hall in anger and scorn. It may not be that our chiefest noble shall so disgrace us."

But Sieur Rudel laughed lightly, and answered her:

"Madame, full oft have I jeopardised my life in your good cause, and I fear no charge of cowardice more than I fear thistle-down."

His words did but increase the fury of the princess, and she brake out in most bitter speech:

"Nay, but it is a kitchen knave we have been honouring unawares, and bidding sit with us at table!"

And straightway she called to her servants and bade them fetch the warden of the castle with the fetters. But the Sieur Rudel laughed again, and said:

"Thus it will be impossible that I leave my dear Solita and voyage perilously to Broye."

Nor any effort or resistance did he make, but lightly suffered them to fetter him, the while the princess most foully missaid him. With fetters they prisoned his feet, and manacles they straitly fastened about his wrists, and they bound him to a pillar in the hall by a chain about his middle.

"There shall you bide," she said, "in shameful bonds until you make promise to voyage forth to Broye. For surely there is nothing so vile in all this world as a craven gentleman."

With that she turned her again to the feast, though little heart she had thereto. But the Sieur Rudel was well content; for not for all the honour in Christendom would he break his word to his dear Solita. Howbeit, the nobles were ever urgent that the princess should set him free, pleading the worshipful deeds he had accomplished in her cause. But to none of them would she hearken, and the fair gentle ladies of the Court greatly applauded her for her persistence—and especially those who had erstwhile dropped their gauntlets that Rudel might bend and pick them up. And many pleasant jests they passed upon the Sieur Rudel, bidding him dance with them, since he was loth to fight. But he paid no heed to them, nor could they provoke him by any number of taunts.

Whereupon, being angered at his silence, they were fain to send to Solita and make their sport with her.

But that Joceliande would not suffer, and, rising, she went to Solita's chamber and entreated her most kindly, telling her that for love of her the Sieur Rudel would not adventure himself at Broye. Not a word did she say of how she had mistreated him, and Solita answered her jocundly for that her lord had held his pledge with her. But when the castle was still, the princess took Solita by the hand and led her down the steps to where Rudel stood against the pillar in the dark hall.

"For thy sake, sweet Solita," she said, "is he bound. For thy sake!" and she made her feel the manacles upon his hands. And when Solita had so felt his bonds, she wept, and made the greatest sorrow that ever man heard.

"Alas!" she cried, "that my dear lord should suffer in such straits. In God's mercy, madame, I pray you let him go! Loyal service hath he done for you, such as no other in the kingdom."

"Loyal service, I trow," replied the princess. "He hath brought such shame upon my Court that for ever am I dishonoured. It may not be that I let him go, without you give him back his word and bid him forth to Broye."

"And that will I never do," replied Solita, "for all your cruelty."

So the princess turned her away and gat her from the hall, but Solita remained with her lord, making moan and easing his fetters with her hands as best she might. Hence it fell out that she who should have comforted must needs be comforted herself, and that the Sieur Rudel did right willingly.

The like, he would say to me, hath often happened to him since, and when he was harassed with sore distress he must needs turn him about to stop a woman's tears; for which he thanked God most heartily, and prayed that so it might ever be, since thus he clean forgot his own sad plight. Whence, meseems, may men understand how noble a gentleman was my good lord the Sieur Rudel.

Now when the night was well spent and drawing on to dawn, Solita, for very weariness, fell asleep at the pillar's foot, and Rudel began to take counsel with himself if, by any manner of means, he might outwit the Princess Joceliande. For this he saw, that she would not have him wed her handmaiden, and for that cause, and for no cowardice of his, had so cruelly entreated him. And when he had pondered a little with himself, he bent and touched Solita with his hands, and called to her in a low voice.

"Solita," he said, "it is in Joceliande's heart to keep us twain each from other. Rise, therefore, and get thee to the good abbot who baptised thee. Ever hath he stood my friend, and for friendship's sake this thing he will do. Bring him hither into the hall, that he may marry us even this night, and when the morning comes I will tell the princess of our marriage; and so will she know that her cruelty is of small avail, and release me unto thee."

Thereupon Solita rose right joyously.

"Surely, my dear lord," said she, "no man can match thee, neither in craft nor prowess," and she hurried through the dark passages towards the lodging of the abbot. Hard by this lodging was the chapel of the castle, and when she came thereto the windows were ablaze with light, and Solita clapped her ear to the door. But no sound did she hear, no, not so much as the stirring of a mouse, and bethinking her

A. E. W. Mason

that the good abbot might be holding silent vigil, she gently pressed upon the door, so that it opened for the space of an inch; and when she looked into the chapel, she beheld the Princess Joceliande stretched upon the steps before the altar. Her coronet had fallen from her head and rolled across the stones, and she lay like one that had fallen asleep in the counting of her beads. Greatly did Solita marvel at the sight, but no word she said lest she should wake the princess; and in a little, becoming afeard of the silence and of the shadows which the flickering candles set racing on the wall, she shut the door quickly and stole on tiptoe to the abbot. Long she entreated him or ever she prevailed, for the holy man was timorous, and feared the wrath of the princess. But at the last, for the Sieur Rudel's sake, he consented, and married them privily in the hall as the grey dawn was breaking across the sea.

Now, in the morning, the princess bid Solita be brought to her, and when they were alone, gently and cunningly she spake:

"Child," she said, "I doubt not thy heart is hot against me for that I will not enlarge the Sieur Rudel. Alas! fain were I to do this thing, but for the honour of my Court I may not. Bound are we not by our wills but by our necessities—and thus it is with all women. Men may ride forth and shape their lives with their good swords; but for us, we must needs bide where we were born, and order such things as fall to us, as best we can. Therefore, child, take my word to heart: the Sieur Rudel loves thee, and thou wouldst keep his love. Let my age point to thee the way! What if I release him? No longer can he stay with us, holding high honour and dignity, since he hath turned him from his knightlihood and avoided this great adventure, but forth with you must he fare. And all day long will he sit with you in your chamber, idle as a woman, and ever his thoughts will go back to the times of his nobility. The clash of steel will grow louder in his ears; he will list again to the praises of minstrels in the banquet-hall, and when men speak to him of great achievements wrought by other hands, then thou wilt see the life die out of his eyes, and his heart will become cold as stone, and thou wilt lose his love. A great thing will it be for thee if he come not to hate thee in the end. But if, of thy own free will, thou send him from thee, then shalt thou ever keep his love. Thy image will ride before his eyes in the van of battles; for very lack of thee he will move from endeavour to endeavour; and so thy life will be enshrined in his most noble deeds."

At these words, with such cunning gentleness were they spoken, Solita was sore troubled.

"I cannot send him from me," she cried, "for never did woman so love her lord—no, not ever in the world!"

"Then prove thy love," said Joceliande again. "A kingdom is given into his hand, and he will not take it because of thee. It is a hard thing, I trow right well. But the cross becomes a crown when a woman lifts it. Think! A kingdom! And never yet was kingdom established but the stones of its walls were mortised with the blood of women's hearts."

So she pleaded, hiding her own thoughts, until Solita answered her, and said:

"God help me, but he shall go to Broye!"

Much ado had the Princess Joceliande to hide her joy for the success of her device; but Solita, poor lass! had neither eyes nor thoughts for her. Forthwith she rose to her feet, and quickly gat her to the hall, lest her courage should fail, before that she had accomplished her resolve. But when she came near to the Sieur Rudel, blithely he smiled at her and called "Solita, my wife." It seemed to her that words so sweet had never as yet been spoken since the world began, and all her strength ebbed from her, and she stood like one that is dumb, gazing piteously at her husband. Again Rudel called to her, but no answer could she make, and she turned and fled sobbing to the chamber of the princess.

"I could not speak," she said; "my lips were locked, and Rudel holds the key."

But the princess spoke gently and craftily, bidding her take heart, for that she herself would go with her and second her words; and taking Solita by the hand, she led her again to the hall.

This time Solita made haste to speak first. "Rudel," she said, "no honour can I bring to you, but only foul disgrace, and that is no fit gift from one who loves you. Therefore, from this hour I hold you quit of your promise and pray you to undertake this mission and set forth for Broye."

But the Sieur Rudel would hearken to nothing of what she said.

"No foul disgrace can come to me," he cried, "but only if I prove false to you and lose your love. My promise I will keep, and all the more for that I see the Princess Joceliande hath set you on to this."

But Solita protested that it was not so, and that of her own will and desire she released him, for the longing to sacrifice herself for her dear lord's sake grew upon her as she thought upon it. Yet he would not consent.

"My word I passed to you when you were a maid, and shall I not keep it now that you are a wife?" he cried.

"Wife?" cried the princess, "you are his wife?" And she roughly gripped Solita's wrist so that the girl could not withhold a cry.

"In truth, madame," replied the Sieur Rudel, "even last night, in this hall, Solita and I were married by the good abbot, and therefore I will not leave her while she lives."

Still Joceliande would not believe it, bethinking her that the Sieur Rudel had hit upon the pretence as a device for his enlargement; but Solita showed to her the ring which the abbot had taken from the finger of her lord and placed upon hers, and then the princess knew that of a surety they were married, and her hatred for Solita burned in her blood like fire.

But no sign she gave of what she felt, but rather spoke with greater softness to them both, bidding them look forward beyond the first delights of love, and behold how all their years to come were the price they needs must pay.

Now, while they were yet debating each with other, came Sir Broyance into the hall, and straightway the princess called to him and begged him to add his prayers to Solita's. But he answered:

"That, madame, I will not do, for, indeed, the esteem I have for the Sieur Rudel is much increased, and I hold it no cowardice that he should refuse a kingdom for his wife's sake, but the sweetest bravery. And therefore it was that I broke off my plea last night and sought not to persuade him."

At that Rudel was greatly rejoiced, and said:

"Dost hear him, Solita? Even he who most has need of me acquits me of disgrace. Truly I will never leave thee while

I live."

But the princess turned sharply to Sir Broyance. "Sir, have you changed your tune?" she said; "for never was a man so urgent as you with me for the Sieur Rudel's help."

"Alas! madame," he replied, "I knew not then that he was plighted to the maiden Solita, or never would I have borne this message. For this I surely know, that all my days are waste and barren because I suffered my mistress to send me from her after a will-of-the-wisp honour, even as Solita would send her lord."

Thereupon Solita brake in upon him:

"But, my lord, you have won great renown, and far and wide is your prowess known and sung."

"That avails me nothing," he replied, "my life rings hollow like an empty cup, and so are two lives wasted."

"Nay, my lord, neither life is wasted. For much have you done for others, though maybe little for yourself, while for her you loved the noise of your achievements must have been enough."

"Of that I cannot tell," he answered. "But this I know: she drags a pale life out behind convent walls. Often have I passed the gate with my warriors, but never could I hold speech with her."

"She will have seen your banners glancing in the sun," said Solita, "and so will she know her sacrifice was good." Thereupon she turned her again to her husband. "For my sake, dear Rudel, I pray you go to Broye."

But still he persisted, saying he would not depart from her till death, until at last she ceased from her importunities, and went sadly to her chamber. Then she unbound her hair and stood gazing at her likeness in the mirror.

"O cursed beauty," she cried, "wherein I took vain pride for my sweet lord's sake—truly art thou my ruin and snare!" And while she thus made moan, the princess came softly into her chamber.

"He will not leave me, madame," she sobbed. Joceliande came over to her and gently laid her hand upon her head and whispered in her ear, "Not while you live!"

For awhile Solita sat silent.

"Ay, madame," she said at length, "even as I came alone to these coasts, so will I go from them;" and slowly she drew from its sheath a little knife which she carried at her girdle. She tried the point upon her finger, so that the blood sprang from the prick and dropped on her white gown. At the sight she gave a cry and dropped the knife, and "I cannot do it" she said, "I have not the courage. But you, madame! Ever have you been kind to me, and therefore show me this last kindness."

"I will well," said the princess; and she made Solita to sit upon a couch, and with two bands of her golden hair she tied her hands fast behind her, and so laid her upon her back on the couch. And when she had so laid her she said:

"But for all that you die, he shall not go to Broye, but here shall he bide, and share my throne with me."

Thereupon did Solita perceive all the treachery of Princess Joceliande, and vainly she struggled to free her hands and to

A. E. W. Mason

cry out for help. But Joceliande clapped her palm upon Solita's mouth, and drawing a gold pin from her own hair, she drove it straight into her heart, until nothing but the little knob could be seen. So Solita died, and quickly the princess wiped the blood from her breast, and unbound her hands and arranged her limbs as though she slept. Then she returned to the hall, and, summoning the warden, bade him loose the Sieur Rudel.

"It shall be even as you wish," she said to him. Wise and prudent had she been, had she ended with that; but her malice was not yet sated, and so she suffered it to lead her to her ruin. For she stretched out her hand to him and said, "I myself will take you to your wife." And greatly marvelling, the Sieur Rudel took her hand and followed.

Now when they were come to Solita's chamber, the princess entered first, and turned her again to my Lord Rudel and laid her finger to her lips, saying, "Hush!" Therefore he came in after her on tiptoe and stood a little way from the foot of the couch, fearing lest he might wake his wife.

"Is she not still?" asked Joceliande in a whisper. "Is she not still and white?"

"Still and white as a folded lily," he replied, "and like a folded lily, too, in her white flesh there sleeps a heart of gold." Therewith he crept softly to the couch and bent above her, and in an instant he perceived that her bosom did not rise and fall. He gazed swiftly at the princess; she was watching him, and their glances met. He dropped upon his knees by the couch and felt about Solita's heart that he might know whether it beat or not, and his fingers touched the knob of Joceliande's bodkin. Gently he drew the gown from Solita's bosom, and beheld how that she had been slain. Then did he weep, believing that in truth she had killed herself, but the princess must needs touch him upon the shoulder.

"My lord," she said, "why weep for the handmaid when the princess lives?"

Then the Sieur Rudel rose straightway to his feet and said:

"This is thy doing!" For a little Joceliande denied it, saying that of her own will and desire Solita had perished. But Rudel looked her ever sternly in the face, and again he said, "This is thy doing!" and at that Joceliande could gainsay him no more. But she dropped upon the floor, and kissed his feet, and cried:

"It was for love of thee, Rudel. Look, my kingdom is large and of much wealth, yet of no worth is it to me, but only if it bring thee service and great honour. A princess am I, yet no joy do I have of my degree, but only if thou share my siege with me."

Then Rudel broke out upon her, thrusting her from him with his hand and spurning her with his foot as she crouched upon the floor.

"No princess art thou, but a changeling. For surely princess never did such foul wrong and crime;" and even as he spake, many of the nobles burst into the chamber, for they had heard the outcry below and marvelled what it might mean. And when Rudel beheld them crowding the doorway, "Come in, my lords," said he, "so that ye may know what manner of woman ye serve and worship. There lies my dear wife, Solita, murdered by this vile princess, and for love of me she saith, for love of me!" And again he turned him to Joceliande. "Now all the reverence I held thee in is turned to hatred, God be thanked; such is the guerdon of thy love for me."

　　　　　A. E. W. Mason

Joceliande, when she heard his injuries, knew indeed that her love was unavailing, and that by no means might she win him to share her siege with her. Therefore her love changed to a bitter fury, and standing up forthwith she bade the nobles take their swords and smite off the Sieur Rudel's head. But no one so much as moved a hand towards his hilt. Then spake Rudel again:

"O vile and treacherous," he cried, "who will obey thee?" and his eyes fell upon Solita where she lay in her white beauty upon the golden pillow of her hair. Thereupon he dropped again upon his knees by the couch, and took her within his arms, kissing her lips and her eyes, and bidding her wake; this with many tears. But seeing she would not, but was dead in very truth, he got him to his feet and turned to where the princess stood like stone in the middle of the chamber. "Now for thy sin," he cried, "a shameful death shalt thou die and a painful, and may the devil have thy soul!"

He bade the nobles depart from the chamber, and following them the last, firmly barred the door upon the outside. Thus was the Princess Joceliande left alone with dead Solita, and ever she heard the closing and barring of doors and the sound of feet growing fainter and fainter. But no one came to her, loud though she cried, and sorely was she afeard, gazing now at the dead body, now wondering what manner of death the Sieur Rudel planned for her. Then she walked to the window if by any chance she might win help that way, and saw the ships riding at their anchorage with sails loose, and heard the songs of the sailors as they made ready to cast free; and between the coast and the castle were many men hurrying backwards and forwards with all the purveyance of a voyage. Then did she think that she was to be left alone in the tower, to starve to death in company of the girl she had murdered, and great moan she made; but other device was in the mind of my ingenious master Lord Rudel. For all about the castle he piled stacks of wood and drenched them with oil, bethinking him that Solita his wife, if little joy she had had of her life, should have undeniable honour in her obsequies. And so having set fire to the stacks, he got him into the ships with all the company that had dwelled within the castle, and drew out a little way from shore. Then the ships lay to and watched the flames mounting the castle walls. The tower wherein the Princess Joceliande was prisoned was the topmost turret of the building, so that many a roof crashed in, and many a rampart bowed out and crumbled to the ground, or ever the fire touched it. But just as night was drawing on, lo! a great tongue of flame burst through the window from within, and the Sieur Rudel beheld in the midst of it as it were the figure of a woman dancing.

Thereupon he signed to his sailors to hoist the sail again, and the other ships obeying his example, he led the way gallantly to Broye.

A. E. W. Mason

A LIBERAL EDUCATION

"So you couldn't wait!"

Mrs. Branscome turned full on the speaker as she answered deliberately: "You have evidently not been long in London, Mr. Hilton, or you would not ask that question."

"I arrived yesterday evening."

"Quite so. Then will you forgive me one tiny word of advice? You will learn the truth of it soon by yourself; but I want to convince you at once of the uselessness—to use no harder word—of trying to revive a flirtation—let me see! yes, quite two years old. You might as well galvanise a mummy and expect it to walk about. Besides," she added inconsistently, "I had to marry and—and—you never came."

"Then you sent the locket!"

The word sent a shiver through Mrs. Branscome with a remembrance of the desecration of a gift which she had cherished as a holy thing. She clung to flippancy as her defence.

"Oh, no! I never sent it. I lost it somewhere, I think. Must you go?" she continued, as Hilton moved silently to the door.

"I expect my husband in just now. Won't you wait and meet him?"

"How dare you?" Hilton burst out. "Is there nothing of your true self left?"

*   *   *   *   *

David Hilton's education was as yet in its infancy. This was not only his first visit to England, but, indeed, to any spot further afield than Interlaken. All of his six-and-twenty years that he could recollect had been passed in a *chalet* on the Scheidegg above Grindelwald, his only companion an elderly recluse who had deliberately cut himself off from communion with his fellows. The trouble which had driven Mr. Strange, an author at one time of some mark, into this seclusion, was now as completely forgotten as his name. Even David knew nothing of its cause. That Strange was his uncle and had adopted him when left an orphan at the age of six, was the sum of his information. For although the pair had lived together for twenty years, there had been little intercourse of thought between them, and none of sentiment. Strange had, indeed, throughout shut his nephew, not merely from his heart, but also from his confidence, at first out of sheer neglect, and afterwards, as the lad grew towards manhood, from deliberate intent. For, by continually brooding over his embittered life, he had at last impregnated his weak nature with the savage cynicism which embraced even his one comrade; and the child he had originally chosen as a solace for his loneliness, became in the end the victim of a heartless experiment. Strange's plan was based upon a method of training. In the first place, he thoroughly isolated David from any actual experience of persons beyond the simple shepherd folk who attended to their needs and a few Alpine guides who accompanied him on mountain expeditions. He kept incessant guard over his own past life,

A. E. W. Mason

letting no incidents or deductions escape, and fed the youth's mind solely upon the ideal polities of the ancients, his object being to launch him suddenly upon the world with little knowledge of it beyond what had filtered through his books, and possessed of an intuitive hostility to existing modes. What kind of a career would ensue? Strange anticipated the solution of the problem with an approach to excitement. Two events, however, prevented the complete realisation of his scheme. One was a lingering illness which struck him down when David was twenty-four and about to enter on his ordeal. The second, occurring simultaneously, was the advent of Mrs. Branscome—then Kate Alden—to Grindelwald.

They met by chance on the snow slopes of the Wetterhorn early one August morning. Miss Alden was trying to disentangle some meaning from the *patois* of her guides, and gratefully accepted Hilton's assistance. Half-an-hour after she had continued the ascent, David noticed a small gold locket glistening in her steps. It recalled him to himself, and he picked it up and went home with a strange trouble clutching at his heart. The next morning he carried the locket down into the valley, found its owner and—forgot to restore it. It became an excuse for further descents. Meanwhile, the theories were wooed with a certain coldness. In front of them stood perpetually the one real thing which had surged up through the quiet of his life, and, lover-like, he justified its presence to himself, by seeing in Kate Alden's frank face the incarnation of the ideal patterns of his books. The visits to Grindelwald grew more frequent and more prolonged. The climax, however, came unexpectedly to both. David had commissioned a jeweller at Berne to fashion a fac-simile of the locket for his own wearing, and, meaning to restore the original, handed Kate Alden the copy the evening before she left. An explanation of the mistake led to mutual avowals and a betrothal. Hilton returned to nurse his adoptive father, and was to seek England as soon as he could obtain his release. Meanwhile, Kate pledged herself to wait for him. She kept the new locket, empty except for a sprig of edelweiss he had placed in it, and agreed that if she needed her lover's presence, she should despatch it as an imperative summons.

During the next two years Strange's life ebbed sullenly away. The approach of death brought no closer intimacy between uncle and nephew, since indeed the former held it almost as a grievance against David that he should die before he could witness the issue of his experiment. Consequently the younger man kept his secret to himself, and embraced it the more closely for his secrecy, fostering it through the dreary night watches, until the image of Kate Alden became a Star-in-the-East to him, beckoning towards London. When the end came, David found himself the possessor of a moderate fortune; and with the humiliating knowledge that this legacy awoke his first feeling of gratitude towards his uncle, he locked the door of the *chalet*, and so landed at Charing Cross one wet November evening. Meanwhile the locket had never come.

* * * * *

After Hilton had left, Mrs. Branscome's forced indifference gave way. As she crouched beside the fire, numbed by pain beyond the power of thought, she could conjure up but one memory—the morning of their first meeting. She recollected that the sun had just risen over the shoulder of the Shreckhorn, and how it had seemed to her young fancy that David had come to her straight from the heart of it. The sound of her husband's step in the hall brought her with a shock to facts. "He must go back," she muttered, "he must go back."

David, however, harboured no such design. One phrase of

hers had struck root in his thoughts. "I had to marry," she had said, and certain failings in her voice warned him that this, whatever it meant, was in her eyes the truth. It had given the lie direct to the flippancy which she had assumed, and David determined to remain until he had fathomed its innermost meaning. A fear, indeed, lest the one single faith he felt as real should crumble to ashes made his resolve almost an instinct of self-preservation. The idea of accepting the situation never occurred to him, his training having effectually prevented any growth of respect for the *status quo* as such. Nor did he realise at this time that his determination might perhaps prove unfair to Mrs. Branscome. A certain habit of abstraction, nurtured in him by the spirit of inquiry which he had imbibed from his books, had become so intuitive as to penetrate even into his passion. From the first he had been accustomed to watch his increasing intimacy with Kate Alden from the standpoint of a third person, analysing her actions and feelings no less than his own. And now this tendency gave the crowning impetus to a resolve which sprang originally from his necessity to find sure foothold somewhere amid the wreckage of his hopes.

From this period might be dated the real commencement of Hilton's education. He returned to the Branscomes' house, sedulously schooled his looks and his words, save when betrayed into an occasional denunciation of the marriage laws, and succeeded at last in overcoming a distaste which Mr. Branscome unaccountably evinced for him. To a certain extent, also, he was taken up by social entertainers. There was an element of romance in the life he had led which appealed favourably to the seekers after novelty—"a second St. Simeon Skylights" he had been rashly termed by one good lady, whose wealth outweighed her learning. At first his gathering crowd of acquaintances only served to fence him more closely within himself; but as he began to realise that this was only the unit of another crowd, a crowd of designs and intentions working darkly, even he, sustained by the strength of a single aim, felt himself whirling at times. Thus he slowly grew to some knowledge of the difficulties and complications which must beset any young girl like Kate Alden, whose nearest relation and chaperon had been a feather-headed cousin not so many years her elder. At last, in a dim way, he began to see the possibility of replacing his bitterness with pity. For Mrs. Branscome did not love her husband; he plainly perceived that, if only from the formal precision with which she performed her duties. She appeared to him, indeed, to be paying off an obligation rather than working out the intention of her life.

The actual solution of his perplexities came by an accident. Amongst the visitors who fell under Hilton's observation at the Branscomes' was a certain Mr. Marston, a complacent widower of some five-and-thirty years, and Branscome's fellow servant at the Admiralty. Hilton's attention was attracted to this man by the air of embarrassment with which Mrs. Branscome received his approaches. Resolute to neglect no clue, however slight, David sought Marston's companionship, and, as a reward, discovered one afternoon in a Crown Derby teacup on the mantel-shelf of the latter's room his own present of two years back. The exclamation which this discovery extorted aroused Marston.

"What's up?"

"Where did you get this?"

"Why? Have you seen it before?"

The question pointed out to David the need of wariness.

"No!" he answered. "Its shape rather struck me, that's all. The emblem of a conquest, I suppose?"

A. E. W. Mason

The invitation stumbled awkwardly from unaccustomed lips, but Marston noticed no more than the words. He was chewing the cud of a disappointment and answered with a short laugh:

"No! Rather of a rebuff. The lady tore her hand away in a hurry—the link on the bracelet was thin, I suppose. Anyway, that was left in my hand."

"You were proposing to her?"

"Well, hardly. I was married at the time."

There was a silence for some moments, during which Hilton slowly gathered into his mind a consciousness of the humiliation which Kate must have endured, and read in that the explanation of her words "I had to marry." Marston took up the tale, babbling resentfully of a nursery prudishness, but his remarks fell on deaf ears until he mentioned a withered flower, which he had found inside the locket. Then David's self control partially gave way. In imagination he saw Marston carelessly tossing the sprig aside and the touch of his fingers seemed to sully the love of which it was the token. The locket burned into his hand. Without a word he dropped it on to the floor, and ground it to pieces with his heel. A new light broke in upon Marston.

"So this accounts for all your railing against the marriage laws," he laughed. "By Jove, you have kept things quiet. I wouldn't have given you credit for it."

His eyes travelled from the carpet to David's face, and he stopped abruptly.

"You had better hold your tongue," David said quietly. "Pick up the pieces."

"Do you think I would touch them now?"

Marston rose from his lounge; David stepped in front of the door. There was a litheness in his movements which denoted obedient muscles. Marston perceived this now with considerable discomfort, and thought it best to comply: he knelt down and picked up the fragments of the locket.

"Now throw them into the grate!"

That done, David took his leave. Once outside the house, however, his emotion fairly mastered him. The episode of which he had just heard was so mean and petty in itself, and yet so far-reaching in its consequences that it set his senses aflame in an increased revolt against the order of the world. Marriage was practically a necessity to a girl as unprotected as Kate Alden; he now acquiesced in that. But that it should have been forced upon her by the vanity of a trivial person like Marston, engaged in the pursuit of his desires, sent a fever of repulsion through his veins. He turned back to the door deluded by the notion that it was his duty to render the occurrence impossible of repetition. He was checked, however, by the thought of Mrs. Branscome. The shame he felt hinted the full force of degradation of which she must have been conscious, and begot in him a strange feeling of loyalty. Up till now the true meaning of chivalry had been unknown to him. In consequence of his bringing up he had been incapable of regarding faith in persons as a working motive in one's life. Even the first dawn of his passion had failed to teach him that; all the confidence and trust which he gained thereby being a mere reflection, from what he saw in Kate Alden, of truth to him. It was necessary that he should feel her trouble first and his poignant sense of that now revealed to him, not merely the wantonness of the perils women are compelled to run, but their consequent sufferings and their endurance in suppressing them.

A. E. W. Mason

A feverish impulse towards self-sacrifice sprang up within him. He would bury the incident of that afternoon as a dead thing—nay, more, for Mrs. Branscome's sake he would leave England and return to his retreat among the mountains. If she had suffered, why should he claim an exemption? The idea had just sufficient strength to impel him to catch the night-mail from Charing Cross. That it was already weakening was evidenced by a half-feeling of regret that he had not missed the train.

The regret swelled during his journey to the coast. The scene he had just come through became, from much pondering on it, almost unreal, and, with the blurring of the impression it had caused, there rose a doubt as to the accuracy of his vision of Mrs. Branscome's distress, which he had conjured out of it. His chivalry, in a word, had grown too quickly to take firm root. It was an exotic planted in soil not yet fully prepared. David began to think himself a fool, and at last, as the train neared Dover, a question which had been vaguely throbbing in his brain suddenly took shape. Why had she not sent for him? True, the locket was lost, but she might have written. The formulation of the question shattered almost all the work of the last few hours. He cursed his recent thoughts as a child's fairy dreams. Why should he leave England after all? If he was to sacrifice himself it should be for some one who cared sufficiently for him to justify the act.

There might, of course, have been some hidden obstacle in the way, which Mrs. Branscome could not surmount. The revelation of Marston's unimagined story warned him of the possibility of that. But the chances were against it. Anyway, he quibbled to himself, he had a clear right to pursue the matter until he unearthed the truth. Acting upon this decision, David returned to town, though not without a lurking sense of shame.

A few evenings after, he sought out Mrs. Branscome at a dance. The blood rushed to her face when she caught his figure, and as quickly ebbed away.

"So you have not gone, after all?" There was something pitiful in her tone of reproach.

"No. What made you think I had?"

"Mr. Marston told me!"

"Did he tell you why?"

"I guessed that, and I thanked you in my heart."

David was disconcerted; the woman he saw corresponded so ill with what he was schooling himself to believe her. He sought to conceal his confusion, as she had once done, and played a part. Like her, he overplayed it.

"Well! I came to see London life, you know. It makes a pretty comedy."

"Comedies end in tears at times."

"Even then common politeness makes us sit them out. Can you spare me a dance?"

Mrs. Branscome pleaded fatigue, and barely suppressed a sigh of relief as she noted her husband's approach. David followed her glance, and bent over her, speaking hurriedly:—

"You said you knew why I went away; I want to tell you why I came back."

"No! no!" she exclaimed. "It could be of no use—of no help

to either of us."

"I came back," he went on, ignoring her interruption, "merely to ask you one question. Will you hear it and answer it? I can wait," he added, as she kept silence.

"Then, to-morrow, as soon as possible," Mrs. Branscome replied, beaten by his persistency. "Come at seven; we dine at eight, so I can give you half-an-hour. But you are ungenerous."

That night began what may be termed the crisis of Hilton's education. This was the second time he had caught Mrs. Branscome unawares. On the first occasion—that of his unexpected arrival in England—he did not possess the experience to measure accurately looks and movements, or to comprehend them as the connotation of words. It is doubtful, besides, whether, had he owned the skill, he would have had the power to exercise it, so engrossed was he in his own distress. By the process, however, of continually repressing the visible signs of his own emotions, he had now learnt to appreciate them in others. And in Mrs. Branscome's sudden change of colour, in little convulsive movements of her hands, and in a certain droop of eyelids veiling eyes which met the gaze frankly as a rule, he read this evening sure proofs of the constancy of her heart. This fresh knowledge affected him in two ways. On the one hand it gave breath to the selfish passion which now dominated his ideas. At the same time, however it assured him that when he asked his question: "Why did you not send for me?" an unassailable answer would be forthcoming; and, moreover, by convincing him of this, it destroyed the sole excuse he had pleaded to himself for claiming the right to ask it. In self-defence Hilton had recourse to his old outcry against the marriage laws and, finding this barren, came in the end to frankly devising schemes for their circumvention. Such inward personal conflicts were, of necessity, strange to a man dry-nursed on abstractions, and, after a night of tension, they tossed him up on the shores of the morning broken in mind and irresolute for good or ill.

*   *   *   *   *

Mrs. Branscome received him impassively at the appointed time. David saw that he was expected to speak to the point, and a growing scorn for his own insistence urged him to the same course. He plunged abruptly into his subject and his manner showed him in the rough, more particularly to himself.

"What I came back to ask you is just this. You know—you must know—that I would have come, whatever the consequence. Why did you not send for me after, after—?"

"Why did I not send for you?" Mrs. Branscome took him up, repeating his words mechanically, as though their meaning had not reached her. "You don't mean that you never received my letter. Oh, don't say that! It can't have miscarried, I registered it."

"Then you did write?"

This confirmation of her fear drove a breach through her composure.

"Of course, of course, I wrote," she cried. "You doubt that? What can you think of me? Yes, I wrote, and when no answer came, I fancied you had forgotten me—that you had never really cared, and so I—I married."

Her voice dried in her throat. The thought of this ruin of two lives, made inevitable by a mistake in which neither shared,

A. E. W. Mason

brought a sense of futility which paralysed her.

The same idea was working in Hilton's mind, but to a different end. It fixed the true nature of this woman for the first time clearly within his recognition, and the new light blinded him. Before, his imagined grievance had always coloured the picture; now, he began to realise not only that she was no more responsible for the catastrophe than himself, but that he must have stood in the same light to her as she had done to him. The events of the past few months passed before his mind as on a clear mirror. He compared the gentle distinction of her bearing with his own flaunting resentment.

"I am sorry," he said, "I have wronged you in thought and word and action. The fact is, I never saw you plainly before; myself stood in the way."

Mrs. Branscome barely heeded his words. The feelings her watchfulness had hitherto restrained having once broken their barriers swept her away on a full flow. She recalled the very terms of her letter. She had written it in the room in which they were standing. Mr. Branscome had called just as she addressed the envelope—she had questioned him about its registration to Switzerland, and, yes, he had promised to look after it and had taken it away. "Yes!" she repeated to herself aloud, directing her eyes instinctively towards her husband's study door. "He promised to post it."

The sound of the words and a sudden movement from Hilton woke her to alarm. David had turned to the window, and she felt that he had heard and understood. The silence pressed on her like a dead weight. For Hilton, this was the crucial moment of his ordeal. He had understood only too clearly, and this second proof of the harm a petty sin could radiate struck through him the same fiery repulsion which had stung him to revolt when he quitted Marston's rooms. He flung up the window and faced the sunset. Strips of black cloud barred it across, and he noticed, with a minute attention of which he was hardly conscious, that their lower edges took a colour like the afterglow on a Swiss rock mountain. The perception sent a riot of associations through his brain which strengthened his wavering purpose. Must he lose her after all, he thought; now that he had risen to a true estimation of her worth? His fancy throned Kate queen of his mountain home, and he turned towards her, but a light of fear in her eyes stopped the words on his lips.

"I trust you," she said, simply.

The storm of his passions quieted down. That one sentence just expressed to him the debt he owed to her. In return— well, he could do no less than leave her her illusion.

"Good-bye," he said. "All the good that comes to us, somehow, seems to spring from women like yourself, while we give you nothing but trouble in return. Even this last misery, which my selfishness has brought to you, lifts me to breathe a cleaner air."

"He must have forgotten to post it," Mrs. Branscome pleaded.

"Yes; we must believe that. Good-bye!"

For a moment he stayed to watch her white figure, outlined against the dusk of the room, and then gently closed the door on her. The next morning David left England, not, however, for Grindelwald. He dreaded the morbid selfishness which grows from isolation, and sought a finishing school in the companionship of practical men.

A. E. W. Mason

THE TWENTY-KRONER STORY

The surgeon has a weakness for men who make their living on the sea. From the skipper of a Dogger Bank fishing-smack to the stoker of a Cardiff tramp, from Margate 'longshoreman to a crabber of the Stilly Isles, he embraces them all in a lusty affection. And this not merely out of his own love of salt water but because his diagnosis reveals the gentleman in them more surely than in the general run of his wealthier patients. "A primitive gentleman, if you like," Lincott will say, "not above tearing his meat with his fingers or wearing the same shirt night and day for a couple of months on end, but still a gentleman." As one of the innumerable instances which had built up his conviction, Lincott will offer you the twenty-kroner story.

As he was walking through the wards of his hospital he stopped for a moment by the bed of a brewer's drayman who was suffering from an access of *delirium tremens*. The drayman's language was violent and voluble. But he sank into a coma with the usual suddenness common to such cases, and in the pause which followed Lincott heard a gentle voice a few beds away earnestly apologising to a nurse for the trouble she was put to. "Why," she replied with a laugh, "I am here to be troubled." Apologies of the kind are not so frequently heard in the wards of an East End hospital. This one, besides, was spoken with an accent not very pronounced, it is true, but unfamiliar. Lincott moved down to the bed. It was occupied by a man apparently tall, with a pair of remorseful blue eyes set in an open face, and a thatch of yellow hair dusted with grey.

"What's the matter?" asked Lincott, and the patient explained. He was a Norseman from Finland, fifty-three years old, and he had worked all his life on English ships. He had risen from "decky" to mate. Then he had injured himself, and since he could work no more he had come into the hospital to be cured. Lincott examined him, found that a slight operation was all the man needed, and performed it himself. In six weeks time Helling, as the sailor was named, was discharged. He made a simple and dignified little speech of thanks to the nurses for their attention, and another to the surgeon for saving his life.

"Nonsense!" said Lincott, as he held out his hand. "Any medical student could have performed that operation."

"Then I have another reason to thank you," answered Helling. "The nurses have told me about you, sir, and I'm grateful you spared the time to perform it yourself."

"What are you going to do?" asked Lincott.

"Find a ship, sir," answered Helling. Then he hesitated, and slowly slipped his finger and thumb along the waist-band of his trousers. But he only repeated, "I must find a ship," and so left the hospital.

Three weeks later Helling called at Lincott's house in Harley Street. Now, when hospital patients take the trouble, after they have been discharged, to find out the doctor's private address and call, it generally means they have come to beg. Lincott, remembering how Helling's simple courtesies had

A. E. W. Mason

impressed him, experienced an actual disappointment. He felt his theories about the seafaring man begin to totter. However, Helling was shown into the consulting-room, and at the sight of him Lincott's disappointment vanished. He did not start up, since manifestations of surprise are amongst those things with which doctors find it advisable to dispense, but he hooked a chair forward with his foot.

"Now then, sit down! Chuck yourself about! Sit down," said Lincott genially. "You look bad."

Helling, in fact, was gaunt with famine; his eyes were sunk and dull; he was so thin that he seemed to have grown in height.

"I had some trouble in finding a ship," he said; and sitting down on the edge of the chair, twirled his hat in some embarrassment.

"It is three weeks since you left the hospital?"

"Yes."

"You should have come here before," the surgeon was moved to say.

"No," answered Helling. "I couldn't come before, sir. You see, I had no ship. But I found one this morning, and I start to-morrow."

"But for these three weeks? You have been starving." Lincott slipped his hand into his pocket. It seemed to him afterwards simply providential that he did not fumble his money, that no clink of coins was heard. For Helling answered,

"Yes, sir, I've been starving." He drew back his shoulders

and laughed. "I'm proud to know that I've been starving."

He laid his hat on the ground, drew out and unclasped his knife, felt along the waist-band of his breeches, cut a few stitches, and finally produced a little gold coin. This coin he held between his forefinger and thumb.

"Forty years ago," he said, "when I was a nipper and starting on my first voyage, my mother gave me this. She sewed it up in the waist-band of my breeches with her own hands and told me never to part with it until I'd been starving. I've been near to starvation often and often enough. But I never have starved before. This coin has always stood between that and me. Now, however, I have actually been starving and I can part with it."

He got up from his chair and timidly laid the piece of gold on the table by Lincott's elbow. Then he picked up his hat. The surgeon said nothing, and he did not touch the coin. Neither did he look at Helling, but sat with his forehead propped in his hand as though he were reading the letters on his desk. Helling, afraid to speak lest his coin should be refused, walked noiselessly to the door and noiselessly unlatched it.

"Wait a bit!" said Lincott. Helling stopped anxiously in the doorway.

"Where have you slept"—Lincott paused to steady his voice—"for the last three weeks?" he continued.

"Under arches by the river, sir," replied Helling. "On benches along the Embankment, once or twice in the parks. But that's all over now," he said earnestly. "I'm all right. I've got my ship. I couldn't part with that before, because it was the only thing I had to hang on to the world with. But I'm all right now."

A. E. W. Mason

Lincott took up the coin and turned it over in the palm of his hand.

"Twenty kroners," he said. "Do you know what that's worth in England?"

"Yes, I do," answered Helling with some trepidation.

"Fifteen shillings," said Lincott. "Think of it, fifteen shillings, perhaps sixteen."

"I know," interrupted Helling quickly, mistaking the surgeon's meaning. "But please, please, you mustn't think I value what you have done for me at that. It's only fifteen shillings, but it has meant a fortune to me all the last three weeks. Each time that I've drawn my belt tighter I have felt that coin underneath it burn against my skin. When I passed a coffee-stall in the early morning and saw the steam and the cake I knew I could have bought up the whole stall if I chose. I could have had meals, and meals, and meals. I could have slept in beds under roofs. It's only fifteen shillings; nothing at all to you," and he looked round the consulting-room, with its pictures and electric lights, "but I want you to take it at what it has been worth to me ever since I came out of the hospital."

Lincott took Helling into his dining-room. On a pedestal stood a great silver vase, blazing its magnificence across the room.

"You see that?" he asked.

"Yes," said Helling.

"It was given to me by a patient. It must have cost at the least L500."

Helling tapped the vase with his knuckles.

"Yes, sir, that's a present," he said enviously. "That *is* a present."

Lincott laughed and threw up the window.

"You can pitch it out into the street if you like. By the side of your coin it's muck."

Lincott keeps the coin. He points out that Helling was fifty-three at the time that he gave him this present, and that the operation was one which any practitioner could have performed.

A. E. W. Mason

THE FIFTH PICTURE

Lady Tamworth felt unutterably bored. The sensation of lassitude, even in its less acute degrees, was rare with her; for she possessed a nature of so fresh a buoyancy that she was able, as a rule, to extract diversion from any environment. Her mind took impressions with the vivid clearness of a mirror, and also, it should be owned, with a mirror's transient objectivity. To-day, however, the mirror was clouded. She looked out of the window; a level row of grey houses frowned at her across the street. She looked upwards; a grey pall of cloud swung over the rooftops. The interior of the room appeared to her even less inviting than the street. It was the afternoon of the first drawing-room, and a *debutante* was exhibiting herself to her friends. She stood in the centre, a figure from a Twelfth-Night cake, amidst a babble of congratulations, and was plainly occupied in a perpetual struggle to conceal her moments of enthusiasm beneath a crust of deprecatory languor.

The spectacle would have afforded choice entertainment to Lady Tamworth, had she viewed it in the company of a sympathetic companion. Solitary appreciation of the humorous, however, only induced in her a yet more despondent mood. The tea seemed tepid; the conversation matched the tea. Epigrams without point, sallies void of wit, and cynicisms innocent of the sting of an apt application floated about her on a ripple of unintelligent laughter. A phrase of Mr. Dale's recurred to her mind, "Hock and seltzer with the sparkle out of it;" so he had stigmatised the style and she sadly thanked him for the metaphor.

There was, moreover, a particular reason for her discontent. Nobody realised the presence of Lady Tamworth, and this unaccustomed neglect shot a barbed question at her breast. "After all why should they?" She was useless, she reflected; she did nothing, exercised no influence. The thought, however, was too painful for lengthened endurance; the very humiliation of it produced the antidote. She remembered that she had at last persuaded her lazy Sir John to stand for Parliament. Only wait until he was elected! She would exercise an influence then. The vision of a *salon* was miraged before her, with herself in the middle deftly manipulating the destinies of a nation.

"Lady Tamworth!" a voice sounded at her elbow.

"Mr. Dale!" She turned with a sudden sprightliness. "My guardian angel sent you."

"So bad as that?"

"I have an intuition." She paused impressively upon the word.

"Never mind!" said he soothingly. "It will go away."

Lady Tamworth glared, that is, as well as she could; nature had not really adapted her for glaring. "I have an intuition," she resumed, "that this is what the suburbs mean." And she waved her hand comprehensively.

"They are perhaps a trifle excessive," he returned. "But then

A. E. W. Mason

you needn't have come."

"Oh, yes! Clients of Sir John." Lady Tamworth sighed and sank with a weary elegance into a chair. Mr. Dale interpreted the sigh. "Ah! A wife's duties," he began.

"No man can know," she interrupted, and she spread out her hands in pathetic forgiveness of an over-exacting world. Her companion laughed brutally. "You *are* rude!" she said and laughed too. And then, "Tell me something new!"

"I met an admirer of yours to-day."

"But that's nothing new." She looked up at him with a plaintive reproach.

"I will begin again," he replied submissively. "I walked down the Mile-End road this morning to Sir John's jute-factory."

"You fail to interest me," she said with some emphasis.

"I am so sorry. Good-bye!"

"Mr. Dale!"

"Yes!"

"You may, if you like, go on with the first story."

"There is only one. It was in the Mile-End road I met the admirer—Julian Fairholm."

"Oh!" Lady Tamworth sat up and blushed. However, Lady Tamworth blushed very readily.

"It was a queer incident," Mr. Dale continued. "I caught sight of a necktie in a little dusty shop-window near the Pavilion Theatre. I had never seen anything like it in my life; it fairly fascinated me, seemed to dare me to buy it."

The lady's foot began to tap upon the carpet. Mr. Dale stopped and leaned critically forward.

"Well! Why don't you go on?" she asked impatiently.

"It's pretty," he reflected aloud.

The foot disappeared demurely into the seclusion of petticoats. "You exasperate me," she remarked. But her face hardly guaranteed her words. "We were speaking of ties."

"Ah, the tie wasn't pretty. It was of satin, bright yellow with blue spots. And an idea struck me; yes, an idea! Sir John's election colours are yellow, his opponent's blue. So I thought the tie would make a tactful present, symbolical (do you see?) of the state of the parties in the constituency."

He paused a second time.

"Well?"

"I went in and bought it."

"Well?"

"Julian Fairholm sold it to me."

Lady Tamworth stared at the speaker in pure perplexity. Then all at once she understood and the blood eddied into her cheeks. "I don't believe it!" she exclaimed.

A. E. W. Mason

"His face would be difficult to mistake," Mr. Dale objected. "Besides I had time to assure myself, for I had to wait my turn. When I entered the shop, he was serving a woman with baby-linen. Oh yes! Julian Fairholm sold me the tie."

Lady Tamworth kept her eyes upon the ground. Then she looked up. She struck the arm of her chair with her closed fist and cried in a quick petulance, "How dare he?"

"Exactly what I thought," answered her companion smoothly. "The colours were crude by themselves, the combination was detestable. And he an artist too!" Mr. Dale laughed pleasantly.

"Did he speak to you?"

"He asked me whether I would take a packet of pins instead of a farthing."

"Ah, don't," she entreated, and rose from her chair. It might have been her own degradation of which Mr. Dale was speaking.

"By the way," he added, "I was so taken aback that I forgot to present the tie. Would you?"

"No! No!" she said decisively and turned away. But a sudden notion checked her. "On second thoughts I will; but I can't promise to make him wear it."

The smile which sped the words flickered strangely upon quivering lips and her eyes shone with anger. However the tie changed hands, and Lady Tamworth tripped down stairs and stepped into her brougham. The packet lay upon her lap and she unfolded it. A round ticket was enclosed, and the bill. On the ticket was printed, *A Present from Zedediah Moss*. With a convulsion of disgust she swept the parcel on to the floor. "How dare he?" she cried again, and her thoughts flew back to the brief period of their engagement. She had been just Kitty Arlton in those days, the daughter of a poor sea-captain but dowered with the compensating grace of personal attractions. Providence had indisputably designed her for the establishment of the family fortunes; such at all events was the family creed, and the girl herself felt no inclination to doubt a faith which was backed by the evidence of her looking-glass. Julian Fairholm at that time shared a studio with her brother, and the acquaintance thus begun ripened into an attachment and ended in a betrothal. For Julian, in the common prediction, possessed that vague blessing, a future. It is true the common prediction was always protected by a saving clause: "If he could struggle free from his mysticism." But none the less his pictures were beginning to sell, and the family displayed a moderate content. The discomposing appearance of Sir John Tamworth, however, gave a different complexion to the matter. Sir John was rich, and had besides the confident pertinacity of success. In a word, Kitty Arlton married Sir John.

Lady Tamworth's recollections of the episode were characteristically vague; they came back to her in pieces like disconnected sections of a wooden puzzle. She remembered that she had written an exquisitely pathetic letter to Fairholm "when the end came," as she expressed it; and she recalled queer scraps of the artist's talk about the danger of forming ties. "New ties," he would say, "mean new duties, and they hamper and clog the will." Ah yes, the will; he was always holding forth about that and here was the lecture finally exemplified! He was selling baby-linen in the Mile-End road. She had borne her disappointment, she reflected, without any talk about will. The thought of her self-sacrifice even now brought the tears to her eyes; she saw herself wearing her orange-blossoms in the spirit of an Iphigeneia.

A. E. W. Mason

Sections of the puzzle, however, were missing to Lady Tamworth's perceptions. For, in fact, her sense of sacrifice had been mainly artificial, and fostered by a vanity which made the possession of a broken romance seem to pose her on a notable pedestal of duty. What had really attracted her to Julian was the evidence of her power shown in the subjugation of a being intellectually higher than his compeers. It was not so much the man she had cared for, as the sight of herself in a superior setting; a sure proof whereof might have been found in a certain wilful pleasure which she had drawn from constantly impelling him to acts and admissions which she knew to be alien to his nature.

It was some revival of this idea which explained her exclamation, "How dare he?" For his conduct appeared more in the light of an outrage and insult to her than of a degradation of himself. He must be rescued from his position, she determined.

She stooped to pick up the bill from the floor as the brougham swung sharply round a corner. She looked out of the window; the coachman had turned into Berkeley Square; in another hundred yards she would reach home. She hastily pulled the check-string, and the footman came to the door. "Drive down the Mile-End road," she said; "I will fetch Sir John home." Lady Tamworth read the address on the bill. "Near the Pavilion Theatre," Mr. Dale had explained. She would just see the place this evening, she determined, and then reflect on the practical course to be pursued.

The decision relieved her of her sense of humiliation, and she nestled back among her furs with a sigh of content. There was a pleasurable excitement about her present impulse which contrasted very brightly with her recent *ennui*. She felt that her wish to do something, to exert an influence, had been providentially answered. The task, besides, seemed to her to have a flavour of antique chivalry; it smacked of the princess undoing enchantments, and reminded her vaguely of Camelot. She determined to stop at the house and begin the work at once; so she summoned the footman a second time and gave him the address. So great indeed was the charm which her conception exercised over her, that her very indignation against Julian changed to pity. He had to be fitted to the chivalric pattern, and consequently refashioned. Her harlequin fancy straightway transformed him into the romantic lover who, having lost his mistress, had lost the world and therefore, naturally, held the sale of baby-linen on a par with the painting of pictures. "Poor Julian!" she thought.

The carriage stopped suddenly in front of a shuttered window. A neighbouring gas-lamp lit up the letters on the board above it, *Z. Moss*. This unexpected check in the full flight of ardour dropped her to earth like a plummet. And as if to accentuate her disappointment the surrounding shops were aglare with light; customers pressed busily in and out of them, and even on the roadway naphtha-jets waved flauntingly over barrows of sweet-stuff and fruit. Only this sordid little house was dark. "They can't afford to close at this hour," she murmured reproachfully.

The footman came to the carriage door, disdain perceptibly struggling through his mask of impassivity.

"Why is the shop closed?" Lady Tamworth asked.

"The name, perhaps, my lady," he suggested. "It is Friday."

Lady Tamworth had forgotten the day. "Very well," she said sullenly. "Home at once!" However, she corrected herself adroitly: "I mean, of course, fetch Sir John first."

A. E. W. Mason

Sir John was duly fetched and carried home jubilant at so rare an attention. The tie was presented to him on the way, and he bellowed his merriment at its shape and colour. To her surprise Lady Tamworth found herself defending the style, and inveighing against the monotony of the fashions of the West End. Nor was this the only occasion on which she disagreed with her husband that evening. He launched an aphorism across the dinner-table which he had cogitated from the report of a divorce-suit in the evening papers. "It is a strange thing," he said, "that the woman who knows her influence over a man usually employs it to hurt him; the woman who doesn't, employs it unconsciously for his good."

"You don't mean that?" she asked earnestly.

"I have noticed it more than once," he replied.

For a moment Lady Tamworth's chivalric edifice showed cracks and rents; it threatened to crumble like a house of cards; but only for a moment. For she merely considered the remark in reference to the future; she applied it to her present wish to exercise an influence over Julian. The issue of that, however, lay still in the dark, and was consequently imaginable as inclination prompted. A glance at Sir Julian sufficed to finally reassure her. He was rosy and modern, and so plainly incapable of appreciating chivalric impulses. To estimate them rightly one must have an insight into their nature, and therefore an actual experience of their fire; but such fire left traces on the person. Chivalric people were hollow-cheeked with luminous eyes; at least chivalric men were hollow-cheeked, she corrected herself with a look at the mirror. At all events Sir John and his aphorism were beneath serious reflection; and she determined to repeat her journey upon the first opportunity.

The opportunity, however, was delayed for a week and

occasioned Lady Tamworth no small amount of self-pity. Here was noble work waiting for her hand, and duty kept her chained to the social oar!

On the afternoon, then, of the following Friday she dressed with what even for her was unusual care, aiming at a complex effect of daintiness and severity, and drove down in a hansom to Whitechapel. She stopped the cab some yards from the shop and walked up to the window. Through the glass she could see Julian standing behind the counter. His hands (she noticed them particularly because he was displaying some cheap skeins of coloured wool) seemed perhaps a trifle thinner and more nervous, his features a little sharpened, and there was a sprinkling of grey in the black of his hair. For the first time since the conception of her scheme Lady Tamworth experienced a feeling of irresolution. With Fairholm in the flesh before her eyes, the task appeared difficult; its reality pressed in upon her, driving a breach through the flimsy wall of her fancies. She resolved to wait until the shop should be empty, and to that end took a few steps slowly up the street and returned yet more slowly. She looked into the window again; Julian was alone now, and still she hesitated. The admiring comments of two loungers on the kerb concerning her appearance at last determined her, and she brusquely thrust open the door. A little bell jangled shrilly above it and Julian looked up.

"Lady Tamworth!" he said after the merest pause and with no more than a natural start of surprise. Lady Tamworth, however, was too taken aback by the cool manner of his greeting to respond at once. She had forecast the commencement of the interview upon such wholly different lines that she felt lost and bewildered. An abashed confusion was the least that she expected from him, and she was prepared to increase it with a nicely-tempered indignation. Now the positions seemed actually reversed; he was looking at her

A. E. W. Mason

with a composed attention, while she was filled with embarrassment.

A suspicion flashed through her mind that she had come upon a fool's errand. "Julian!" she said with something of humility in her voice, and she timidly reached out her little gloved hand towards him. Julian took it into the palm of his own and gazed at it with a sort of wondering tenderness, as though he had lighted upon a toy which he remembered to have prized dearly in an almost forgotten childhood.

This second blow to her pride quickened in her a feeling of exasperation. She drew her fingers quickly out of his grasp. "What brought you down to this!" She snapped out the words at him; she had not come to Whitechapel to be slighted at all events.

"I have risen," he answered quietly.

"Risen? And you sell baby-linen!"

Julian laughed in pure contentment. "You don't understand," he said. For a moment he looked at her as one debating with himself and then: "You have a right to understand. I will tell you." He leaned across the counter, and as he spoke the eager passion of a devotee began to kindle in his eyes and vibrate through the tones of his voice. "The knowledge of a truth worked into your heart will lift you, eh, must lift you high? But base your life upon that truth, centre yourself about it, till your thoughts become instincts born from it! It must lift you still higher then; ah, how much higher! Well, I have done that. Yes, that's why I am here. And I owe it all to you."

Lady Tamworth repeated his words in sheer bewilderment. "You owe it all to me?"

"Yes," he nodded, "all to you." And with genuine gratitude he added, "You didn't know the good that you had done."

"Ah, don't say that!" she cried.

The bell tinkled over the shop-door and a woman entered. Lady Tamworth bent forward and said hastily, "I must speak to you."

"Then you must buy something; what shall it be?" Fairholm had already recovered his self-possession and was drawing out one of the shelves in the wall behind him.

"No, no!" she exclaimed, "not here; I can't speak to you here. Come and call on me; what day will you come?"

Julian shook his head. "Not at all, I am afraid. I have not the time."

A boy came out from the inner room and began to get ready the shutters. "Ah, it's Friday," she said. "You will be closing soon."

"In five minutes."

"Then I will wait for you. Yes, I will wait for you."

She paused at the door and looked at Julian. He was deferentially waiting on his customer, and Lady Tamworth noticed with a queer feeling of repugnance that he had even acquired the shopman's trick of rubbing the hands. Those five minutes proved for her a most unenviable period. Julian's sentence,—"I owe it all to you"—pressed heavily upon her conscience. Spoken bitterly, she would have given little heed to it; but there had been a convincing sincerity in the ring of his voice. The words, besides, brought back to her

Sir John's uncomfortable aphorism and freighted it with an accusation. She applied it now as a search-light upon her jumbled recollections of Julian's courtship, and began to realise that her efforts during that time had been directed thoughtlessly towards enlarging her influence over him. If, indeed, Julian owed this change in his condition to her, then Sir John was right, and she had employed her influence to his hurt. And it only made her fault the greater that Julian was himself unconscious of his degradation. She commenced to feel a personal responsibility commanding her to rescue him from his slough, which was increased moreover by a fear that her persuasions might prove ineffectual. For Julian's manner pointed now to an utter absence of feeling so far as she was concerned.

At last Julian came out to her. "You will leave here," she cried impulsively. "You will come back to us, to your friends!"

"Never," he answered firmly.

"You must," she pleaded; "you said you owed it all to me."

"Yes."

"Well, don't you see? If you stay here, I can never forgive myself; I shall have ruined your life."

"Ruined it?" Julian asked in a tone of wonder. "You have made it." He stopped and looked at Lady Tamworth in perplexity. The same perplexity was stamped upon her face. "We are at cross-purposes, I think," he continued. "My rooms are close here. Let me give you some tea, and explain to you that you have no cause to blame yourself."

Lady Tamworth assented with some relief. The speech had

an odd civilised flavour which contrasted pleasantly with what she had imagined of his mode of life.

They crossed the road and turned into a narrow side-street. Julian halted before a house of a slovenly exterior, and opened the door. A bare rickety staircase rose upwards from their feet. Fairholm closed the door behind Lady Tamworth, struck a match (for it was quite dark within this passage), and they mounted to the fourth and topmost floor. They stopped again upon a little landing in front of a second door. A wall-paper of a cheap and offensive pattern, which had here and there peeled from the plaster, added, Lady Tamworth observed, a paltry air of tawdriness to the poverty of the place. Julian fumbled in his pocket for a key, unlocked the door, and stepped aside for his companion to enter. Following her in, he lit a pair of wax candles on the mantelpiece and a brass lamp in the corner of the room. Lady Tamworth fancied that unawares she had slipped into fairyland; so great was the contrast between this retreat and the sordid surroundings amidst which it was perched. It was furnished with a dainty, and almost a feminine luxury. The room, she could see, was no more than an oblong garret; but along one side mouse-coloured curtains fell to the ground in folds from the angle where the sloping roof met the wall; on the other a cheerful fire glowed from a hearth of white tiles and a kettle sang merrily upon the hob. A broad couch, piled with silk cushions occupied the far end beneath the window, and the feet sank with a delicate pleasure into a thick velvety carpet. In the centre a small inlaid table of cedar wood held a silver tea-service. The candlesticks were of silver also, and cast in a light and fantastic fashion. The solitary discord was a black easel funereally draped.

Julian prepared the tea, and talked while he prepared it. "It is this way," he began quietly. "You know what I have always believed; that the will was the man, his soul, his life,

A. E. W. Mason

everything. Well, in the old days thoughts and ideas commenced to make themselves felt in me, to crop up in my work. I would start on a picture with a clear settled design; when it was finished, I would notice that by some unconscious freak I had introduced a figure, an arabesque, always something which made the whole incongruous and bizarre. I discovered the cause during the week after I received your last letter. The thoughts, the ideas were yours; better than mine perhaps, but none the less death to me."

Lady Tamworth stirred uneasily under a sense of guilt, and murmured a faint objection. Julian shook off the occupation of his theme and handed her some cake, and began again, standing over her with the cake in his hand, and to all seeming unconscious that there was a strain of cruelty in his words. "I found out what that meant. My emotions were mastering me, drowning the will in me. You see, I cared for you so much—then."

A frank contempt stressing the last word cut into his hearer with the keenness of a knife. "You are unkind," she said weakly.

"There's no reproach to you. I have got over it long ago," he replied cheerily. "And you showed me how to get over it; that's why I am grateful. For I began to wonder after that, why I, who had always been on my guard against the emotions, should become so thoroughly their slave. And at last I found out the reason; it was the work I was doing."

"Your work?" she exclaimed.

"Exactly! You remember what Plato remarked about the actor?"

"How should I?" asked poor Lady Tamworth.

"Well, he wouldn't have him in his ideal State because acting develops the emotions, the shifty unstable part of a man. But that's true of art as well; to do good work in art you must feel your work as an emotion. So I cut myself clear from it all. I furnished these rooms and came down here,—to live." And Julian drew a long breath, like a man escaped from danger.

"But why come here?" Lady Tamworth urged. "You might have gone into the country—anywhere."

"No, no, no!" he answered, setting down the cake and pacing about the room. "Wherever else I went, I must have formed new ties, created new duties. I didn't want that; one's feelings form the ties, one's soul pays the duties. No, London is the only place where a man can disappear. Besides I had to do something, and I chose this work, because it didn't touch me. I could throw it off the moment it was done. In the shop I earn the means to live; I live here."

"But what kind of a life is it?" she asked in despair.

"I will tell you," he replied, sinking his tone to an eager whisper; "but you mustn't repeat it, you must keep it a secret. When I am in this room alone at night, the walls widen and widen away until at last they vanish," and he nodded mysteriously at her. "The roof curls up like a roll of parchment, and I am left on an open platform."

"What do you mean?" gasped Lady Tamworth.

"Yes, on an open platform underneath the stars. And do you know," he sank his voice yet lower, "I hear them at times; very faintly of course,—their songs have so far to travel; but I hear them,—yes, I hear the stars."

Lady Tamworth rose in a whirl of alarm. Before this crazy

exaltation, her very desire to pursue her purpose vanished. For Julian's manner even more than his words contributed to her fears. In spite of his homily, emotion was dominant in his expression, swaying his body, burning on his face and lighting his eyes with a fire of changing colours. And every note in his voice was struck within the scale of passion.

She glanced about the room; her eyes fell on the easel. "Don't you ever paint?" she asked hurriedly.

He dropped his head and stood shifting from one foot to the other, as if he was ashamed. "At times," he said hesitatingly; "at times I have to,—I can't help it,—I have to express myself. Look!" He stepped suddenly across the room and slid the curtains back along the rail. The wall was frescoed from floor to ceiling.

"Julian!" Lady Tamworth cried. She forgot all her fears in face of this splendid revelation of his skill. Here was the fulfilment of his promise.

In the centre four pictures were ranged, the stages in the progress of an allegory, but executed with such masterful craft and of so vivid an intention that they read their message straightway into the heart of one's understanding. Round about this group, were smaller sketches, miniatures of pure fancy. It seemed as if the artist had sought relief in painting these from the pressure of his chief design. Here, for instance, Day and Night were chasing one another through the rings of Saturn; there a swarm of silver stars was settling down through the darkness to the earth.

"Julian, you must come back. You can't stay here."

"I don't mean to stay here long. It is merely a halting-place."

"But for how long?"

"I have one more picture to complete."

They turned again to the wall. Suddenly something caught Lady Tamworth's eye. She bent forward and examined the four pictures with a close scrutiny. Then she looked back again to Julian with a happy smile upon her face. "You have done these lately?"

"Quite lately; they are the stages of a man's life, of the struggle between his passions and his will."

He began to describe them. In the first picture a brutish god was seated on a throne of clay; before the god a man of coarse heavy features lay grovelling; but from his shoulders sprang a white figure, weak as yet and shadowy, but pointing against the god the shadow of a spear; and underneath was written, "At last he knoweth what he made." In the second, the figure which grovelled and that which sprang from its shoulders were plodding along a high-road at night, chained together by the wrist. The white figure halted behind, the other pressed on; and underneath was written, "They know each other not." In the third the figures marched level, that which had grovelled scowling at its companion; but the white figure had grown tall and strong and watched its companion with contempt. Above the sky had brightened with the gleam of stars; and underneath was written, "They know each other." In the fourth, the white figure pressed on ahead and dragged the other by the chain impatiently. Before them the sun was rising over the edge of a heath and the road ran straight towards it in a golden line; and underneath was written, "He knoweth his burden."

Lady Tamworth waited when he had finished, in a laughing expectancy. "And is that all?" she asked. "Is that all?"

"No," he replied slowly; "there is yet a further stage. It is unfinished." And he pointed to the easel.

"I don't mean that. Is that all you have to say of these?"

"I think so. Yes."

"Look at me!"

Julian turned wonderingly to Lady Tamworth. She watched him with a dancing sparkle of her eyes. "Now look at the pictures!" Julian obeyed her. "Well," she said after a pause, with a touch of anxiety. "What do you see now?"

"Nothing."

"Nothing?" she asked. "Do you mean that?"

"Yes! What should I see?" She caught him by the arm and stared intently into his eyes in a horror of disbelief. He met her gaze with a frank astonishment. She dropped his arm and turned away.

"What should I see?" he repeated.

"Nothing," she echoed with a quivering sadness in her voice. "It is late, I must go."

The white figure in each of those four pictures wore her face, idealised and illumined, but still unmistakably her face; and he did not know it, could not perceive it though she stood by his side! The futility of her errand was proved to her. She drew on her gloves and looking towards the easel inquired dully, "What stage is that?"

"The last; and it is the last picture I shall paint. As soon as it is completed I shall leave here."

"You will leave?" she asked, paying little heed to his words.

"Yes! The experiment has not succeeded," and he waved a hand towards the wall. "I shall take better means next time."

"How much remains to be done?" Lady Tamworth stepped over to the easel. With a quick spring Julian placed himself in front of it.

"No!" he cried vehemently, raising a hand to warn her off. "No!"

Lady Tamworth's curiosity began to reawaken. "You have shown me the rest."

"I know; you had a right to see them."

"Then why not that?"

"I have told you," he said stubbornly. "It is not finished."

"But when it is finished?" she insisted.

Julian looked at her strangely. "Well, why not?" he said reasoning with himself. "Why not? It is the masterpiece."

"You will let me know when it's ready?"

"I will send it to you; for I shall leave here the day I finish it."

They went down stairs and back into the Mile-End road. Julian hailed a passing hansom, and Lady Tamworth drove westwards to Berkeley Square.

The fifth picture arrived a week later in the dusk of the afternoon. Lady Tamworth unpacked it herself with an odd foreboding.

It represented an orchard glowing in the noontide sun. From the branches of a tree with lolling tongue and swollen twisted face swung the figure which had grovelled before the god. A broken chain dangled on its wrist, a few links of the chain lay on the grass beneath, and above the white figure winged and triumphant faded into the blue of the sky; and underneath was written, "He freeth himself from his burden."

Lady Tamworth rushed to the bell and pealed loudly for her maid. "Quick!" she cried, "I am going out." But the shrill screech of a newsboy pierced into the room. With a cry she flung open the window. She could hear his voice plainly at the corner of the square. For a while she clung to the sash in a dumb sickness. Then she said quietly: "Never mind! I will not go out after all! I did not know I was so late."

ABOUT THE AUTHOR

 **Alfred Edward Woodley Mason** (7 May 1865 Dulwich, London - 22 November 1948 London) was a British author.

He studied at Dulwich College and graduated from Trinity College, Oxford in 1888.

His first novel, A Romance of Wastdale, was published in 1895. He is the author of more than twenty books, among them The Four Feathers, originally published in London in 1902. His next successful work was At The Villa Rose (1910), where he introduced his French detective, Hanaud.

Mason was elected as a Liberal Member of Parliament for Coventry in the 1906 general election. He served only a single term in Parliament, retiring at the next general election in January 1910.

Mason rose to the rank of major during the First World War serving with The Manchester Regiment and the Royal Marine Light Infantry. His military career included work in naval intelligence, serving in Spain and Mexico, where he set up counter-espionage networks on behalf of the British government.

He died in 1948 while working on a non-fiction book about Admiral Robert Blake.

A. E. W. Mason

Choose from Thousands of 1stWorldLibrary Classics By

A. M. Barnard	Booth Tarkington	Edward Everett Hale
Ada Leverson	Boyd Cable	Edward J. O'Biren
Adolphus William Ward	Bram Stoker	Edward S. Ellis
Aesop	C. Collodi	Edwin L. Arnold
Agatha Christie	C. E. Orr	Eleanor Atkins
Alexander Aaronsohn	C. M. Ingleby	Eleanor Hallowell Abbott
Alexander Kielland	Carolyn Wells	Eliot Gregory
Alexandre Dumas	Catherine Parr Traill	Elizabeth Gaskell
Alfred Gatty	Charles A. Eastman	Elizabeth McCracken
Alfred Ollivant	Charles Amory Beach	Elizabeth Von Arnim
Alice Duer Miller	Charles Dickens	Ellem Key
Alice Turner Curtis	Charles Dudley Warner	Emerson Hough
Alice Dunbar	Charles Farrar Browne	Emilie F. Carlen
Allen Chapman	Charles Ives	Emily Bronte
Alleyne Ireland	Charles Kingsley	Emily Dickinson
Ambrose Bierce	Charles Klein	Enid Bagnold
Amelia E. Barr	Charles Hanson Towne	Enilor Macartney Lane
Amory H. Bradford	Charles Lathrop Pack	Erasmus W. Jones
Andrew Lang	Charles Romyn Dake	Ernie Howard Pie
Andrew McFarland Davis	Charles Whibley	Ethel May Dell
Andy Adams	Charles Willing Beale	Ethel Turner
Angela Brazil	Charlotte M. Braeme	Ethel Watts Mumford
Anna Alice Chapin	Charlotte M. Yonge	Eugene Sue
Anna Sewell	Charlotte Perkins Stetson	Eugenie Foa
Annie Besant	Clair W. Hayes	Eugene Wood
Annie Hamilton Donnell	Clarence Day Jr.	Eustace Hale Ball
Annie Payson Call	Clarence E. Mulford	Evelyn Everett-green
Annie Roe Carr	Clemence Housman	Everard Cotes
Annonaymous	Confucius	F. H. Cheley
Anton Chekhov	Coningsby Dawson	F. J. Cross
Archibald Lee Fletcher	Cornelis DeWitt Wilcox	F. Marion Crawford
Arnold Bennett	Cyril Burleigh	Fannie E. Newberry
Arthur C. Benson	D. H. Lawrence	Federick Austin Ogg
Arthur Conan Doyle	Daniel Defoe	Ferdinand Ossendowski
Arthur M. Winfield	David Garnett	Fergus Hume
Arthur Ransome	Dinah Craik	Florence A. Kilpatrick
Arthur Schnitzler	Don Carlos Janes	Fremont B. Deering
Arthur Train	Donald Keyhoe	Francis Bacon
Atticus	Dorothy Kilner	Francis Darwin
B.H. Baden-Powell	Dougan Clark	Frances Hodgson Burnett
B. M. Bower	Douglas Fairbanks	Frances Parkinson Keyes
B. C. Chatterjee	E. Nesbit	Frank Gee Patchin
Baroness Emmuska Orczy	E. P. Roe	Frank Harris
Baroness Orczy	E. Phillips Oppenheim	Frank Jewett Mather
Basil King	E. S. Brooks	Frank L. Packard
Bayard Taylor	Earl Barnes	Frank V. Webster
Ben Macomber	Edgar Rice Burroughs	Frederic Stewart Isham
Bertha Muzzy Bower	Edith Van Dyne	Frederick Trevor Hill
Bjornstjerne Bjornson	Edith Wharton	Frederick Winslow Taylor

Friedrich Kerst
Friedrich Nietzsche
Fyodor Dostoyevsky
G.A. Henty
G.K. Chesterton
Gabrielle E. Jackson
Garrett P. Serviss
Gaston Leroux
George A. Warren
George Ade
Geroge Bernard Shaw
George Cary Eggleston
George Durston
George Ebers
George Eliot
George Gissing
George MacDonald
George Meredith
George Orwell
George Sylvester Viereck
George Tucker
George W. Cable
George Wharton James
Gertrude Atherton
Gordon Casserly
Grace E. King
Grace Gallatin
Grace Greenwood
Grant Allen
Guillermo A. Sherwell
Gulielma Zollinger
Gustav Flaubert
H. A. Cody
H. B. Irving
H.C. Bailey
H. G. Wells
H. H. Munro
H. Irving Hancock
H. R. Naylor
H. Rider Haggard
H. W. C. Davis
Haldeman Julius
Hall Caine
Hamilton Wright Mabie
Hans Christian Andersen
Harold Avery
Harold McGrath
Harriet Beecher Stowe
Harry Castlemon
Harry Coghill
Harry Houidini

Hayden Carruth
Helent Hunt Jackson
Helen Nicolay
Hendrik Conscience
Hendy David Thoreau
Henri Barbusse
Henrik Ibsen
Henry Adams
Henry Ford
Henry Frost
Henry James
Henry Jones Ford
Henry Seton Merriman
Henry W Longfellow
Herbert A. Giles
Herbert Carter
Herbert N. Casson
Herman Hesse
Hildegard G. Frey
Homer
Honore De Balzac
Horace B. Day
Horace Walpole
Horatio Alger Jr.
Howard Pyle
Howard R. Garis
Hugh Lofting
Hugh Walpole
Humphry Ward
Ian Maclaren
Inez Haynes Gillmore
Irving Bacheller
Isabel Cecilia Williams
Isabel Hornibrook
Israel Abrahams
Ivan Turgenev
J.G.Austin
J. Henri Fabre
J. M. Barrie
J. M. Walsh
J. Macdonald Oxley
J. R. Miller
J. S. Fletcher
J. S. Knowles
J. Storer Clouston
J. W. Duffield
Jack London
Jacob Abbott
James Allen
James Andrews
James Baldwin

James Branch Cabell
James DeMille
James Joyce
James Lane Allen
James Lane Allen
James Oliver Curwood
James Oppenheim
James Otis
James R. Driscoll
Jane Abbott
Jane Austen
Jane L. Stewart
Janet Aldridge
Jens Peter Jacobsen
Jerome K. Jerome
Jessie Graham Flower
John Buchan
John Burroughs
John Cournos
John F. Kennedy
John Gay
John Glassworthy
John Habberton
John Joy Bell
John Kendrick Bangs
John Milton
John Philip Sousa
John Taintor Foote
Jonas Lauritz Idemil Lie
Jonathan Swift
Joseph A. Altsheler
Joseph Carey
Joseph Conrad
Joseph E. Badger Jr
Joseph Hergesheimer
Joseph Jacobs
Jules Vernes
Julian Hawthrone
Julie A Lippmann
Justin Huntly McCarthy
Kakuzo Okakura
Karle Wilson Baker
Kate Chopin
Kenneth Grahame
Kenneth McGaffey
Kate Langley Bosher
Kate Langley Bosher
Katherine Cecil Thurston
Katherine Stokes
L. A. Abbot
L. T. Meade

L. Frank Baum
Latta Griswold
Laura Dent Crane
Laura Lee Hope
Laurence Housman
Lawrence Beasley
Leo Tolstoy
Leonid Andreyev
Lewis Carroll
Lewis Sperry Chafer
Lilian Bell
Lloyd Osbourne
Louis Hughes
Louis Joseph Vance
Louis Tracy
Louisa May Alcott
Lucy Fitch Perkins
Lucy Maud Montgomery
Luther Benson
Lydia Miller Middleton
Lyndon Orr
M. Corvus
M. H. Adams
Margaret E. Sangster
Margret Howth
Margaret Vandercook
Margaret W. Hungerford
Margret Penrose
Maria Edgeworth
Maria Thompson Daviess
Mariano Azuela
Marion Polk Angellotti
Mark Overton
Mark Twain
Mary Austin
Mary Catherine Crowley
Mary Cole
Mary Hastings Bradley
Mary Roberts Rinehart
Mary Rowlandson
M. Wollstonecraft Shelley
Maud Lindsay
Max Beerbohm
Myra Kelly
Nathaniel Hawthrone
Nicolo Machiavelli
O. F. Walton
Oscar Wilde

Owen Johnson
P.G. Wodehouse
Paul and Mabel Thorne
Paul G. Tomlinson
Paul Severing
Percy Brebner
Percy Keese Fitzhugh
Peter B. Kyne
Plato
Quincy Allen
R. Derby Holmes
R. L. Stevenson
R. S. Ball
Rabindranath Tagore
Rahul Alvares
Ralph Bonehill
Ralph Henry Barbour
Ralph Victor
Ralph Waldo Emmerson
Rene Descartes
Ray Cummings
Rex Beach
Rex E. Beach
Richard Harding Davis
Richard Jefferies
Richard Le Gallienne
Robert Barr
Robert Frost
Robert Gordon Anderson
Robert L. Drake
Robert Lansing
Robert Lynd
Robert Michael Ballantyne
Robert W. Chambers
Rosa Nouchette Carey
Rudyard Kipling
Saint Augustine
Samuel B. Allison
Samuel Hopkins Adams
Sarah Bernhardt
Sarah C. Hallowell
Selma Lagerlof
Sherwood Anderson
Sigmund Freud
Standish O'Grady
Stanley Weyman
Stella Benson
Stella M. Francis

Stephen Crane
Stewart Edward White
Stijn Streuvels
Swami Abhedananda
Swami Parmananda
T. S. Ackland
T. S. Arthur
The Princess Der Ling
Thomas A. Janvier
Thomas A Kempis
Thomas Anderton
Thomas Bailey Aldrich
Thomas Bulfinch
Thomas De Quincey
Thomas Dixon
Thomas H. Huxley
Thomas Hardy
Thomas More
Thornton W. Burgess
U. S. Grant
Upton Sinclair
Valentine Williams
Various Authors
Vaughan Kester
Victor Appleton
Victor G. Durham
Victoria Cross
Virginia Woolf
Wadsworth Camp
Walter Camp
Walter Scott
Washington Irving
Wilbur Lawton
Wilkie Collins
Willa Cather
Willard F. Baker
William Dean Howells
William le Queux
W. Makepeace Thackeray
William W. Walter
William Shakespeare
Winston Churchill
Yei Theodora Ozaki
Yogi Ramacharaka
Young E. Allison
Zane Grey